REPUBLICAN
LIKE
ME

REPUBLICAN

LIKE

★ ★

ME

HOW I LEFT THE LIBERAL BUBBLE AND LEARNED TO LOVE THE RIGHT

KEN STERN

HARPER

An Imprint of HarperCollinsPublishers

HarperCollins books may be purchased for educational, business, or sales promotional use. For information, please email the Special Markets Department at SPsales@harpercollins.com.

FIRST EDITION

Designed by William Ruoto

Library of Congress Cataloging-in-Publication Data

Names: Stern, Ken, author.

Title: Republican like me : a lifelong Democrat's journey across the aisle / Ken Stern.

Description: First edition. | New York, NY : Broadside Books, [2017] | Includes bibliographical references and index.

Identifiers: LCCN 2017021668 | ISBN 978-0-06-246078-3

Subjects: LCSH: Political culture—United States. | Conservatism—United States. | Republican Party (U.S. : 1854-) | Stern, Ken, 1963-

Classification: LCC JK1726 .S745 2017 | DDC 320.520973—dc23 LC record available at https://lccn.loc.gov/2017021668

17 18 19 20 21   LSC   10 9 8 7 6 5 4 3 2 1

For Hobart Street

CONTENTS

Introduction. 1

1 The Fellowship of the Pig 21

2 The Party of God 53

3 The Basket of Deplorables 89

4 The Grand Coal Party 115

5 The Party of Science?. 143

6 The Greatest Society 171

7 The Party of the Press 205

8 The End and the Beginning 237

Acknowledgments. 251

Notes 253

Index 285

INTRODUCTION

You never really understand a person until you consider things from his point of view.

—ATTICUS FINCH, IN *TO KILL A MOCKINGBIRD*

Hobart Street is just a single block, but it is long enough to have three rough geographic areas: Hi-Ho, for the area at the top of the hill near Mount Pleasant Street; Lo-Ho, at the bottom of the hill bordering Irving Street; and Mid-Ho, in between. I live in Mid-Ho.

Today, the Mount Pleasant neighborhood is tranquil and stately, populated by so many young families that it is occasionally referred to as "Mount Stroller." But the area has had its ups and downs over the years. It was first developed about one hundred years ago and, even though the neighborhood sits only three miles north of the White House, Mount Pleasant was originally conceived and marketed as a suburb, its modest elevation offering an allegedly cool respite from the heat of the D.C. swamp. If you walk around Mount Pleasant and adjoining areas today, with its gracious row homes and stately embassies, you would be forgiven for thinking of its history as one unbroken line of financial prosperity. But that is not the case. Like many parts of the city, and like many cities in this country, Mount Pleasant experienced considerable

1

"white flight" during the 1960s and 1970s, those whites replaced largely by lower-income blacks and Central American immigrants. The neighborhood struggled for decades, with the nadir being the Mount Pleasant riots of 1991, which consisted of three days of protesting, looting, and burning of police cars. Mount Pleasant has undergone an accelerating re-gentrification over the last twenty years, which has resulted in a cultural and economic mix that is a significant part of the neighborhood's charm: trendy Thai restaurants abutting bodegas, big-box stores looming over Salvadoran fast-food places. There is a little something for everyone, which is why Mount Pleasant is often described as "diverse" and "eclectic," and we like it that way.

Our commitment to diversity is pretty complete when it comes to black, white, and brown, and to the rainbow colors of the gay pride flag, but it falls a little short when it comes to red and blue. The neighborhood is astonishingly Democratic and liberal. Hillary Clinton received 92.5 percent of the vote in the 2016 general election and Jill Stein outpolled Donald Trump in my precinct by a narrow margin (74 votes to 70). During 2016, it was always very easy to spot a Bernie Sanders or a Black Lives Matter yard sign, but good luck finding one for Bush or Kasich, let alone Trump or Cruz.

In the past, I never paid much attention to the political homogeneity of Hobart Street, other than a joke here or there with my neighbors. Hobart Street and the Mount Pleasant neighborhood aren't all that different from the wider city and, let's face it, I fit in rather well, being a lifelong Democrat married to a Democratic staffer on Capitol Hill. It all seemed pretty natural, until Porchfest.

Say what you want about Hobart Street, but it has a lot of team spirit. Every Halloween the street is closed to traffic and kids from miles around come here, certainly attracted by the efficient access to candy provided by row homes and perhaps by the "dead baby house," a neighbor who strings baby dolls in various bloody poses and drops them down on the trick-or-treaters as they approach the front porch (I said we have team spirit, not good taste). Porchfest is the other main festival of the Hobart social calendar, our annual block party held each June. Virtually every house on the block contributes something: a food stand, music, home-brewed beer, a slip-and-slide for the kids. My wife, Beth, stays up all night baking cookies, which she cuts variously into the shape of the Washington Monument, the Capitol Building, and a map of the District of Columbia. Some she decorates herself, but others are left unfrosted so that the kids can wield the icing tubes like junior Jackson Pollocks. They do that with uncommon enthusiasm, if not complete coordination. For days afterward, our front steps look like the victim of a food-coloring balloon prank.

The highlight of Porchfest is the annual parade, which is always led by a marching band, a fire truck from the local firehouse, the same vintage convertible that appears each Porchfest and then is not seen again on Hobart Street for the rest of the year, and all the kids on the block, some riding bikes or scooters, others tunelessly playing musical instruments, or in the case of my nine-year-old son, Nate, randomly throwing a baseball up in the air. It's all hopelessly chaotic, like a band in which all the musicians are playing from different sheet music, and it's all wonderful. And every year the parade starts with the children reciting the "Hobart Street Pledge." I always loved the Pledge, at least the concept of it, that in our increasingly entropic world we share a community, an identity, a home here on Hobart Street. I loved the Pledge, that is, until I bothered to listen to the words, which I discovered one year go something like this: "I pledge allegiance to Hobart Street Northwest. . . . Gay or straight, woman or man, all are welcome on Hobart Street—except for Republicans."

The end of the Pledge was meant to be all good fun, I suppose, except for the fact that it reflects an uncomfortable truth: as much as my neighbors on Hobart Street speak to the values of diversity and tolerance, they have no real interest in viewpoint diversity. I have tried, episodically and unsystematically, to find a Republican on Hobart Street. They must be there: our precinct is 94 percent Democratic, an astonishing number on its face, but that must mean there is still that 6 percent somewhere. It's simple to find Democrats: Bernie banners? Yes. Hillary bumper stickers? Sure. Black Lives Matter yard signs? Plenty of them. An "Everybody SUCKS, We're Screwed 2016" sign that pops up right after the election? You bet. But evidence of support for Bush, Kasich, Cruz, Carson, or Trump? No, no, no, no, and hell no. I posted a plea on our local message board, Nextdoor Mt. Pleasant, for information on any Republicans on Hobart Street, and was met with a stony silence. At one point I thought I would hit pay dirt with my neighbor Richard, mostly because I knew him to be entirely dismissive of liberal orthodoxy, but it turns out that Richard is just dismissive by nature. When I finally cornered him, he confessed that he hasn't voted for a Republican for president since 1992. I heard tale of a Republican who used to live on Hobart Street, but that's as close as I ever came.

Truth be told, in its political homogeneity, Hobart Street is not all that unusual. During the 2016 election, the *Washington Post* asked Virginia voters whether they had any family members or close friends who were supporting the opposing candidate. Fifty-four percent of Trump supporters and 60 percent of Clinton supporters reported that they had no family members and no close friends who were planning to vote for the other side.[1] It is an extraordinary thing, if you think about it for a moment. Virginia was a closely contested state, swinging back and forth on election night, ultimately going to Hillary Clinton by just five points. But

4

somehow a majority of Virginians had managed to arrange their friends and family to be entirely politically compatible. Amazing as it is, I must confess that it was the same for me as well, but at least I have the excuse of living in a single-party neighborhood.

The truth is that my neighbors don't really want Republicans among them, because they fear and dislike them. Over the past two years, from time to time, I have conducted an informal and resolutely unscientific poll of neighbors and guests on our street, asking them: "Would you say the Republican Party's policies are so misguided that they threaten the nation's well-being, or would you not go that far?" Almost uniformly, and almost always without hesitation, they have answered yes; when I have pushed harder and urged reflection, they have affirmed their strongly held belief that Republicans as a group do form a real threat to the health of the United States.

That may make the good people of Hobart Street seem parochial and perhaps a bit paranoid, and maybe they are, but it does not make them unusual. In fact, the partisanship reflected on Hobart Street is completely in tune with the rest of the country. The question I have asked of my neighbors is the same question that the Pew Research Center has used for the past twenty years to get a handle on political polarization in America. Pew carefully designed the "threat to the nation's well-being" question to suggest that a positive answer is a substantial, maybe even daring, statement against the other party and perhaps the democratic process. Yet the number of people answering "yes" has risen at a frightful clip in recent years, nearly doubling since 2004.[2] But it has gotten worse. More than half of Democrats (55 percent) say the Republican Party makes them "afraid," while 49 percent of Republicans say the same about the Democratic Party. Among those highly engaged in politics—those who say they vote regularly and either volunteer for or donate to campaigns—fully 70 percent of Democrats and 62 percent of Republicans say they are afraid of the other party. Since these figures come from polls taken in June 2016, well before the misery of the Clinton–Trump square dance, these numbers likely underrepresent partisan animosity, and perhaps significantly so. In this atmosphere, it is hardly surprising that my neighbors on Hobart Street are unwelcoming to Republicans.[3]

The Pew data may be the most arresting, but it is by no means the only data pointing to our growing polarization. The American National Election Studies (ANES), an academic poll that has been conducted for decades, has also shown rising antipathy toward the opposite party for the better part of a half century.[4] In 1988, the share of people who felt "very coldly" toward the other party was about 40 percent. By 2004 that had risen to about 60 percent and by 2012 to about 80 percent. The numbers are interesting—perhaps even sobering—by themselves, but their real relevance is revealed by comparison to the other fault lines of American society. The "warmth" gap between Democrats and Republicans is now greater than the gap between blacks and whites and the gap between Protestants and Catholics.[5] Even in the most fundamental and personal matters, the political divide is taking the place of race, religion, and class—once the key flash points in American society—as a specification for marriage. In 1960, parents were asked whether they would be "displeased" if their children married outside their political party. Only 5 percent said yes. In 2010, American parents were asked if they would be "upset," a slightly higher bar, and fully 40 percent objected to interparty marriages.[6] What was probably a bizarre question half a century ago is now becoming a standard qualifying requirement for marriage, the new "guess who's coming to dinner."

It seems ridiculous to suggest, as I just did, that partisan biases could be stronger than racial bigotry, the cleavages that have in many ways defined our country since inception. It just can't be. But in 2015, two political scientists, Shanto Iyengar of Stanford and Sean Westwood, now of Dartmouth, both well-known researchers on issues related to polarization, decided to try to find out how partisan biases carried over to behaviors outside of politics and then compare them to racial biases. To do this they designed a simple but clever experiment. They crafted résumés of two fictitious high school seniors who were described as competing for a college scholarship, and asked a little more than 1,000 people to award the scholarship based only on information presented in the paper résumé. The résumés had three variables: first, the two competing students would have either a 3.5 or a 4.0 GPA, both scholarship worthy but different enough for comparison purposes; second, the students could be differentiated by political affiliation (Arthur Wolfe, president of the Young Republicans Club and member of the bowling team, or Jeremy O'Neill, president of the Young Democrats Club and member of the Art Club); or third, the competing students could have either a stereotypically African American name and association (Jamal Washington, president of the African American Student Association) or a stereotypically white, Anglo-Saxon name and association (Arthur Wolfe, president of the Future Investment Bankers Club).

The results of the study were stunning. When the résumé featured only the political party distinctions, about 80 percent of Democrats and Republicans awarded the scholarship to their copartisan. This held true whether or not their political "teammate" had the higher GPA—when the Republican student was more qualified, Democrats chose him only 30 percent of the time. Republicans were even more partisan. When the Democratic applicant sported the higher GPA—and remember, that was the only discernible difference beyond party—Republicans still chose the Democrat only 15 percent of the time.

It is quite horrible and reads like a modern form of racism, and indeed, according to Iyengar and Westwood, the pull of political party is stronger than racial identity. When they pitted candidates against each other with only racial markers differentiating the two applicants, they found mixed evidence of bias: when the candidates were equally qualified, about 78 percent of African Americans chose the candidate of the same race, and only 42 percent of European Americans did the same, which actually suggests, at least on a coin-flip basis, that whites were giving a small advantage to black candidates, or perhaps just thought that anyone who was the head of the Future Investment Bankers Club was a completely unworthy dink. When the candidate of the other race had a higher GPA, 45 percent of African Americans and 71 percent of European Americans chose him.[7] These numbers suggest some steering due to race, particularly among blacks who want to give a leg up to other blacks, but not even close to the numbers around political discrimination.

When the residents of Hobart Street said that Republicans were not welcome, they weren't kidding: they don't want to live near them, they sure don't want to marry them, and apparently they don't even want them to get a decent education.

★　★　★

We may dislike the other side, but we are not nearly as different from them as we like to think we are. There is a large body of evidence, all rather depressing, that demonstrates the limits of our knowledge and the frailty of our political decision making. In general, our view of policy and ideology is driven by signaling; that is, our political perspective is often shaped by what others are suggesting we should think rather than by any careful and independent consideration of the issues. The research on this goes a long way back and mostly suggests that political scientists like to fuck with voters. In 1975, for instance, a University of Cinncinati political scientist named George Bishop and his colleagues undertook an extensive research project on the "Public Affairs Act of 1975." In a series of phone surveys and face-to-face interviews, the researchers queried voters on whether the act should be repealed or amended and found that somewhere between 20 percent and 40 percent were willing to venture an opinion on the matter, despite the fact that the Public Affairs Act of 1975 was entirely a creature of Bishop's imagination.[8] In 2013, YouGov, working with the *Huffington Post*, updated Bishop's research and took it one step futher. Like Bishop, they started with the question "some people say" that the Public Affairs Act should be repealed, and received similar results, with about 15 percent of the population willing to offer their thoughtful view on this nonexistent law. But that's where it gets interesting: when YouGov varied the question to state that "President Obama says" the act should be repealed, support for its repeal rose modestly among Democrats, but opposition to its repeal among Republicans skyrocketed, from 3 percent to 39 percent. And when the question was altered to assert that congressional Republicans advocated repeal, Democrats rose to its defense, with a substantial minority, some 28 percent, instantly converting to the role of staunch defenders of the Public Affairs Act.[9]

You can have all sorts of fun with these things, and many people have. In 2015, the *Huffington Post* asked people to react to the notion that "President Obama has praised the idea of universal health care." Democrats were wildly supportive, with more than 80 percent agreeing, and Republicans were particularly unethusiastic, with less than 20 percent agreeing. When the question was changed to say that Donald Trump has praised the idea (as in fact he once did), Democratic support immediately dropped in half, while Republican support more than doubled. This dynamic is not just limited to political science games. When it was originally introduced, Common Core was one of those increasingly rare policies that drew support from across the political spectrum. As recently as 2013, it had incredible public support, at about 83 percent, but, around then, the Tea Party, licking its wounds from its 2012 electoral disaster, latched on to the concept as an example of unwarranted federal intrusion on local governance, even though Common Core from inception was a state-driven initiative. Support for the idea quickly plummeted, so by 2016 only 35 percent of Republicans were willing to support Common Core. But when you describe what Common Core is—standards for reading and math that are the same across the states—without mentioning the "Common Core" brand, support among Republicans instantly pops up to more than 50 percent and strong opposition largely disappears, from 34 percent to 14 percent. Lest you think this is a Republican folly, the same dynamic holds true for Democrats, though a little less strongly, probably because Common Core is not an identity issue for Democrats.[10]

You can go on all day with this stuff. Kentuckians are pretty negative on the Affordable Care Act, opposing it by a margin of 47–33 percent, but they are reasonably positive on Kynect (33 percent pro and only 29 percent con), despite the fact that they are for all intents and purposes the same thing.[11] When they think that affirmative action is "Obama endorsed," Democrats favor it by huge margins over Republicans, 64–15. When it is Trump's affirmative action, that gap virtually disappears, to 45–33 percent. And it's not like affirmative action is a new or obscure concept, having first been implemented in an executive order by President John F. Kennedy in 1961. Nonetheless, these are complicated issues, and most of us are far too uncertain and far too inexpert to render truly independent judgments on these matters, so we tend to follow the signals of the people we have been trained to trust.[12]

And once people cleave to their partisan position, it is difficult to shake them with the facts. In 2005, a team from the University of Michigan conducted a series of experiments to determine the effect of false and correct facts on political views. In their experiment, participants were given mock news stories, each of which contained a demonstrably false, though widely believed, claim made by a political figure: that there were weapons of mass destruction (WMD) found in Iraq, that the Bush tax cuts led to increased federal government revenues, and that the Bush administration had imposed a total ban on stem cell research. After the false information was given, the researchers then presented a specific correction for each piece of misinformation, and measured the effect of the correction on study participant views.

In most cases, the new and factually correct information did have a significant impact on people's views, but perhaps not what the researchers expected, or at least hoped for. Rather remarkably, when conservatives heard the corrective information on WMD and taxes, they felt even *more* strongly about their previously established positions. In effect, the new information, even though it did not support their position, reinforced and strengthened their views, the more so with those who possessed strongly held views on the subject already. The impact on liberals was similar, though a little less dramatic: the corrected information simply did not move their views at all, as they apparently simply ignored the nonconforming fact that the Bush administration's restrictions on stem cell research were not total. It is a remarkable, and truly scary, piece of research, and even if it doesn't explain it, it certainly describes our partisan behaviors now.

★ ★ ★

In recent years, Daniel Patrick Moynihan's famous statement, "You are entitled to your opinion, but not to your own facts," has gained considerable currency. There are of course truths and falsehoods in this world, and we regrettably live in a world now of routine creative fact-making. But putting aside for the moment those who make a habit, or in some cases a business, of intentionally fabricating information, we need to understand how slippery facts are. When we identify with a team, it changes how we perceive the world, not just opinions but the facts as well. Some of the foundational work on how "team spirit" changes our understanding of facts comes from the world of sports, and the research on this dates back more than half a century, to 1951 and a particularly compelling football match between Dartmouth and Princeton. Today no one, perhaps not even their respective alumni, pays much attention when Dartmouth and Princeton square off, but sixty-five years ago, college sports were far from the oversize industrial activity they are today and Ivy League football still counted. Princeton came into the game undefeated and its star player, Dick Kazmaier, was up for All-America honors. But a Dartmouth player broke Kazmaier's nose early in the second quarter and the game degenerated into a rough affair: one Dartmouth player was carted off with a broken leg, and both teams engaged in an unusual amount of dirty play both during and after the game. The controversy around the game dragged on for several weeks, with the respective student newspapers, the *Daily Princetonian* and the *Dartmouth*, placing blame for the injuries and for the extracurricular activities on the other squad.

It's inconsequential stuff in hindsight and would have been soon forgotten except for the fact that two prominent researchers, Albert Hastorf of Dartmouth and Hadley Cantril of Princeton, took an interest in the game, and especially why the students of the respective schools seemed to have such differing understandings of the situation. They obtained film of the game and showed it to groups of students from both schools, and they found wildly different interpretations of the game from both sets of students. The Princeton students saw dirty play and by an overwhelming majority blamed Dartmouth for it. The Dartmouth students saw a tough, hard-nosed game with both sides equally engaged.

It is something of a puzzle. The students saw the same game, and reviewed the same film, and it is not as if the Dartmouth and Princeton students were of widely different backgrounds and perspectives. You could have swapped the student bodies one day and no one would have been much the wiser. But everyone brought, even within the very limited flavor pack of the Ivy League of the 1950s, differing motivations, and that shaped their understanding of what they saw.

Hastorf and Cantril concluded from their research that the game was like a social event, where there was no shared experience; everyone brought their own biases to the game and interpreted events through their own preconceptions. There was no single event and thus no single truth to the event. "For the 'thing' simply is *not* the same for different people whether the 'thing' is a football game, a presidential candidate, Communism or spinach" (emphasis in original).

It is much the same in politics, as Hastorf and Cantril themselves noted in passing.[13] We tend to think of the 2016 campaign or any other political experience as a single event but in reality it is nothing like that. Even a single three- or four-hour football game is a complex affair, comprising a television broadcast, social media, running commentaries from friends, family, and television personalities, and different experiences and aspirations. Seen in this light, it is not at all surprising that essentially interchangeable populations at Dartmouth and Princeton could still come away with vastly different understandings of what happened.

Now take that and turn a three-hour football game into an eighteen-month, sprawling, media-soaked presidential campaign and it is virtually inconceivable that anyone could have a shared experience. And think about how different the encounter is when you are a laid-off factory worker from Youngstown, Ohio, versus a tech entrepreneur from Silicon Valley: different history, different identities, different language, different conversation circles, and different rooting interests. The comment that I heard most frequently during the campaign from friends, from the media, and from people I talked to for this book was: "I don't understand how they don't see [Trump/Clinton] like I do." The real question is how could they *not* see things differently from each other.

★   ★   ★

Our polarization is abetted not only by media and group psychology but by how we are organizing ourselves. In 2008, journalist Bill Bishop wrote a remarkably insightful book called *The Big Sort*, which focused on how Americans are increasingly self-selecting into cities and even neighborhoods that are politically and socially congenial to them. Liberals move to Austin; conservatives go to Dallas. In some places, you can draw a red line (or a blue line, if you prefer) that separates Democratic and Republican areas and make easy predictions about where people will live. Milwaukee County is extremely liberal and Democratic, but as soon as you cross the invisible dividing line into suburban Washington, Waukesha, and Ozaukee counties, you will be in some of the most conservative counties in the state. When you get down to the molecular level, the neighborhood ward, you can see the sorting even more. According to a 2014 study, there is a 44 percent chance that you now live in an "extreme ward," a neighborhood that deviated from the national norm in one direction or the other by more than 20 percent. In the abstract, it is hard to know whether 44 percent is a big number or not, so let's put this in historical perspective. In less than a generation, the number of extreme wards in the Milwaukee area has almost doubled, a major social change in how we organize ourselves. Just like the Virginians who somehow arranged their friends and family in such a way to be politically compatible, so we now organize our neighborhoods to support this political segregation. We are like electrons, in close orbit around the same core, but our paths never cross.[14]

It is not limited of course to Milwaukee, and the sorting that Bill Bishop observed in the mid-2000s is dramatically on the rise. In 1992, well into the era of polarization, roughly 1,100 counties accounting for 32 percent of the national vote were categorized as "landslide counties," that is, counties that one presidential candidate won by a gap larger than 20 percent. By 2016 that number had exploded to about 2,500 counties, amounting to about 60 percent of the vote and representing 197 million Americans. Increasingly, the Democratic and Republican parties are occupying different spheres of the United States.[15] And the divide is not just state-to-state or county-to-county; it is increasingly rural versus urban, secular versus evangelical, white versus the multicultural coalition of the Democrats. Odds are that more than ever, when it comes to politics, the people around you think like you, act like you, and vote like you.

★   ★   ★

All this research that we have been punching through for the last few pages shows how we have divided ourselves into partisan bubbles and the impact that has on our sense of self and our sense of the world. As other bonds of identity have weakened in American

life—religion and membership in labor unions, for example—
the draw and meaning of political parties as social identity has
strengthened. The parties have become stalking horses for identity, and their successes have become more and more important
to our own sense of self-worth.

Our increased polarization reflects many different things:
our geographic sorting, our partisan media environment, the
increased saliency of party to identity in modern life, and the
fact that the political parties have become more uniform in their
ideologies. What I have not mentioned in that list, though, is an
increasing gap among Americans over policies, and that is because that increasing gap does not exist. If you look at Americans'
views on key issues—abortion, immigration, environment, gay
rights, taxes, size of government, and on and on—they haven't
changed very much over the years, even as we have become angrier about them all. The person who has studied this the most
closely, a Stanford political scientist named Morris Fiorina, has
noted, "[i]f one thinks about polarization in terms of positions
on specific policy issues, one would expect to see a decline in the
center and a lumping up of people on the extremes. We do not
have long time series of attitudes toward particular policy issues
since they rise and fall on the national agenda, but on most issues, attitudes continue to cluster in the middle rather than lump
up on the extremes."[16] It leads to a fascinating insight. We are
becoming angrier and more polarized not because of increasing
issue disagreement but because we are increasingly participating
in groupthink. When all the people you know, when all the people in your political sect agree with you, it becomes easy to relax
in the certainty that you and your cohort are right, and the other
side is not just wrong, but also taking a long, slow bubble-bath in
the sea of craziness. When we don't know the other side, when we
don't hear from them, when we don't talk to them, when we can

demonize them to our heart's content, there are just no brakes on our sense of self-righteousness. Polarization is increasing because polarization is increasingly easy.

★   ★   ★

I have watched the increasing polarization of our country with growing concern but, even as a longtime partisan, I have been forced to acknowledge that my views are too parochial, too absent of any exposure to the "other side." The Hobart Street Pledge was a wake-up call for me, in that it signaled that something was wrong with the insularity of my comfortable little world. If I thought that the country should be less polarized, and Lord knows I do, I would have to start with being less polarized myself.

Republican Like Me is a book about what happens when a liberal sets out to look at issues from a conservative perspective. As is the case for most people in this day and age, much of my political information is gained in the confirmation process: listening to the pundits and politicians from "my side," filtering information to find all the facts that support the undoubtedly excellent Democratic position, and engaging with a social cohort that will relentlessly reinforce the righteousness of my views. For this book, I will change all that. I will spend the year getting outside my liberal bubble, by traveling across Red America, getting my information from conservative sources, and, to the best of my ability, giving them the benefit of the doubt.

My inquiry will go beyond the issues, like gun control or poverty programs, to challenge the instinctual beliefs that are driving our politics, chief among them the idea that history is on our side and that all would be better if we could tutor those benighted Republicans about the facts. And, so goes the line of thought, if that missionary work fails, it will not be because of honest disagreements but due to the fact that Republicans have wayward values or are just plain angry that they are living in the twenty-first century. It is the ethic of our time to cast the political process not as a good-faith debate over ideas but as a clash of right versus wrong. I intend to challenge that as much as I can.

That is easy to write, but hard to do. You see, liberal views were practically imprinted on me from birth. My mother was the authoritative political voice in our home—a Roosevelt Democrat, and a frequent volunteer for the campaigns of ill-fated candidates. (Handing out election day brochures for the likes of George McGovern, Jerry Brown, Frank Mankiewicz, and Lanny Davis are among my formative memories.) She had (and still has) strong partisan views and little tolerance for Republicans, and these views have not mellowed with age. On a recent visit home, Grandma Viv, as she is now known, proudly displayed a monograph titled *The Best Ideas from the Republican Party Over the Past 100 Years.* One hundred and twenty blank pages. Hilarious stuff. My father wisely never claimed a political party and refused to discuss his private voting habits; I suspected him of being a closeted Republican, but he always had the good sense to deny it.

Even after leaving my childhood home, I have been surrounded by Democrats. I went to schools (Haverford College, Yale Law School) that are beehives of liberal affiliation and beliefs. I did my turn in Democratic politics, spending more than a year working on the reelection campaign for Bill Clinton and almost a decade running National Public Radio (NPR), where rumor has it that you might find a Democrat or two. I've already described the liberal views of Hobart Street and it's pretty much the same once you walk into my house: Beth is a Democratic staff member for a U.S. Senate committee, and young Nate is dedicated in equal parts to the Washington Nationals and the Democratic Party. Political diversity is not much appreciated in my house.

As you might expect from my résumé, I have always been a straight-line Democratic voter, though under duress I will admit voting for Republican Carol Schwartz in her myriad failed campaigns against Mayor for Life Marion Barry. I may not be as reflexively partisan as some, but I detest Fox News, and the very sight of Mitch McConnell's hound-dog, jowly face irritates me.

But I have decided to leave that all behind. Not the wife and kid, mind you, but the committed dedication to the Democrats, their candidates, and their issues. These pages are full of facts and data to attest to the relatively thin differences between Republicans and Democrats, but deep down, I have long suspected that I wouldn't like many Republicans if I mixed with them on a regular basis. But I am choosing to find out. That means spending time with Fox, and Breitbart, and Mark Levin, listening to commentary I have avoided for much of my life. It means going to evangelical church for the first time, hunting in Texas, standing in pit row at a NASCAR race, and hanging out at Tea Party meetings. It also means tracking down conservative policy experts at places like the Manhattan Institute, the American Enterprise Institute, and other parts of the Republican ideas factory.

I planned to do all this with an open mind and an open heart, but I had no idea how much it would open my eyes.

1

THE FELLOWSHIP OF THE PIG

In England, if you commit a crime, the police don't have a gun and you don't have a gun. If you commit a crime, the police will say, "Stop, or I'll say stop again."

—ROBIN WILLIAMS

But if someone has a gun and is trying to kill you . . . it would be reasonable to shoot back with your own gun.

—THE DALAI LAMA

To my left, Joe yells, "Pigs, Ken, pigs! Right in front of you." I start up from my reverie, and see two fat pigs, one brown and one black, charging toward me. I raise up my shotgun, snug it in tight to my shoulder as I've been taught, ready for the big kick that everyone has warned me about. I fire, and a big puff of dirt kicks up behind the larger, black pig. The pig squeals, and cuts to its left. I reload, hastily shoulder the gun once again, and fire, missing for a second time. My pig, as I have already begun to think of him, is now in full flight, and I have barely time enough to squeeze off one more shot before he is out of range. I fire for a third time, and this time he squeals with something sounding more like pain than fear, but he keeps on running down the hill, perhaps a touch slower than before.

"I think you got him!" yells Mack, who takes off, sprinting down the hill in hot pursuit. I am a bit dubious, figuring that I have given the pig only a good fright, but I trudge off slowly after Mack, shotgun dangling from my side. My hunting trip to the Independence Ranch in Gonzales, Texas, is now in its sixth hour, but this is the first time that I have fired my gun all day. And truth be told, outside of a hastily arranged trip to a skeet-shooting range outside of D.C. in preparation for my visit to Texas, this is the first time I have ever fired any gun at all.

I have long had settled views on gun control, despite the fact that I had only the sketchiest knowledge about guns, gun statistics, and the science of violent crimes. Living in Washington, D.C., I am surrounded by people with guns. We have the highest density of armed law enforcement in the world: D.C. police, U.S. Capitol Police, uniformed Secret Service, U.S. Park Police, Homeland Security police—and that does not even count military and FBI personnel who are endemic to the city. But other than that, by and large I have been able to go through life fairly confident that the other people around me are probably not armed. To the extent that I have given it any thought, I would have said that's the way it should be: people with badges have guns, people without should not.

But guns and gun regulation are increasingly a cleavage issue in American life, reflective of politics, geography, and culture, and I am convinced that understanding the other side means grappling with the uniquely American gun culture and the uniquely American gun problem. Easier said than done. My bubble is not just a liberal bubble; it is a cultural bubble as well. There just aren't a whole lot of hunters, gun collectors, survivalists, or military personnel, for instance, hanging around Hobart Street or NPR or Yale Law School, and I don't think I have ever heard anyone in my circle carry on about "Second Amendment rights," other than to argue that the Founders meant to confer rights on militias, not every yahoo who practices saying "go ahead, punk, make my day" in front of a mirror.

I confess that I have never seen much utility in private gun ownership, but I am willing to try to clear my mental slate and see guns from a different point of view. So let's start with the most obvious facts: America is awash in guns, in excess of 300 million guns by most estimates, enough to arm every man, woman, child, and baby in this country. And we have a murder rate that well exceeds virtually every developed country, some 25 times the United Kingdom, for instance, and roughly on a par with Equatorial Guinea, Uzbekistan, and Belarus, to name a few comparison points that should make us all proud.

If your understanding of gun violence in the United States is dictated principally by news coverage (or worse, by social media), you would understandably think that mass shootings using assault weapons, and accidental deaths, especially of small children, are the dominant form of gun violence. You would also be badly mistaken. Gun deaths in the United States come from two sources, almost exclusively: suicides, and urban violence involving handguns. In 2013, there were 21,335 firearm-related suicides in the United States, 63 percent of all firearm deaths.[1] Let's pause on this for a second, because it is a shockingly high component of gun violence. While gun homicide has decreased substantially in the last decade, gun suicide has increased slightly over the same time period, and, if there is a gun violence epidemic, it is at the juncture of alcohol, mental illness, white working-class despair (we will come to that later), and firearm access. There are no doubt important public policy aspects of suicide by gun, which frankly far too few people talk about, but they are clearly distinct from the larger gun control debate.

But what we are talking about is gun homicides, and the numbers in that category are in their own way equally surprising. Of gun homicides, a significant majority (about 60 percent) take place in our urban centers, are typically concentrated in poor areas, and are overwhelmingly associated with gangs and drugs.[2] And those crimes are quite different from the typical mass shootings (though there may be mass shootings among them) that fuel so much of our concern about gun safety. These crimes are almost always committed with handguns, since handguns are ubiquitous, cheap, and easier to conceal, a key attribute in urban crime, and those guns are almost always obtained through the black market or through friends or family.[3] Because there are so many ways to obtain guns in a weapons-saturated market, restrictive ownership laws, such as in Chicago, have never really reduced violence; however, better policing, smarter drug control laws, and shared economic success have. It's not that guns don't kill people—try shooting someone without one—but controlling gun violence often has less to do with the guns themselves than you might initially think.

What's left after removing suicides and urban crime is comparatively small, a grab bag of some 4,000 to 5,000 deaths that include the occasional rural and suburban murder, accidental shootings, and mass shootings. Let us not minimize the impact of several thousand deaths, especially when they come in large clusters, but let's also put them in perspective in a nation of more than 300 million people. The amount of reporting on accidental gun deaths among children is significant, understandably so, but perspective is important. "[A]ccording to the U.S. Consumer Product Safety Commission (CPSC), 346 children under age five drowned in bathtubs between 2006 and 2010. By contrast, only ninety-four children under five died from accidental gunshots over the same period. That is a difference of nearly a factor of four. In fact, more children under five died from drowning in bathtubs than children under ten or even fifteen from accidental gun shots (174 and 298 respectively)."[4]

Because much of the public debate on guns has been fueled by reports of mass shootings, and specifically mass shootings that take place outside the less affluent parts of our urban centers, there is great attention on "assault weapons" in general and on the AR-15, a semiautomatic rifle manufactured originally by ArmaLite, in particular. The AR-15 has at once widespread notoriety and widespread popularity.

It is the most popular rifle in America, coveted because it is lightweight, easy to operate, has interchangeable parts, and reminds many people of the guns they had in the military. It is notorious because it has become the weapon of choice of mass murderers, deployed at Sandy Hook, San Bernardino, and Aurora, and it has proven, even in semiautomatic mode, to be an extremely efficient weapon. The vast majority of people use the gun for hunting, range shooting, and competitive shooting. And, despite its menacing look and pedigree, it is not different in operation from other rifles, though it is versatility, ease of use, and adaptability that has made it particularly attractive to gun lovers and mass murderers alike. On the surface, given the notoriety of the AR-15, banning it and its cousins such as the SIG Sauer MCX (used in Orlando) would be a logical decision, except they are used for illegal purposes rather infrequently outside of a few mass-casualty events.[5] Rifles of all types are implicated in only about 4 percent of all gun murders, with the AR-15 being present in some unidentified subset of those. To put that in perspective, about six times more people are killed each year with knives than with rifles, and Colonel Mustard with the candlestick is decidedly more dangerous—almost twice as many people were killed in 2014 with a blunt instrument as with any type of rifle, let alone an AR-15.

The AR-15 guns are unquestionably effective tools, but they are neither unique nor irreplaceable as killing machines. You could ban the sale of new AR-15s in this country tomorrow—I would not be bothered a whit if you did—but it would make no discernible difference in the overall homicide rate or in the severity of mass killings. That's not really an opinion. Sales of assault weapons were banned in the United States from 1994 to 2003 with little effect on homicides. The most authoritative study on the assault rifle ban came in 2004 from Christopher Koper, a criminologist then at the University of Pennsylvania. "In general we found, really, very, very little evidence, almost none, that gun violence was becoming any less lethal or any less injurious during this time frame. So on balance, we concluded that the ban had not had a discernible impact on gun crime during the years it was in effect."[6] Koper did hold open the possibility that an extension of the ban could someday produce a small reduction in shootings, and perhaps that would have happened, but it is very difficult in light of the facts to conceive of the Assault Weapons Ban as a meaningful part of any effort to reduce gun violence in this country.

I have always looked at the gun problem and assumed that there is a "commonsense" solution if the gun lobby would just get out of the way and people would just screw their heads on right. Like most Americans, I still support efforts to improve the efficacy of the background-check system, but I now understand them to be common sense but not solutions—and potentially distractions from the core social questions of economic despair and shuttered opportunity, which plague both poor minority neighborhoods and the white working class alike.

Over the past year, I have from time to time posted the most mild-mannered of comments on Facebook, suggesting that the gun issue is more complex than one might think. I am not exactly

fearless on social media, anxious about the cultural disapproba-
tion that comes with conservative views in my circles. My posts
have been exceptionally mealy-mouthed, timid suggestions that
the gun issue is tricky or perhaps a particular *National Review* article is "worth a look." My reading suggestions have not been well
received. My liberal friends have rather disdainfully rejected the
facts offered, not usually with their own facts but with the statement that we just need to get on with doing "something." This
would seem to suggest that people who don't agree with policy for
window dressing's sake are somehow hunky-dory with thousands
of gun deaths every year. It is a little window into the sanctimony
of some liberals, and I don't like it very much.

Virtually all of the guns used in mass-murder situations in the
past decade were lawfully obtained, and could have been lawfully
obtained under proposed laws, such as the extension of background checks to private sales (eighteen states already do so). The
Aurora, Newtown, and Orlando shootings were all committed
with lawfully obtained guns, or with guns taken from licensed
owners. And it is just not credible to think that restricting private
sales at places like gun shows will substantially reduce urban violence. The most recent, though admittedly still dated, surveys of
prisoners, which were undertaken back in the 1990s, indicate that
only about .6 percent of guns obtained by criminals were from
gun shows.[7] I'm not terribly impressed with surveys like this, but
I don't have any reason to dispute the conclusions: that there are
just too many lawful and unlawful ways to obtain a gun to believe
that new restrictions will make a material impact on outcomes.
And even if new laws reduced gun transactions in a meaningful
way, people would still continue to steal guns at a frightful rate.
Somewhere between 300,000 and 600,000 guns are stolen each
year, enough to cover every gun-related crime in the country, several times over.[8]

One of the key arguments for gun control is the unfavorable comparison between gun violence in the United States and in other developed countries. As President Obama noted in 2015, "What we also have to recognize is, is that our homicide rates are so much higher than other industrialized countries. I mean by like a mile. And most of that is attributable to the easy ready availability of firearms, particularly handguns."[9] And it is true; out of the 35 countries of the Organisation for Economic Co-operation and Development (OECD), the United States ranks 31st in homicide rates, though gun proponents hasten to note that the United States is far safer than Russia, Mexico, and Brazil and a little safer than Latvia, none of which is likely to be bulletin-board material for our national tourism agency. And what is most disturbing is that we are not even a close 31. Our homicide rate is ten times the rate in Japan and three times the rate in Canada, for instance. It's truly depressing stuff, unless you are planning to move to England, where the writer Bill Bryson recently reported, in all seriousness, and with some satisfaction, that you are more likely to be killed by walking into a wall than by being murdered.[10] I've pondered that statement quite a bit, trying to figure out what impels so many Britons to rush into walls, presumably headfirst, at speeds high enough to kill themselves, and haven't found any adequate explanation, but the sentiment expressed by Bryson is still true: England is an amazingly safe place. There were only 573 murders in all of England and Wales in 2015 (Chicago by itself is on pace to hit about 700 in 2017) and only about 40 of those murders were with firearms.

I couldn't find statistics to confirm Bryson's running-into-walls comparison, but it is true that in England you are about twice as likely to die from falling out of or through a building as you are to be killed with a gun, and about six times more likely to die from "malaise or fatigue."[11]

Those numbers are deeply satisfying to gun control advocates—and to the Brits as well, I should think—but it's not clear what they mean for the United States. Gun control advocates link the low murder rate in England, for example, to the 1997 Firearms Act, which effectively outlawed private ownership of handguns, but in truth the homicide rate in England was low long before the Firearms Act and it has actually increased modestly since 1997. And the relationship between the number of guns and murder rates is not always very clear. If you are to believe the Small Arms Survey, countries like Russia and Brazil have relatively low firearms ownership rates, but apparently all those guns are in the hands of killers and thieves, and high-ownership countries like Switzerland and Finland have comparatively low murder rates.

Switzerland, for instance, is awash in guns—a "gun in every closet" is integral both to the national defense plan and the national culture—and there is roughly one gun for every two people in the country. And yet the murder rate is pleasingly low, not so different from England itself. It is not that there is no relationship between gun availability and homicide rates—of course there is—but the story of violence and the means of controlling it are far more complicated and nuanced than advocates on either side of the story would have us believe.

I started off this process thinking, as do many of my political coreligionists, that reducing gun violence is simply a matter of will, and of overcoming the Neanderthals at the National Rifle Association (NRA).[12] But I have learned that it is not, and that if we really want to reduce gun violence, we should be focusing not first upon the weapons but on a lot of things around it: poverty, drugs, race, addressing mental illness, opportunity, and gangs, to name just a few.

★   ★   ★

Before I had ever dreamed of shooting a hog in Texas, I had spied a quote from Michael Needham, head of Heritage Action for America, decrying the isolation of Washington and New York elites from the "awesomeness of middle America."[13] In days past, I would have ignored the statement or dismissed it as some sort of reverse cultural superiority complex. But now I was intrigued. If I didn't live in "real America" or even "normal America,"[14] where could I go to find it? If you google "awesome America," you are directed to things like the Boll Weevil Monument in Enterprise, Alabama, or the Pez Candy company's headquarters in Orange, Connecticut, both of which sound pretty fantastic but neither of which is exactly what I was looking for. So I turned to Tucker Carlson, the Fox News host and the founding editor in chief of the conservative news site the *Daily Caller*. When I asked him, he immediately boomed, "Go shoot pigs in Texas. It will be fantastic!" I do recognize the rich irony in getting Middle America cultural advice from Needham, the son of a Wall Street investment banker, and Carlson, a scion of big media, a fancier of bow ties, and the son of Dick Carlson, a political operator so capable that he landed the job of ambassador to the Seychelles, the only lawful way to get a paid tropical vacation from the U.S. government. But sometimes you can find wisdom from the unlikeliest of sources, and Tucker's counsel sounded inspired to me.

Late on a January evening, I fly into Houston's George Bush Intercontinental Airport and encounter my first blast of Middle America awesomeness, an endless line at the Thrifty rental counter. The line stretches through a series of switchbacks and well past midnight. By the time I reach the counter, my plan to rent a pickup truck has melted into a weary desperation for anything with four wheels. Without any protest, I meekly accept the ignominy of a minivan instead and drive off into Houston to collapse in the guest room of my friends John and Anne.

It is a little bit of an indication of my regional and social isolation that for much of my life John Clutterbuck was as close to Middle America as I would typically come. We were roommates at Yale Law School and John is now a prosperous corporate lawyer operating out of a glass tower in downtown Houston. He is a connoisseur of wines and a lover of music that is neither country nor western, but he is still a son of Texas, and that has always brought with him some cultural differences, including a learned dislike for the casual intolerance of many of our Ivy League friends and their assumptions of political, moral, and regional superiority. In law school, none of us would have ever been caught dead saying anything against blacks or Hispanics or Jews or gay people, but rubes, southerners, white trash, hillbillies, and Republicans were all fair game. It rankled.

And then there are the guns. Like most people in Texas, John had grown up around guns and hunting, and understood them as part of life, so he was naturally a bit surprised coming east for college to find guns marked as evidence of social deviance and a propensity for violence. I had hoped to recruit John to come pig hunting with me, but he had demurred, telling me that he would only hunt birds these days. John is only partially awesome.

Leaving Houston behind, the next morning I pilot my minivan west on Interstate 10 toward Gonzales and the Independence Ranch. Next to me in a small duffel bag is an orange cap and a Day-Glo orange "hunting vest" that I had bought the week before. It reads "construction crew," not fearsome hunter, but there are limited hunting apparel options when your store of choice is the Target in downtown D.C.

I pull into the gravel parking lot in front of the rough-hewn log cabin that passes for an office at the ranch. A small group of hunters are clustered outside the office, waiting for the hunt to begin. Naturally enough, everyone has a rifle, either grasped loosely in their hands or slung over the shoulder, but more puzzling to me is the fact that most people also have a pistol as well, tucked into belts or nestled into leg, back, or shoulder holsters. You're only going to piss off a 150-pound hog with a pistol, so its utility on the hunt is a bit of a mystery to me.

Over the course of the day, I ask several people about the pistols, and the answers come back somewhere between a fashion statement and a shrug. Mack, who turns out to be a uniform sales rep from Houston, puzzles on the question for a bit and then confesses that he carries a pistol because everyone carries one: "It's America. It's Texas. You carry a gun." Since I come from a social circle where gun ownership is rare and is more associated with murder than with outerwear, I'm a little startled by it all. No one else is. It turns out that many of the people I meet at Independence Ranch learned to shoot some form of firearm starting at the age of five or six (a fact that still amazes and scares me a bit), and guns are no more a point of special notice to them than an iPhone is to most kids today. Rob, a retired police officer from Odessa, Texas, confesses to me that he didn't learn to shoot until he was thirteen, but he has made up for his early life embarrassment with later life enthusiasm: he now owns some ninety guns, and enough ammo by his own estimation to last a year and a half. If you are ever puzzled at the mathematics of gun ownership, where the percentage of people owning guns has declined steadily (from 51 percent in 1977 to just 36 percent today)[15] but the number of guns in circulation has risen precipitously (from less than 250 million in 1996 to more than 300 million today), the answer lies with hoarders like Rob, who buy up guns the same way my mother-in-law buys up Christmas ornaments. Three percent of adults own half the guns in this country, which works out to somewhere between 17 and 25 guns per person for this group, depending upon your data set,[16] but by any count, it is a heck of a lot of guns for anyone who only has two hands. It's a bit unsettling to envision millions of mini-arsenals spread across the country, and it all seems fairly ridiculous to me. But in fact, there is very little evidence to suggest that this group of gun collectors plays an outsize role in gun violence in America.

I'm apparently the only one at Independence Ranch who finds Rob's firearms cache particularly worthy of comment. The others' greater familiarity with guns is one piece of it; the second is that everyone is convinced that owning a gun, or guns, or lots of guns is the key to personal safety. Time and time again I'm told that you can't count on the government for protection, that in a moment of immediate need and slowing 911 response times, "a gun in your hand is better than a cop on the phone." It's not "don't mess with Texas," it is really "don't mess with an armed Texan." This view is reflected in a concept known as defensive gun use (DGU), the lawful use of a weapon to defend yourself against attack. I ask everyone whether they have ever had to use their gun to defend themselves, but as it turns out, DGUs usually happen to someone else.[17]

Joe, a former soldier who now, like Mack, sells uniforms, offers me the mutual assured destruction approach to guns: "I haven't used my gun because everyone in Texas is armed, so no one wants to take the risk. It's a lot safer that way. You don't see any mass shootings in Texas." It's a core belief of the gun crowd, but it's not remotely true. Texas has had roughly its proportionate share of such tragedies over the years, or about 7 of the 81 mass killings that have taken place in the United States over the last thirty-five years. This includes the shooting that many credit with touching off the modern wave of mass shootings. The incident began on August 1, 1966, when ex-marine Charles Whitman killed his wife and mother, climbed the twenty-seven stories of the central clock tower at the University of Texas at Austin, and picked off fourteen more victims before he was gunned down by police.

We all draw different lessons from events like the Austin shooting. In the movie classic *Full Metal Jacket*, Gunnery Sergeant Hartman, played by R. Lee Ermey, himself a former Marine sergeant, extols the virtues of the Austin shooter:

> **HARTMAN:** Do any of you people know who Charles Whitman was? None of you dumbasses know? Private Cowboy?
>
> **PRIVATE COWBOY:** Sir, he was that guy who shot all those people from that tower in Austin, Texas, sir!
>
> **HARTMAN:** That's affirmative. Charles Whitman killed twelve people from a twenty-eight-story observation tower at the University of Texas from distances up to four hundred yards. . . .
>
> **HARTMAN:** Do any of you people know where these individuals learned to shoot? Private Joker?
>
> **PRIVATE JOKER:** Sir, in the Marines, sir!
>
> **HARTMAN:** In the Marines! Outstanding! Those individuals showed what one motivated Marine and his rifle can do! And before you ladies leave my island, you will be able to do the same thing!

Hartman's view of the Austin shooting is, one might hope, peculiar to him and to director Stanley Kubrick, but the tragedy of that day is a good example of how people of different backgrounds draw very different lessons from the same rough set of facts. For many, Austin is a cautionary tale around private gun ownership. But for gun rights advocates, who are legion in Texas, there is another side of the story. As Whitman blasted away at targets down below, dozens of students and civilians from around town grabbed their guns and rushed to the scene, returning fire at him. While many of the volunteer rescue brigade themselves posed a safety hazard, spraying bullets in an undisciplined fashion that threatened civilians and police alike, at least one civilian, a manager at a nearby campus bookstore, was deputized on the spot and was part of the small group of officers who rushed up the tower's stairwell and ultimately gunned down Whitman. The legend of the civilian militia of Austin contributed to the recent legislative success to extend open-carry rights at public universities and colleges in Texas. That includes the flagship campus at Austin, where the law went into effect exactly fifty years to the day after the Whitman shooting spree.[18]

Joe's view that more guns means less crime is, as it turns out, an article of faith among many gun owners, and one of the great dividing lines in the gun debate. I confess that before this year, I didn't even know that the relationship between guns and crime would be an open question. Guns for me were associated almost solely with criminality—murder, rape, and robbery—so the math should be easy: more guns equals more crime, fewer guns, less crime, and it would strain credibility to think otherwise. But the issue is not so clear, as it turns out. In 1997, two University of Chicago researchers, John Lott and David Mustard, published a peer-reviewed paper in the *Journal of Legal Studies* that argued that right-to-carry laws (RTCs) had a dampening effect on major crime.[19] The paper developed not a behavioral argument but rather a sophisticated econometric model built on crime data from every county in the United States from 1977 to 1992. Based on their model, Lott and Mustard concluded that when citizens were authorized to carry concealed handguns, criminals made self-preservation decisions to avoid violent crimes where they might encounter an armed victim, and instead would self-select into property crimes involving stealth, where they could more easily avoid potentially deadly encounters with legally authorized gun owners. With a specificity that only economists could possibly muster, they argued that if states that did not have right-to-carry laws had chosen to adopt them on masse in 1992, they would have been spared 1,570 murders, 4,177 rapes, and more than 60,000 aggravated assaults in that one year alone.

To say that the "more guns, less crime" thesis caused a stir would be quite an understatement. Half of liberal academia, it seemed, or at least the economist and criminologist end of it, set out immediately to challenge and disprove Lott and Mustard's theory. Dozens of papers were published that questioned virtually every aspect of the model, from its cherry-picking of years, to the accuracy of the data sources, to coding and data entry mistakes and faulty analysis.[20] Many studies, in replicating Lott and Mustard's work (to their credit, the pair widely shared their data), came to the conclusion that concealed-carry laws have no effect, one way or the other, and some went ever further, seeing a statistical relationship between concealed-carry laws and an increase in violent crimes, at least in some categories.[21] It was all ugly enough, as fights among researchers go. Lott, who had held research positions at Chicago, the University of California, Los Angeles, Yale Law School, and Wharton, and who had been the chief economist for the U.S. Sentencing Commission, was effectively drummed out of academia for his heretical views.

Eventually the National Research Council (NRC) decided to put an end to all this disagreement, and in 2003 pulled together sixteen top experts to evaluate Lott and Mustard's research. Great hope was placed on this group to firmly resolve the debate. Their long-awaited report, which came out in 2004, failed wonderfully in that regard. Fifteen members of the committee concluded that the voluminous back-and-forth was for all intents and purposes useless, since seemingly minor adjustments to the statistical models could completely change results and there was far too much "statistical imprecision" in the analysis[22] to warrant any meaningful policy conclusions, one way or the other. Only the great Harvard criminologist James Q. Wilson dissented from this majority view, arguing that the evidence demonstrates that "RTC laws do in fact help drive down the murder rate," and that even the critics of right-to-carry laws have been at most able to demonstrate an absence of positive impact, rather than being able to show a negative consequence. It wasn't the repudiation of Lott and Mustard that many wanted, but neither was it an endorsement of their views, leaving us in the limbo as to whether more guns mean more crime. Sadly, the intervening years have only brought more academic papers and more debate. The only certainty here in all this is that conservatives will find data to support their preexisting views and liberals will do exactly the same.

All this has contributed to increasingly polarized views on gun issues. Democrats have heard the news about mass killings and concluded that gun ownership in society puts people's safety at risk (59 percent), while 74 percent of Republicans believe that gun ownership does more to protect people from becoming crime victims.[23] These attitudes are influenced of course by access to different media channels, but they reflect a cultural difference as well. With Republicans coming from rural areas in higher proportions and tending to be more comfortable with handling weapons, they understandably are more inclined to view them as effective defensive tools. The fact that both views have plausible justifications makes the situation only more complicated.

And yet, as with so many issues, if you dig down, you will see that despite the differences, there is considerable common ground. Even during the highly polarized 2016 elections, both sides expressed strong support for increasing background checks on gun show and private sales (90 percent for Clinton supporters, 75 percent for Trump supporters); preventing people with mental illnesses from buying guns (roughly 82–83 percent for both groups); and barring gun purchases for people on the no-fly list (80 percent for Clinton supporters, 72 percent for Trump supporters). Opinions begin to diverge when it gets to creating a federal database of gun owners, bans on high-capacity ammo clips, and on assault-style semiautomatic weapons. Don't get me wrong: people on different sides of the partisan divide see guns very differently. Still, even accepting that, there are surprisingly strong areas of agreement.

★   ★   ★

A week before my trip to Texas, I had called Paul, the owner of Independence Ranch, to book my hunt. I carefully explained to him my lack of hunting and shooting experience, and the fact that I would need to rent or borrow a gun.

> **PAUL:** It's $100 to rent the gun, $200 for the day of shooting.
> **KEN:** Okay, but can someone walk me through the use of the gun?
> **PAUL:** If you have $100 to rent the gun, and $200 for the day of shooting, I sure can.
> **KEN:** Sure, no problem.
> **PAUL:** Good, see you then. (click)

It turns out that Paul is short not just on words but on memory as well. When I remind him of our conversation, he is showily annoyed that I lack firearms training. He bangs noisily around, looking for an extra gun, then finally produces a shotgun and tells me to go outside and figure out how to use it. I grumble something about this is the way people end up shooting a foot off, but fortunately another hunter takes pity and shows me how to break open and load the gun. All this is captured on video, which I watch later, amazed at what can only be described as my steely-eyed determination to fuck up each and every step of the process.

Everyone else is clustering into hunting groups, so I ask Paul how I might join one of them. He bestows a contemptuous expression on me and proclaims that I am far too much of a novice to hunt with others. He has a plan: to take me to a single spot in the woods, order me not to move, and let the pigs come to me. It's a terrible plan, certainly not an awesome one, and not what I came to Texas for, but I don't want to start off my trip by arguing with a belligerent, heavily armed man. We clamor into his golf cart and putt-putt slowly into the woods.

Paul finally pulls over next to a wide dirt path. There is nothing notable about this spot, just a small clearing among the trees, but it must pass for a hunting blind, since there is already a folding chair set up next to the path. Paul points me to the chair and gravely instructs me not to wander off, as I might be mistaken for prey. After he pulls away, I plop down in my chair, waiting for the rush of pigs that Paul assures me will soon be coming. Big, angry, dangerous pigs. It is not how I imagined it, hunting from the relative ignominy of a folding chair, but it is my first taste and I am alert for any sign of pigs, ready to swiftly shoulder the gun, sight down the barrel, and bag me a hog or two. In my research for the trip, and my conversations with hunters, I'd repeatedly heard that hog hunting was more than a little dangerous, that if you didn't hit a 150-pound hog just right, a misplaced shot would just turn that mean, hard-running hog into a pig with a vendetta, so there was a little frisson of fear and self-doubt that puckered underneath my anticipation. But as it turns out, frissons have term limits. Thirty minutes of staring at unmoving dirt turns my anticipation into a chilled, bone-deep boredom. What was I thinking? I don't remember, but it was probably something like,

Screw this, I'd rather risk getting shot by Dick Cheney. I wander out into the woods, looking for other hunters.

Fortunately, no one mistakes me for the world's only upright, Day-Glo pig and I soon make new friends. It turns out, once you are liberated from hunting purgatory, Independence Ranch is quite a lovely place for a stroll: the trees are high and thick, a peaceful silence hangs over the place, and except for the occasional and distant sounds of gunfire, it is all terribly tranquil. Spread to my right is C.J., and to my left is his eight-year-old son, Isaac. Somewhere out farther in the woods is C.J.'s father, who is later introduced to me only as "Paps." The three of them have driven fourteen hours from their home in Georgia two days before and will be making the long drive home tonight. We've been walking the woods for at least an hour, and it has had all the drama of a walk from my office to the local sandwich shop, except that trip holds out the promise of some food at the other end. We've seen a few troops of pigs in the distance, running fast and always the wrong way, but not nearly close enough to even contemplate a shot. It doesn't bother C.J. or Isaac, since the day before, in young Isaac's evocative words, they had already "shot the shit out of a bunch of pigs." But I am antsy, concerned that I will go through my day without any real action.

After a while, C.J. goes off to find Paps, leaving me to stalk pigs alone with Isaac. You might think it is a risk, leaving your young son with an armed stranger, but it seems natural amid the comfortable camaraderie of the hunt. In truth, it is Isaac who quickly establishes leadership in our two-man band. When I keep forgetting basic rules of gun safety, like swinging the gun in his direction every time I turn to talk to him, it is little Isaac who gently reminds me to keep the gun pointed toward the ground at all times. Fortunately, he takes a bit of a shine to me, perhaps because he perceives me as just another kid, albeit a rather large, bald, and apparently dim-witted one who has trouble grasping the simplest rules of hunting. We walk together for the balance of the morning, never getting close enough to the pigs to take a shot, but sharing hunting stories as men do, though we are short a man and I have no hunting stories to tell. Isaac does have some nice stories about his hunting trips with his father and grandfather, though they all devolve at some point into shooting the shit out of things. To see a kid like Isaac handle himself in this way is remarkable to see. I love my son, Nate. He is a whiz at math and a walking encyclopedia of baseball history. But I wouldn't trust the kid with a particularly pointy stick, let alone a loaded rifle.

★　★　★

Over the last decade, there has been a stunning rise in the number of people authorized to carry guns. In 2007, only about 4.6 million Americans had concealed-handgun permits, and I say "only" advisedly because 4.6 million is a whole mess of people. But by 2011, the U.S. Government Accountability Office would estimate more than 8 million permits, and by June 2016, the number had skyrocketed to more than 14.5 million. And it is likely that this number is significantly understated, because it doesn't include people from the ten states—plus nearly all of Montana—that authorize concealed carry without any government license at all.

With so many guns in legal circulation, in houses, in cars, in purses, in hidden holsters, you might expect from time to time an occasional misuse of them, a gunfight at the Golden Corral restaurant, perhaps. But it is rarely the case. Gun permit holders turn out to be a rather law-abiding group. The ever-present Lott has analyzed the felony and misdemeanor records of gun permit holders in a few key states where such data is available (Florida and Texas) and concluded that members of the general public are 222 times more likely to be convicted of crimes than permit holders, and even police officers are six times more likely to be convicted of crimes than permit holders. Even if you are inclined, which I am, to discount Lott's findings significantly, it still is a rather impressive record of legal observance.

We plainly have a major gun violence problem in this country, but liberals seem fairly obsessed with condemning lawful gun owners, and can't seem to acknowledge that the evidentiary base for most of their remedies can only be generously described as limited. Go ahead, reenact the Assault Weapons Ban, implement enhanced registration requirements over private sales of guns, and outlaw large-size magazines. Frankly, like most Americans I'm all for it, but I am not deluding myself anymore that these changes will have any meaningful impact on the homicide or suicide rates in this country. Ultimately, these debates are a diversion from more important opportunities to think about how to reduce violence in this country. I once asked John Lott, somewhat in exasperation: if every gun control scheme was destined to fail, then what would work to reduce gun homicides? Without a pause, Lott said, "Legalize drugs."

Last year, the *New York Times* ran a series of articles called the "Daily Toll," a chronicle of the gun problem in America. I am reading one of the articles, "What 130 of the Worst Shootings Say About Guns in America," as I write this.[24] Six months ago, I might have seen what the authors want me to see: a series of horrific, senseless deaths, aided and abetted by lax gun laws. Call it motivated reasoning, call it greater knowledge, call it brainwashing by John Lott, but I read it a bit differently now. I still see the horror of putting guns in the hands of the mentally ill, and hope that the types of increased background checks that most Americans—gun owners and gun opponents alike—still agree on might deter a few terrible crimes. But I also wonder why the authors don't point out (or bury deep in the article) the fact that very few attempts at gun control in the United States have shown any real success: the background check system is marred by millions of false positives, the Assault Weapons Ban is generally agreed not to have worked, and any motivated killer can get his or her hands on a gun in this country. There are two narratives at work here, both with some considerable merit, and both with some terrible flaws. You can find one of those narratives at work in places like the *New York Times*; you can find the other one at work in Chantilly, Virginia.

★   ★   ★

It's a crisp late winter morning when I pull into the parking lot of the Dulles Expo Center in Chantilly. I am by myself for this visit, my friend Kent having declined the trip to the Nation's Gun Show in favor of joining his wife on a garden tour, perhaps in the hopes of digging up his genitals. Even in the parking lot, I feel a bit out of place: my Subaru Liberalmobile barely squeezing in among the rows of pickup trucks, many of them sporting tires that tower over my car. And, sadly, our Subaru lacks a distinctive bumper sticker like "Yes, I am driving this way just to piss you off" or a great license plate like "relodn" or any of the other myriad warning signs that suggest you might not want to get in a road rage duel with this driver.

Gun shows are big business, though no one seems to know quite how big. Estimates range from about 2,000 a year (U.S. Bureau of Alcohol, Tobacco, Firearms and Explosives, still aka the ATF) to more than 5,000 a year (National Association of Arms Shows). The Nation's Gun Show, spread out before me at the Expo Center, brags of 1,300 exhibitors and one and a half miles' worth of display tables. That is known, in Boolean algebra, as a fuckload of guns.

But it's not just guns. The first thing that jumps out at me, beyond the overwhelming scale of it all, is that guns are just one item out of many for sale: knives, swords, bulletproof vests, tear gas, Gatling guns (for those who have $40,000 and a couple of years to go through the licensing process), crossbows, blowguns, holsters, ammo, purses designed for concealed guns, T-shirts, yard signs, and targets shaped like Hillary Clinton, to name just a small portion of the show's inventory. And Pied Piper Pickles, quite delicious. Say what you want about gun nuts, but they know a fine pickle.

And there is the politics. It is pretty clear to me even before I go that the gun show is more than just a movable department store for guns and related merchandise. On the Showmasters (the company that puts on the Nation's Gun Show) website, appearing where we old-timers would call "above the fold" and ahead of such critical details as the dates of upcoming shows, are two telling quotes. One is from Hillary Clinton: "The Supreme Court is wrong on the Second Amendment. And I am going to make that case every chance I get." The other is from Ronald Reagan: "Freedom is never more than one generation away from extinction. We didn't pass it to our children in the bloodstream. It must be fought for, protected, handed on for them to do the same." It is a pretty neat summary of the political orientation of Showmasters, a view that guns are not just about self-protection but a measure to defend liberty against tyranny, in particular government tyranny. That theme runs through the show, but it also runs through American politics. In 2003, during the first term of President George W. Bush, Gallup started polling Americans on the question, "Do you think that the federal government poses an immediate threat to the rights and freedoms of ordinary citizens, or not?" In the first year of the poll, 30 percent of Americans said they believed their own government posed an immediate threat, but by 2015, that number had risen dramatically to 49 percent.[25] It is really an extraordinary thing in a democracy to have fully half the public view their elected government as an occupying power. It is an area in which there is a strong partisan divide. In 2015, 65 percent of all Republicans agreed with the statement, compared to only 32 percent of Democrats. When I first saw the polling, I merely shrugged, thinking that of course Republicans are more skeptical and hostile to central government than Democrats are. But this, as it turns out, is more a measure of polarization than of political philosophy. During the George W. Bush administration, it was Democrats who viewed government as a threat, and the crossover happened immediately upon Obama assuming office. I will bet you a peck of Pied Piper's Pickles that the numbers are changing again right now along with the new administration. Either way, you can't miss the sentiment in Chantilly: guns are an insurance policy against government overreach, a means to protect American freedoms against the threat of a tyrannical government.[26]

The array of guns is staggering, but I am drawn to the peripherals. I stop at a table displaying an array of bulletproof vests, some with Kevlar, some with ceramic plates. A sign announces that Congress, at the behest of Senator Dianne Feinstein of California (featured in a photo with Hillary Clinton), is on the verge of banning private ownership of military-grade body armor, and it urges purchase now. The claim is not even remotely close to true, but the threat seems to be working as multiple customers swarm the table. As I finger the vests, I make small talk with the salesclerk, asking whether business is good or not.

"Really good," she tells me. "People don't know what way the country is going."

"Which way the country is going? What do you mean?"

She gives me a knowing look. "You know, after Baltimore."

It's a consistent theme: Baltimore, Ferguson, and Black Lives Matter are evidence of American entropy, of the country spinning out of control, of it pulling apart. It is not entirely surprising to hear this view at the body armor booth. You don't need body armor for hunting, unless the deer have geared up in some unexpected fashion. You can't even use it for daily self-defense purposes, unless you plan to wear it around the house, or around town as an undergarment. You buy it if you fear the black gangs surging out of the city or the black helicopters landing in your town square.

There is an ugly and angry iconography spread across the Nation's Gun Show. Some of it is pro-gun or pro-Trump, but mostly it is anti: anti-Obama, anti-Democrat, anti-urban, anti-neighbor. I can buy a cutout of Hillary Clinton to use for target practice (I don't), a T-shirt that reads "Hitler, Stalin, Castro, Pol Pot, Idi Amin, and Obama," or a yard sign that says "No Trespassing. I Own Firearms and a Backhoe." The easy camaraderie of the pig hunt has been replaced by the paranoia of the coming revolution.

Some of that attitude has a distinct regional and ethnic flavor. The myth of the Confederacy hangs heavy over the gun show, and I don't think it is because we are just down the road from the place that earned "Stonewall" Jackson his nickname, at the First Battle of Bull Run. There are Confederate flags, of course, and there is also a brisk business in the art of John Paul Strain, whom you might call the Thomas Kinkade of the southern war set. I'm ushered over to a painting of Nathan Bedford Forrest leading a retreat of soldiers from the Confederate debacle at Fort Donelson. Forrest's modern reputation has been cemented by the fact that he was one of the founders and leaders of the Ku Klux Klan, though I am hastily assured by one of the sales staff that he founded the organization to "fight the carpetbaggers and left the KKK within three years when things started to go bad." Given the context, I am somewhat relieved she feels compelled to distance us from the KKK. Many of Strain's paintings reflect themes of dignity and bravery in the face of long odds and certain defeat. It is this story, rather than the more obvious narrative of race and class, that seems to fit in the broader self-image of the gun set: nobility in the face of the overwhelming power of the central government; honor and independence.

This theme of the gun rights movement shows up in lots of different places, from the iconography of the Don't Tread on Me flags that dot gun shows across the country to the positioning of the NRA, whose flagship magazine is titled *America's 1st Freedom*. In 1998, Charlton Heston, at the time the newly named president of the NRA, gave a speech that has since become famous among gun rights activists. "I say that the Second Amendment is, in order of importance, the first amendment. It is America's First Freedom, the one right that protects all the others. . . . Because there is no such thing as a free nation where police and military are allowed the force of arms but individual citizens are not." He labeled the right to bear arms "the right we turn to when all else fails."[27] The thing is, if you judge by Chantilly, enough people are beginning to think that all else is indeed failing, and that, absent Donald Trump, it will soon be every man for himself. It shows up in a lot of places, like the "prepper" movement, where tens of thousands of people are getting ready to bug out when the shit hits the fan. Go to any prepper website and you will find useful advice on the right gun to buy, how to filter rainwater from a barrel, and how to hide your money so that the bankers won't find it (hint: in the walls of your house if you can handle the carpentry, or by geocaching in a remote location if you can handle the technology; otherwise, just bury it in your yard).

47

I was inclined on my first visit to a gun show to be more than a little freaked out by this group, but in truth there is no particular evidence that the people I encountered at the Nation's Gun Show are any more socially unfit than the next group. The people buying guns at gun shows aren't by and large the people committing crimes; many of the attendees (and sellers) are ex-military or ex–law enforcement and have certainly given more for their country than most. They have just come to the conclusion that the country is pulling apart, that their place in the scheme of things is increasingly fragile and uncertain. It worries me for them as much as about them, and makes me a little bit sad for them as well. Except for that guy selling Nazi paraphernalia—Afrika Korps T-shirts, books about the wonders of the Luftwaffe, movies, if you can trust the cover art, featuring busty women sprawled across the top of Panzer tanks. He can kiss my ass.

★　★　★

The funny thing is, the fears of the people wearing Kevlar vests and the gun control alarmists are equally unfounded. Murder rates, and crime overall, have fallen sharply in this country over the last forty years. Homicides peaked in 1980, at a rate of 10.2 per 100,000 people, and starting in the early 1990s, began to drop steadily until 2014, when the number stabilized at less than half of the 1980 rate, at 4.5 per 100,000.[28] It is an incredible change, akin to sparing the lives of roughly 18,000 people per year. Firearms-related killings have increased modestly recently but even that appears to be a temporal oddity in the long, steady decline of violent crimes in the United States.

There are a number of plausible explanations for this decline, but taking guns off the streets is not one of them. Americans own more guns than ever before: as murders and violent crimes declined, the number of privately owned firearms increased, from about 240 million in 1996 to well over 300 million today.[29] The explanations vary for the decline in murders and violent crimes generally. Some are pretty straightforward: better policing, higher incarceration rates, better job opportunities for young people, a decline in drugs and drug-related violence. There are even more exotic theories, including the decline of unwanted babies after *Roe v. Wade* and new federal safety rules that reduced lead exposure in children (and resulting lead-induced violent behavior), though both of these theories, disappointingly enough to those of us who love complex social science arguments, have been largely rejected by the National Academy of Sciences.[30] And of course, the acolytes of John Lott will argue that the decline is not in spite of, but rather due to the proliferation of guns, though as we have already seen, there is not conclusive evidence for that, either.[31]

Whatever the cause of this decline, the American public is blithely unaware of this historic drop. In fact, most Americans believe the exact opposite. In a Pew Research Center poll in 2013, 56 percent of respondents said that homicides had increased since 1990, 26 percent said that they had stayed about the same, and only 12 percent realized that murder rates had dropped over that period.[32] I'm willing to knock Americans for their ignorance on virtually any subject, but here they get a bit of a pass. Modern news is built around "if it bleeds, it leads," and cable news now gives wall-to-wall coverage around even the possibility of an "active shooter." All of this has left the American public with a distinct sense of vulnerability and a belief that murders generally, and mass murders in particular, are a spreading plague of modern times. Some of that is just a ratings grab, but some of it is also agenda driven. Any reader of Breitbart would be forgiven if they thought that illegal immigrants have been on an extended murder rampage (they haven't) or that the Obama years were a period of unprecedented lawlessness (they weren't). And many in the mainstream media have been guilty of flogging the risk to society of assault weapons, and seem to have only discovered the declining murder rate once President Trump began talking of "American carnage."

It is exceptionally easy for me to buy a gun, and it is regrettably easy for a convicted criminal to get one as well on the black market. The one and only group that has a hard time obtaining firearms in this country is the law-abiding poor, especially the urban poor. Since the Supreme Court in 2008 affirmed an individual right to own guns, in the case of *District of Columbia v. Heller*, legislatures and courts have generally widened the rules around ownership and right to carry. However, some jurisdictions, mostly major cities, have pursued a path of technical compliance with *Heller* while still trying to make it as procedurally difficult as possible to obtain a gun. There is, for instance, only one federally licensed seller of guns in all of D.C., and fees for registering a handgun in the city can easily top $150. And in Chicago, if you want to buy a gun, you are required to complete a gun range safety course, which sounds reasonable enough, except that the nearest shooting range is outside the city and it is illegal to transport weapons on public transportation. That requirement hasn't led to a reduction in gun violence in Chicago—quite the contrary—and it is not much of a barrier to getting a gun if you are wealthy enough to own a car, or if you are not overly concerned with legality. But it is a bit of a barrier to those who are neither, meaning that the only people who don't have ready access to guns in the poorest sections of one the most violent cities in the United States are those who actually need them the most.

Gun ownership is increasingly concentrated on men who own multiple weapons, but there is another story, too. Between 2007 and 2015, the number of permits held by women grew by

270 percent, and women now hold more than a quarter of all concealed-carry permits. A whole new industry, albeit a small one, has emerged around women gun owners. At the Nation's Gun Show in Chantilly, I was encouraged at one kiosk to buy Beth a purple handbag with a special internal holster for a concealed pistol. I toyed with the idea for a moment, but I toy with a lot of different ways to annoy Beth, and ultimately decided against it. Even if you are hostile to guns, however, and even if you are not in the market to buy a concealed carry purse from Gun Goddess online, you might still agree with me that it is probably a net positive to break a male monopoly on guns and spread ownership to those in society most at risk of victimization.[33]

★ ★ ★

In the afternoon, with Paps, C.J., and Isaac starting their long drive back home, I join the group of uniform salesmen from Houston. If my morning hunt was a nice fulfilment of demographic stereotypes—me and three crackers from Georgia—the afternoon is the equivalent of a demographic bar joke: a black man, a Hispanic, a Croatian immigrant, and a Jew from Washington, D.C., head out on a pig hunt. Despite our superficial differences, there is an easy amiability among us as we walk the hunting trails, but it is still not the hunting experience I had imagined. Unlike the morning, we have multiple shooting opportunities. But for several hours, I never get off a shot, because they are much quicker with their rifles, often downing a pig or two before I finish fumbling with the safety switch. But they want me to get my trophy, too, and Joe's warning to me is the invitation to finally take my shot. Half a mile down the road, I finally catch up with Mack, now kneeling over a dead, 120-pound hog. I don't have any real evidence that this was the same pig I had fired at minutes before, but everyone—including me—wants me to share in the day's bounty. I suspend disbelief, accept credit for the kill, and exchange earnest handshakes with my hunting mates. It feels good, not because I care for the trophy, but because I have shared the experience with my hunting buddies. Isaac would have been proud of me, and I can luxuriate for a bit in the awesomeness of the hunt.

2

THE PARTY OF GOD

Every day people are straying away from the church and going
back to God.

—LENNY BRUCE

M y seat is high in the rafters of the Edward Jones Dome,
affording me a bird's-eye view of the thousands of people
cheering and dancing below. The arena was formerly the
home of the St. Louis Rams, once known as the "Greatest Show on Turf," but today the big stage is occupied by a very
different show, this one featuring Michelle Higgins, a preacher
from Ferguson, Missouri. And quite the show it is: for twenty-
five sweaty minutes, Higgins preaches, sings, and lectures about
the challenges of race in America, all while a backup cast of four
women, clad in Black Lives Matter T-shirts, sing and dance along
with her. It's an accusatory presentation, focusing on the failure
of society to grapple with the plight of young African Americans,
and it is hard for me to follow, with all the ellipses connecting the
singing, dancing, and lecturing parts, but logical flow is somewhat beside the point here. This show is about passion, commitment, and purpose, and that spills all over the thousands of young
people arrayed before the stage. And they are eating it up.

This could have been, but wasn't, a Bernie Sanders rally or a

Netroots Nation convention, assuming that liberal bloggers would look up from their screens long enough to take in a performance like this. Rather it was a Christmas break gathering known as Urbana, a triennial conclave of about 15,000 college-age evangelicals. It is not where I would typically be this time of year, or any time of year for that matter. I have successfully dodged organized religion for much of my life. I did go to Hebrew school when I was young, barely skating through Mr. Rip's class on a thin sheet of insolence and apathy but, aside from births, marriages, deaths, and tourism, I have rarely been inside a church or a synagogue for almost forty years. And if I wanted a cold start in religion, I wouldn't have picked evangelicals, since according to *Footloose* and other important sociological studies that I have relied on for my sense of the evangelical community, they are all narrow-minded, intolerant, and out of step with the modern world.

If I am to be honest, it is mostly the excruciating boredom of religious services that has kept me away. I have, on rare occasion, accompanied my in-laws to Catholic services at St. Anastasia (which I try to get Nate to call St. Anesthesia, but it hasn't taken yet), and the creaky, slow-moving service drives me crazy. I always end up trying to quietly amuse myself with my phone, but never quietly enough to avoid nasty glances and that pursed-lips look from Beth. I don't get a lot of return invitations.

But if you are going to try to understand Republicans in America, churches, especially evangelical churches, are a good place to start. There are a lot of evangelicals in America—Pew conservatively estimates that 25.4 percent[1] of the population, or 81 million Americans, are evangelicals—and, at least for the white majority, they almost always vote Republican. White evangelicals went 79 percent for Romney in 2012,[2] and despite speculation on whether evangelicals would rally behind a crude, thrice-married candidate, voted similarly for Trump in 2016.

In early 2016, Charles Murray, the conservative political scientist, constructed a quiz for PBS titled "Do You Live in a Bubble?" The quiz, based upon Murray's book *Coming Apart*, reflects his view that there is a new upper class entirely disconnected from the experiences of the average white American and the broader American culture. Predictably, the Internet exploded over Murray's quiz—whether it was adequately scientific (it's not) and whether there is such a thing anymore as the "average white American" (there's not)—but Murray's underlying point was nonetheless valid. We as a society are increasingly divided by geography, media, association, income, religion, and culture and, even in an era of both lightning-fast information and rapid transit, seem to know less and less about each other—and seem increasingly disinclined to learn more.

If you define living inside the bubble as doing poorly on the test, I came closer to the bottom than I would care to admit, and would have done worse if my television viewing habits hadn't always been a bit mass market (oh, *Big Bang Theory*, I do love you). The questions cover a range of topics, such as have you ever bought any Avon products (no), have you ever bought domestic beer to stock your own fridge (yes, of course), have you in the last month voluntarily hung out with someone smoking cigarettes (hell no), and did you win a high school varsity letter for something other than chess club or debate team (you can get a varsity letter for chess club? I was ripped off). There are many at least superficially trivial questions like these, but one of the most important questions is, "Have you ever had a close friend who was an evangelical Christian?" It's rather an extraordinary question, since evangelicals account for so much of the American population and, even recognizing significant regional biases, it would seem, just on the numbers, difficult to go through life without befriending an evangelical even if you tried really hard.[3] I got a check mark on the question from at least one boyhood friend, but admittedly my interactions with American evangelicalism have been brief and superficial. I'm betting a lot of people I know don't even get that close.

Finding common ground with Republicans means understanding evangelicals, and that is why I find myself talking with John Inazu, a gentle, scholarly professor of law at Washington University in St. Louis. Inazu occupies an unusual perch, one that straddles both the secular world and the evangelical community. As a prominent evangelical, he has a front-row seat on the tensions inside the evangelical community, as evangelicals try to grapple at different speeds with the rapid-fire changes in American culture and values. He tells me that older evangelicals especially struggle with shifting mores, and often lack the explicit vocabulary to even communicate on difficult social evolutions. And their uncertain footing on rapid changes often leads them to react in fearful and harsh ways. As he tells me this, Inazu is in fact driving through flat America, from Indiana to his home in St. Louis, and he exclaims as he passes a billboard that reads "If God is worshipped again, God will protect America." We laugh together, a little uncertainly, about the nuttiness of all this, but he quickly adds that younger evangelicals are rather different, still religious, still culturally conservative, but more comfortable with gay and transgender rights and the multicultural face of the new America.

Misunderstanding, though, runs in both directions. As a professor at Washington University, Inazu has one foot planted firmly in the secular world, though that foot gets frequently trod upon as he faces almost comic ignorance of many of his colleagues on the evangelical community. He tells of working with a fellow faculty member for several months on a project and afterward having her comment to him with genuine puzzlement, "I don't get you. You are a religious person and yet you care about poor people," a statement made without any recognition that in the United States it is more often than not religious people and religious organizations that are running the soup kitchens and homeless shelters and refugee resettlement programs, not law professors at fashionable universities with endowments approaching $7 billion.

Inazu is painfully aware of the insularity of portions of the evangelical community, and their clashes with modernity, but it is more than matched, in his experience, by a rising intolerance and outright ignorance of liberal elites toward religious communities. Inazu tells me that if I am going to write about American evangelicals, I am going to have to meet them in their churches and communities, not just rely on the good word of Kevin Bacon and John Lithgow. It makes sense, and that is why I find myself just weeks later swaying along with thousands of evangelical youth at one of the most unusual concerts of my life.

If I don't know what to expect at Urbana, I certainly knew some things not to expect—starting with the sex, drugs, liquor, and other liberties that thousands of unsupervised college students might typically exercise. They may be young, and have tattoos, and can tell the differences—unlike me—among Machine Gun Kelly, gnash, and Drake, but it is still a conservative group; if you poll them informally, as I did, on abortion and the proper distribution of authority to solve social issues between government and church, you will get typically conservative answers. But that's what I wanted to talk about. What they wanted to talk about were the social issues of concern to their generation: Black Lives Matter, which dominated the conversation, even though very few of them were black (though an extraordinarily large number of attendees were of Asian descent); issues of social justice and economic inequality; and the refugee problem—not how to build a wall, but how to extend a helping hand to those displaced by the bitter wars in the Middle East, Africa, and elsewhere. Surely somewhere in Urbana people were having a conversation about how to block access to the local abortion clinic, or lamenting moral decline in America, or some such typical conservative conference banality, but it sure wasn't obvious to me or to the people who put together the conference agenda.

All the social issues were secondary, however, to the subject of mission, how to spread the "good news" of Jesus. Bringing more people to Christ is what gives evangelicalism its name, so there will always be tensions around appropriate forms of outreach, but in fact most spreading of the good news focuses on demonstrating the love of Jesus by doing what he commanded: helping the poor, the infirm, the powerless, and the people who live in the shadows. The work of most missions takes place not in acts of religious conversion but through helping the sick in hospitals, by feeding the poor, sheltering the homeless, by teaching farming and animal husbandry in and by helping bring clean water to remote villages. Meeting thousands of kids who want to do such things makes me feel a bit ashamed of my preconceived notions of evangelicals.

The heroes of Urbana were not Ted Cruz, or Ralph Reed, or even James Dobson. Rather, it was people like Glenn Chapman, who leads no political movement and has no particular political agenda. Chapman and his wife, Rita, run what is grandly called the Baptist University in Congo (UNIBAC), which turns out to be a one-room schoolhouse offering pastoral training, agricultural skills, and teacher training. Kikongo itself is a small, amazingly isolated rural town some two hundred miles from the capital, Brazzaville, and it is where the Chapmans have made their home for the last thirty years. To read Chapman's online journal is to get a window into a world most of us can hardly believe still exists, and a place where most Americans would struggle to last thirty hours, never mind thirty years. I didn't meet Chapman at Urbana, but instead met another member of American Baptist International Ministries. He wasn't interested in telling me about the peculiarities of life in the Congo, but instead wanted to show me a video highlighting how the Chapmans bring education, training, and a little bit of entertainment from village to village. The transportation system in western Congo is at best limited and at worst nonexistent. The nearest airport to Kikongo lies 110 miles to the northwest, in Kalemie, and many villages can be typically reached only by lengthy and difficult journey by foot or by boat. I suppose Chapman does some of both, but his preferred means of conveyance is a small "powered parachute." A powered parachute, for those of you who are neither aviation fans nor have a death wish, looks like pieces of a playground jungle gym bent into the shape of an egg just big enough to hold one or maybe two people. The egg sits on three wheels and has a small engine sufficient to drive forward fast enough to inflate a parachute, somehow lift off from the earth, and thereafter glide forward at speeds of 20 to 25 miles per hour. If you ask me, the whole contraption looks like a very bad idea, especially if you are flying over dense, uninhabited jungle, but if you ask the people of these tiny, isolated western Congo villages, it must no doubt seem like a miracle to see Chapman slowly descend out of the sky in his motorized steel egg.[4] Every time Chapman flies his parachute, in my mind, it is a smacking rebuke to Inazu's colleague at Washington University School of Law who was puzzled by the good intentions of religious people.

Don't get me wrong. The bubble works both ways, and it's clear to me that not all evangelicals have the cultural tools necessary to connect with a middle-aged, liberal, secular Jew. As I walk through the exhibit hall, I spy the booth of the Chosen People Ministries, team motto: "bringing the message to the original messengers." Zero chance that I would pass this by. As the name suggests, Chosen People Ministries, which has been around for well over a century, is a conversion ministry aimed at the Jewish people. It can't be an easy job—I've never converted anyone in my family on anything—but at least they have a strategy: the nice young lady at the table tells me her approach is "to get them talking. Jews like to talk a lot." Later, in thumbing through the organizational handbook, I discover that her use of the term *Jew* violates language guidance. "The term *Jew* is often said in a derogatory fashion by a non-Jewish person; for example, 'He tried to Jew me down.'" Color me delighted at the cultural sensitivity. It's a reminder to me that evangelicalism feels a little different when you are on the other end of the Jesus pitch. I'm doubtful that all the young people gathered in Urbana, eager as they are to share the good news, will understand that feeling.

★   ★   ★

Over the last year, my perception of the evangelical community has changed rather dramatically. I'm not the only person who has had such a conversion experience, if I can appropriate that term, which is why I find myself sitting across a desk from Sam Adams. That desk is in a small office of the World Resources Institute, where Adams runs a U.S. climate initiative program. He is pleasant and welcoming, but with a hint of reserve, and nothing in his office reveals the fact that he is something of an historic figure in American politics, the first openly gay mayor of a major U.S. city, Portland, Oregon. Adams has more reason than most to be skeptical, even antagonistic, to the evangelical community. Growing up gay in a family of "tough Montanans," he stayed in the closet because in his family and community "there's a premium on being tough and strong, and being a queer and a faggot wasn't strong." Over the years, he tells me, his views of evangelicals were often shaped by stories he heard about the evangelical community, in particular the outsize attention paid by the press to the tiny but horribly hate-filled congregation of Westboro Baptist Church.[5] But it was also informed by more substantial, direct observation.

Because of Portland and Eugene, home of the University of Oregon, we tend to associate Oregon with cultural progressivism, but the state is far more politically diverse, with many deeply conservative areas lying to the east of the Cascades. Not so many years ago, the state was a test bed for the use of the ballot initiative process to suppress gay rights. In 1988, the Oregon Citizens Alliance (OCA), a conservative Christian political action group founded by a former evangelical missionary, successfully introduced Ballot Measure 8, a rollback of the governor's executive order banning discrimination based upon sexual orientation in state government. Even though Measure 8 was ultimately ruled unconstitutional by the Oregon Court of Appeals, its electoral success encouraged the OCA to ramp up its attack on gay rights. In 1992 the group sponsored Measure 9, an extraordinary and wide-ranging assault on the gay community. Measure 9 was chillingly titled "Government Cannot Facilitate, Must Discourage Homosexuality, Other Behaviors," and would have eliminated all civil rights protections for gay and lesbians; it would have further required Oregon schools to "assist in setting a standard for Oregon's youth that recognizes homosexuality, pedophilia, sadism and masochism as abnormal, wrong, unnatural, and perverse and that these behaviors are to be discouraged and avoided."[6] I suppose, if you want to look on the bright side, that it is a signal of how far we've come in a relatively short period of time. Still, it's also a bitter reminder of the dangerous animus that still exists in some corners of the conservative world.[7]

Despite the shocking harshness of Measure 9, the OCA, based on its recent successes, had some expectation of victory, and the landslide defeat of Measure 9 was a turning point in Oregon's relationship with the gay community. Suffice it to say that Adams, who worked in politics through Measure 9 and the OCA's subsequent and ultimately futile efforts to implement similar initiatives on a county level, had plenty of reasons to be hostile toward the evangelical community, so it should be a bit of a stunner when Adams peers across his desk at me and says, "I was the victim of misperceptions" about the evangelical community, and "my views now of evangelicals are shaped by how much we agree."

It's not really a surprise to me, in truth, because I have come to talk to him about his relationship with Kevin Palau, a prominent Oregon evangelical leader. Palau, along with his father, Luis, leads a large Portland church group, a notable distinction in and of itself, since Portland revels in its reputation as the most "unchurched" city in America. But the writ of the Palaus runs much farther than Portland. Luis Palau has for decades led one of the most influential ministries in Latin America, hosting a daily Spanish radio show carried by 880 stations in twenty-five countries. The senior Palau is still known as the Billy Graham of Latin America, though, unlike Graham, he has a reputation for avoiding politics and divisive social issues.

Shortly after winning election as mayor, Adams was startled to receive a phone call from Kevin Palau asking for a meeting. There wasn't an obvious cause for the meeting between an openly gay mayor and an evangelical religious leader who did much of his work outside the city. Adams agreed to the meeting assuming that it was a courtesy call in connection with an upcoming Christian festival that the Palaus would be holding in Portland.

Adams was partially right: it was about the festival. But it was not purely a courtesy call. Palau had an idea. He wanted to create a new "day of service" and he wanted Adam's input on the best way to make a difference in Portland. Adams pondered the question and then offered the suggestion that the Palaus could focus their efforts on two local schools—Jefferson and Roosevelt—that were badly in need of some attention. But Adams also expressed a concern: knowing that a core belief of evangelicals is the personal obligation to spread the good news, as I myself discovered years later at Urbana, he told Kevin Palau that he would sanction the activity only if the Palaus agreed not to use this day of public service to proselytize in any shape or form. Kevin Palau hastily assured him that this was not the purpose and offered his cell phone number, to be shared with school officials in case problems were encountered.

Adams, as he told me that day in the World Resources Institute, remembered the conversation as pleasant but one that he gave little thought to afterward. To the extent that he had any expectations at all, they were that a small number of people would show up, put in an hour or two, and then leave, perhaps all the while congratulating themselves on their public-spiritedness. But when the day came, Adams started getting phone calls from school officials at both Roosevelt and Jefferson, letting him know that something rather unexpected was happening, that the turnout was much larger and the effort more intensive than anyone had expected.

Late in the day, Adams decided to see for himself, and he drove out to Roosevelt, a high school that serves a low-income, hard-pressed neighborhood in North Portland. Portland, when you get right down to it, is a pretty small city, so Roosevelt is not too far length-wise from the hipster coffee bars and artists galleries that have made the city such a magnet, but economically and spiritually, they are on different planets. It was a school and a neighborhood, as Adams had indicated to Palau, that was badly in need of a makeover.

When Adams showed up at Roosevelt, he was astonished

to find not just a handful of people, but busloads of volunteers pulled from one hundred churches around the area, standing on ladders, chipping at paint, pulling up weeds from underneath the dilapidated football stands. They had been doing this since the early hours of the morning. And Adams realized that none of these people had any connection with Roosevelt: they weren't from the neighborhood, their kids didn't go to Roosevelt, and the odds that they knew anyone from the immediate community were remote at best. But there they were with the Palaus, working away until the dwindling light made further effort impossible. Adams was not just impressed, he was intrigued. As an incoming mayor, he knew he had a problem, one not unique to Portland, but still keenly felt: rising demands for city services, static or even dwindling resources, and a need for innovative solutions to solve that bad math.

Several weeks later, reunited onstage with Kevin Palau, Adams made an impromptu challenge to the Palaus and to the audience of evangelicals gathered at the festival: don't rest on a single day of service. Turn it, at the least, into an annual affair, one that would at least build some continuing connection with the city and the community. As it turns out, the offer was a welcome one for Kevin Palau, as he had been looking for new ways to energize and engage his own community. Highly religious Americans are substantially more likely to volunteer than less religious people, almost twice as much on a weekly basis,[8] and the ethic of service is deeply engrained in the evangelical culture. Nonetheless, Palau had a problem: the evangelical community had become "known for what we were against, not what we were for." It was a problem that a relatively small number of evangelicals, like those who had started the OCA, had created, but it lay heavy on Palau in secular, skeptical Portland. Palau knew that if he could not create a new partnership with the public, could not showcase the real core values of his community, then he could never build the trust that is the condition precedent to spreading the gospel. Put another way, no one would want to hear from evangelicals if they were simply known as the people who hated gays.

With that in mind, in the summer of 2008, Palau set out to answer Adams's call and mobilize more than 15,000 evangelical parishioners from around the area, and to create hundreds of partnerships across churches, schools, governmental organizations, and nonprofits. It was no small feat, requiring unity of purpose from what ultimately became four hundred independent churches, and overcoming the suspicions of secular organizations. As Palau told me, the number one concern he heard was to make sure that all this was not merely a pretense for proselytizing. Over and over again, Palau would reassure people that the evangelicals would not evangelize. He appointed himself a one-man firehouse, ready to respond if glass, or in this case people's sensibilities, were ever broken. Fortunately for Palau, in eight years of giving out his cell phone number, his phone has never rung with a single complaint, making him the Maytag repairman of church services.

Palau began that summer focusing on programs that he knew well: hunger, homelessness, health care, and education. Roosevelt High School was to be a particular focus. It was a school built for 1,600 students, but attendance had dropped all the way to 450, because anyone who could get their kids out of Roosevelt did so as fast as possible. Roosevelt could not even field a football team, not because of lack of student interest, but because the stands were falling down and the school lacked funding to rehabilitate its facilities. Palau worked out a relationship between Roosevelt and Southlake Church, an evangelical megachurch located twenty miles away in the prosperous suburb of West Linn. That relationship began tentatively, with another day of service, but quickly blossomed beyond that. Neil Lomax, a parishioner at Southlake and a former NFL quarterback, arranged for funding from Nike to rehabilitate the field and restart the football program—a program that he eventually joined as the team's offensive coordinator. The outreach coordinator from Southlake began to assist with a variety of social service programs, so much so that she became almost a daily presence on the Roosevelt campus. Eventually the school's principal, having overcome initial reservations, suggested that the church open an office in the school, an acknowledgment of what had become a de facto permanent presence. Southlake readily agreed, and now funds two full-time positions at Roosevelt, running the food pantry, clothing closet, and Head Start program.

Roosevelt today is still a challenged school in a challenged neighborhood. Test scores and graduation rates are still chronically and depressingly low, but the school as an institution is growing and thriving in ways that would have seemed unthinkable in 2009. Let's not overstate the role of Southlake in that equation. There have been plenty of other factors at work as well: in 2010, the Obama administration made a $7.7 million grant to Roosevelt as part of an effort to turn around Oregon schools, with the funding going to new computers, extra counselors to help guide students on the path to college, and a parent-involvement specialist, to give a partial list. And the city of Portland itself has made substantial investments in rebuilding the school, completely refurbishing the physical plant and spending $5 million on a new "makerspace," as well as separate investments in new science, technology, engineering, and math (STEM) classrooms. But at the same time let's not underestimate the impact of the Southlake relationship: a new sense of purpose, a lot of extra hands to help a school administration overwhelmed by daily challenges, and the realization that people beyond the four walls of the school care. It all matters.

If this were a movie, we'd all know how the football story would play out. We'd see the first inept practice—out-of-shape players, botched plays, exasperated coaches—and wonder whether this could all possibly work. The team would struggle badly at first, but, overcoming adversity, ultimately rise to victory, bringing pride and honor to a beleaguered community. Portland is not Hollywood, though it has more than a few things in common, including now the story of Roosevelt High, because that is exactly what happened. After going 0-9 in 2009, the team became a perennial contender, even winning the Portland Interscholastic League title in 2013, beating its cross-town rival Jefferson to win its first title in eighteen years and only its second championship since 1951. A football game is of course just that, a game, but nothing better symbolized the turnaround at Roosevelt, from an institution in free fall, slated to be closed, to a school now on the rise once again.

The effort begun by Palau and Adams, now known as City Serve, has expanded significantly. From 100 churches, the program has grown to 400; from 15,000 people, it has expanded to 28,000 regular volunteers. In recent years Palau has opened up governmental partnerships in foster care and in combating juvenile sex trafficking. Each time, rather than launching new, separate, and uncoordinated initiatives, the churches have chosen to support existing efforts, providing more manpower and support to often badly overstretched agencies. Foster care, an area where evangelicals have traditionally played an outsize role, is a prime example. In addition to continuing the practice of serving as foster care families, church volunteers now work in a variety of foster care agency offices, providing physical and moral support to the employees who chronically feel overloaded and underappreciated. As with the schools, this all has quickly moved from a series of ad hoc projects to permanent, though still volunteer, presences inside foster care agency offices.

Adams is long gone from public office but he and Palau remain the odd couple of this enterprise: Adams a liberal Democrat, Palau a conservative Republican; one strongly for gay rights and pro-choice, the other staunchly pro-life and socially conservative. But that has not kept them from finding common cause. Adams has learned of the fallacies that have pitted us against each other: "If we disagree, we must hate each other. If the media portrays us, certain aspects of us or certain individuals hating each other, then that must be true for everybody. . . . There are things we don't agree on as a liberal Democrat and as an evangelical leader. . . . We can agree to disagree on gay marriage and disagree on abortion but we probably agree on eight out of ten things that are important to society. . . . So we can act together genuinely in our communities on those eight of ten and break out of the trap that has been built around us." Adams and Palau, and the city of Portland, are better for that. When Adams ran into personal controversy as mayor, he turned first to the Palaus for support and knowledge, because he has learned that the humanity and common purpose that unite us are stronger than the politics that occasionally divide us.

★ ★ ★

When you live in a bubble, it is easy to think poorly of evangelicals. My experiences at Urbana and with Kevin Palau and Sam Adams have encouraged me to think rather differently about evangelicals, as more than those intolerant people who hate gays.

Events like Urbana, which bring together thousands of people from around the world, don't happen without a strong organizational backbone. In the case of Urbana, that comes from a campus Christian fellowship group called InterVarsity. Before Urbana, I had never heard of InterVarsity, even though it has a long and distinguished history. It was founded in 1941 in the United States but its roots trace back to a gathering at Cambridge University in 1877. The organization boasts of more than 1,100 chapters on college campuses around the country and countless affiliations overseas. Its modest public profile comes from the modest nature of its work: Bible studies, student-led worship, occasional presentations on topics of spiritual interest, and missions. It is a private organization helping students do decidedly private things.

We all know that our public space has become a competition for attention, a race to see who can say the loudest and most obnoxious things. People have figured out that outrage, disparagement, and insults all work. We are angry all the time. So it was not all that surprising for me to learn at Urbana that even a private group like InterVarsity, which takes no political positions, has become the source of substantial institutional attacks, at places like Vanderbilt and the University of Michigan, among others. In 2014 the InterVarsity group was kicked off campus at Vanderbilt, because it would not comply with a new nondiscrimination policy, one designed, in the words of the administration, to ensure that there are no second-class citizens at the school. It's hard to dispute such a lofty goal, until you realize that the school requires student organizations to admit everyone, regardless of their suitability to the organization. That means the black student association has to admit white students, the College Democrats would have to welcome Donald Trump supporters, even women's rape support groups would be required to admit men. The principal groups exempted from the policy are fraternities and sororities, which says more about the pecking order at Vanderbilt than anything else.[9]

InterVarsity ran afoul of this all-comers policy not because it wasn't willing to admit everyone into their fellowship—it was—but because it insisted that the leadership of each chapter adhere to the doctrinal teaching of the group. It doesn't seem much of a stretch to say that if you want to lead a Bible study organization, you might want to believe in the Bible. That Bible of course covers a vast range of ideas and principles, many treated as heretical and offensive at different times in history, but at Vanderbilt and elsewhere, universities have seemingly reduced the entire evangelical worldview to one important, but doctrinally peripheral, belief: that sexual congress be limited to the confines of heterosexual marriage. As it turns out, though the rules at Vanderbilt and elsewhere were articulated in neutral terms, it appeared to many to intentionally punish InterVarsity for its conservative views on homosexuality. As the leader of the Vanderbilt chapter then wrote in *Christianity Today*:

> If religious groups required set truths or limited sexual autonomy, they were bad—not just wrong but evil, narrow-minded, and too dangerous to be tolerated on campus. It didn't matter to them if we were racially or politically diverse, if we cared about the environment or built Habitat homes. It didn't matter if our students were top in their fields and some of the kindest, most thoughtful, most compassionate leaders on campus. There was a line in the sand, and we fell on the wrong side of it.[10]

I still disagree entirely with the evangelical view on sexual congress (though I always get a bit of a thrill from writing out "sexual congress"), but I have even less sympathy, if that is possible, for an educational institution like Vanderbilt, which appears so eager to define evangelicals by that single issue, regardless of their other contributions to the community and whatever the other values of the organization. Mother Teresa (who was pedestrian in her adherence to Catholic doctrine and extraordinary in her love for all) could have shown up at Vanderbilt and been barred from a formal presentation, despite a lifetime of apparently miraculous service, because she held views on abortion and gay marriage contrary to the norm on campus. The actions of Vanderbilt reflect not only intolerance of competing views—a wholly dislikable attribute for an educational institution—but also a foolish impulse to define some 80 million Americans in a single way.

I wish that I could say that I have been immune from these same tendencies, but I can't. I scored better on the Charles Murray test because my high school friend Tom Goering was an evangelical. We went to school together in McLean, Virginia, a tony suburb of Washington, D.C. As is the way of most sixteen-year-old boys, my friends and I ridiculed each other incessantly for one thing or another. As for Tom, his failing, according to the norms of our group, was his participation in a "cult," the oh-so-clever formulation we retreated to incessantly. It's not that Tom was above the fray—he was as nasty as any of us—but I know it must have hurt. It was supposed to. Deep into writing this book, I hunted down Tom, whom I hadn't spoken to in twenty-five years, and he paused a bit when I asked him what it felt like to be the odd religious one in the group: "The thing I remember most is that I had [our mutual friend] Greg on a prayer list, because that is what I was taught to do, to pray for our friends, not to convert them but out of love for them. But Greg saw the list, and got really angry about it, and I remember being hurt and confused." It is a tiny refutation of my theory that if you know someone from the other side, you won't hate as much, but maybe there is a different rule for sixteen-year-old boys.

From one angle, you might consider Tom's life safely evangelical: a stop at Wheaton College, a career spent almost entirely at A. C. Nielsen doing project management, deep involvement in his church and its mission work, and fairly predictable conservative views on social issues. But if you dig just a little deeper, it looks a little different. One daughter struggled to reconcile her same-sex attraction with her own deep conservative religious convictions and finally heard God say, "Stop asking my opinion on that one topic. I am bigger than that." Tom never thought of himself as a Bible thumper on these questions but had to struggle with his own innate conservatism on these issues. His better angels won, and he sent me a copy of her blog post detailing her struggle, with the simple notation "Proud of my kid." His other daughter is a social worker serving the homeless; his wife works to help Muslim immigrants assimilate into their community. A lot to be proud of, cult or no cult.

★   ★   ★

It's a sweaty, late summer day, the hot corona of the sun clipping the edges of the buildings at Liberty University. It is a pretty campus and the sun gives it a certain celestial glow, or at least the school administration would like you to think of it in that way.

Liberty was founded by Jerry Falwell Sr., the man who a good quarter century after his heyday still defines for many the very notion of evangelical intolerance and spite in America. I was officially there to meet the current president of Liberty, Jerry Falwell Jr., but unofficially it was to be a highlight of my "Places I Am Pretty Sure I Should Hate Tour." By now, having been to Urbana, met with Palau and Adams, and spent time in numerous evangelical churches, I was a little more tentative in my dislike for Liberty and was intrigued when John Inazu described it to me as "surprisingly nuanced," a phrase I would not ordinarily associate with the Falwells.

Liberty has the reputation of being "Bible Boot Camp," but I quickly discover that much of the campus has been stripped of obvious religious orientation. The principal shrine on campus is not Thomas Road Church, where Jerry Sr. cut his pastoral teeth and where his other son, Kevin Falwell, now preaches, but the massive football and baseball complex that towers over campus. There is a different accent at the school than in the past. When Jerry Sr. was president of the university, his office was a jumble of religious and political iconography, a testament to the intertwined threads of his life. I, on the other hand, meet with Junior in a whitewashed postmodern office suite that is notable only for its lack of personality. Only the sign over the door, EXECUTIVE OFFICES, hints even blandly at the purpose of the place. It is not an accident. The school has grown in recent decades not because of evangelical passion but because it has become an online powerhouse, supporting some 60,000 distant students, in decidedly nonreligious topics such as psychology and sports management.

Jerry Jr. himself is a study in how far the apple can roll from the tree: while his father was brash and bold, a larger-than-life figure who reveled in boisterous and sometimes even violent pranks, Junior is careful and a little dull, as befits a lawyer trained at the University of Virginia. Jerry Sr. was notorious for his animosity toward the gay community, once referring to it as a "vile and satanic system," and for his eagerness to purge the idea of acceptance of gays from public life, so I am more than a little curious to gauge the attitudes of his namesake. But he just shrugs and says that there is "no question we have lots of gay students," as if it were the most natural thing in the world. Students, according to Falwell, are more interested in talking about Second Amendment issues and abortion and national defense, and they accept homosexuality as just part of the world. And it's clear right away that Falwell himself is not all that interested in the topic. He is not a moral leader, but rather an institution builder. The pace of our conversation quickens when we start talking about the school's $1.8 billion endowment ("it took Harvard 350 years to get that far, we did it in forty") and the rapid growth of the school's online enrollment. Liberty is now less of an evangelical school than a major university with an evangelical orientation. It is no accident that the one decoration in the otherwise featureless conference room is a congratulatory letter from Father Theodore Hesburgh, the longtime president of the University of Notre Dame, because Falwell sees Notre Dame and Brigham Young University as his inspiration, schools that have reached beyond their narrow religious roots to become major educational institutions.

Doctrinally, Liberty has not changed much over the last decade: curfews have been relaxed and skirts shortened, but the core strictures of social conservatism remain unaltered. But attitudinally, the place, like other corners of the evangelical world, has changed substantially in a few short years. It is not only the accepted presence of gay students but the fact that students at Liberty are questioning authority in ways that are far more similar to mainline schools than to the hierarchy of devotional schools. In the immediate month following my visit, students erupted against Jerry Jr. first for his support of the Trump presidential bid and then for his hiring of a new athletic director who had been implicated in the Baylor sexual assault scandal. Watching from afar, it was rather clear that while Jerry Jr. relished the transitions at Liberty, he was enjoying far less the diminishment of pastoral authority. Don't get me wrong, no one would confuse Liberty with Oberlin, but the character of the school, and evangelicalism, is different than it was just a handful of years ago.[11]

But while the modern reputation of evangelicals remains largely fixed from the Jerry Sr. days, the views and activities of the evangelical movement is undergoing a slow renovation. That change, slow but steady, is captured in leadership changes within the movement. James Dobson forged a reputation at Focus on the Family for outspoken criticism of what he described as the homosexual agenda, which in his understanding included support for special privileges for gays, overturning laws against pedophilia, and the indoctrination of children through public education. Dobson made Focus on the Family a key institutional player in the evangelical movement, and Jim Daly, his successor at the organization, holds many of the same doctrinal views as Dobson. But he shares none of the rough edges and obsessions that Dobson and his generation had. When I talk with him, he says that his predecessors treated homosexuality as some type of "super sin" and erred in their obsession with the issue. He speaks with pride of his partnership with Denver gay activist Ted Trimpa on sex-trafficking legislation and tells me that his priority is solving real social problems, pointing to the two apartment blocks that New Life Church, Daly's home church in Colorado Springs, have recently bought for single mothers. It is, in Daly's view, a switch from telling to doing, from lecturing people on God's edicts to demonstrating God's love through good works.

Priorities and attitudes matter enormously, which is why Daly reads differently than Dobson, but their interpretation of scripture that homosexuality is a sin is probably pretty much in alignment. That remains the prevailing view in the evangelical community, but even that view is beginning to show cracks. As American views have shifted generally on the topic, a number of prominent evangelicals have begun to shift their stance as well. Within the last year, three large evangelical megachurches—EastLake Community Church in Seattle, GracePointe Church in Nashville, and City Church in San Francisco—have come out with policies supporting full inclusion and affirmation of LGBT people.

The congregation at Wilshire Baptist Church in Dallas voted 577 to 367 to welcome gays as full participants in the church after its pastor declared his "judgment . . . that God is doing something beautiful here. I'm going to err on the side of love and grace."[12]

Gay evangelical groups have sprung up to push for greater acceptance of gay rights and gay families, and even institutions like
Liberty University, created to hold the line against modern values,
have become, if not quite models of modern tolerance, accepting
of gay students.

Change has come quickly at places like Liberty. A decade ago,
Kevin Roose, a Brown University student and author who spent a
semester undercover at Liberty, could write favorably of the general tolerance and diversity within the Liberty community, except
when it came to acceptance of homosexuality, which was treated
with locker room insults and the offering of pastoral restorative
therapy:

> This semester, I've developed a numbness to homophobia.
> I don't like it, but it's unavoidable when you're in a climate
> like this, where homosexuality is talked about at near-
> Tourettic frequency. Every day, I've heard someone worry-
> ing about gay people, praying for gay people, talking about
> the scientific evidence against the alleged "gay gene." I've
> heard ten times as many conversations about homosexual-
> ity at Liberty than I ever heard any place where gay people
> existed in the open. . . . I'm utterly convinced that . . . [a]
> Martian, invited to Liberty, would take one look around
> this campus and say, "What is it, what can it possibly be
> about two dudes kissing?"[13]

If that same Martian appeared today, that would no longer
be his takeaway. He might take notice of the general prohibitions
against kissing and wonder what is the great harm in locking lips,
but his reports back to the mother ship would likely focus on
general chasteness, not homophobia.

The changes in the evangelical culture reflect not only the

broader culture but also a generational shift. Younger evangelicals are far more accepting of gay rights, and it is no accident that Ryan Meeks, the head pastor at EastLake Church, is all of thirty-eight years old. And with social and generational change has come cracks in the doctrinal wall. Books like James Brownson's *Bible, Gender, Sexuality: Reframing the Church's Debate on Same-Sex Relationships* have put forth a case that the Bible does not in fact prohibit homosexual relationships, as evangelical leaders have maintained for generations, but instead favors the "common bond of shared kinship" of any stable monogamous relationship, regardless of gender orientation. While acknowledging the gender complementarity of Genesis 2:24, which is the centerpiece of the traditionalist argument on the subject of homosexuality, Brownson argues that what God wanted for Adam was a stable, long-lasting relationship that could be consecrated forever before God. The biblical proscriptions against homosexuality thus are not about long-term monogamous commitments but against the exploitative, lustful, and transactional practices in Roman times that Jesus observed and decried. The sexually differentiated couple is thus *blessed* to "be fruitful and multiply," but they are not commanded to do so. The character of marriage and kinship in the Bible, Brownson argues, is not about the physical differences that promote procreation but about the moral strength and stability of the relationships. I am certainly not going to be the one to referee the theological arguments around Brownson's book and others like it, and certainly there have been many challenges from traditionalists on the topic, but suffice it to say that these interpretations are now giving a textual fig leaf, so to speak, to those within the evangelical community inclined to support gay rights and acceptance within the church.[14]

The slow change in attitude is not just anecdotal observation. Over the last fifteen years, support for same sex marriage among evangelicals has more than doubled, from 13 percent in 2001 to 27 percent in 2016. The growth percentage among evangelicals is more than any other religious group in America measured by the Pew Research Center: Catholics, White Mainstream Protestants, Black Protestants, and even the Unaffiliated. In fact, the approval rate of same-sex marriage has grown faster among evangelicals than any group measured by Pew: faster than among whites, blacks, young people, old people, Democrats, Republicans, and Independents, among men and women, and among liberals and conservatives, just to name a few. And even these numbers underweight the rapid change in attitudes, since there was virtually no change in evangelical attitudes on same-sex marriage in the first six years of polling. But if you mark it from the day Jerry Falwell Sr. died in 2007, the numbers have just about doubled in less than a decade. It is of course much easier to show large percentage increases from such a small base, so let's not overstate the case, but at the same time, the change is real and it should indicate to us that the evangelical community is a more complicated, diverse, and changing place than many of us have been led to believe.[15]

Many evangelicals have made the long journey toward inclusion and affirmation, but it is a trip that is still fraught with insult and anger. It is easy for me to support gay marriage; how could I not, when virtually everyone I know supports it and my neighbors two doors down are David and Steve, and their cute daughter, Sydney? It is, on the other hand, an act of courage to publicly support gay marriage when your peer group, your audience, or your customers have an entirely different perspective. In 2016, evangelical author Jen Hatmaker and her husband, Pastor Brandon Hatmaker, publicly announced their support for same-sex marriage and their belief in the equal sanctity of LGBT relationships. It is not a view they came to naturally or easily. As Brandon detailed on Facebook:

We started with scripture (Again, please assume a ton of prayer). For more than a year we studied every version of every verse in the Bible that appeared to discuss "homosexuality." We studied the Greek. We studied the Hebrew. We read every commentary we could find related specifically to the related passages. . . . Every verse in the Bible that is used to condemn a "homosexual" act is written in the context of rape, prostitution, idolatry, pederasty, military dominance, an affair, or adultery. It was always a destructive act. It was always a sin committed against a person. And each type of sexual interaction listed was an abuse of God's gift of sex and completely against His dream for marriage to be a lifelong commitment of two individuals increasingly and completely giving themselves to one another as Christ did for the church.[16]

The Hatmakers' statements were acts of courage and came with a price: not just the rather unchristian comments they received from some of their peers but the decision by LifeWay Christian Stores, a large Southern Baptist book seller, to drop all of Jen Hatmaker's books from inventory. As the data shows, the momentum is on the side of change and inclusion, but change comes slowly and often painfully when you are talking about reinterpreting a two-thousand-year-old text. The evangelical community in the United States remains deeply conservative and often irritably uncomfortable with many aspects of modernity.

After Wilshire Baptist voted for inclusion, the Baptist General Convention of Texas started proceedings to evict it and another similarly affirming church from the organization for not being in "harmonious cooperation" with the broader organization. But change is nonetheless coming: slow, halting, episodic, but really. Approval of same-sex marriage, let alone acceptance of LGBT rights, is now a mainstream, if distinctly minority, view within the evangelical community, and may be even more than that if you add in the many evangelicals who still disapprove of gay marriage but accept it, like divorce, as a fact of modern life.

★   ★   ★

Over the last three decades, the evangelical community has been loudly vocal with its concerns about the decay of the traditional family unit. Many people have quite understandably, and frequently correctly, dismissed much of this as poorly designed camouflage for bigotry and as a device for reasserting Christian privilege. Indeed, much of the vitriol from the Falwells and the Dobsons and the Schlaflys (though she was not an evangelical) came not from thoughtful concern but from confusion and bewilderment from a rapidly changing world. But whatever the reason—and I am surprised as any of you to be writing this—and whatever the logic or emotion that got them there, the predictions they made about the collapse of the American family have proven to be at least partially right, with enormous negative consequences for society.

The two-parent family in the United States has deteriorated with astonishing speed, in ways different from the rest of the world. Of the thirty-five countries in the Organisation for Economic Co-operation and Development that collectively comprise much of the developed world, the United States has by far the highest rate of single-parent households, with more than 25 percent of all children living in them, approximately three times as many, for instance, as in Italy and Greece.[17] In 1960, single mothers accounted for only 5.3 percent of births. By 1980, that number had swelled to 18.9 percent. By 2014, it had ballooned to 40.2 percent. Even those children born into traditional two-parent families are increasingly facing fluid situations. Three in ten children under the age of six now experience some type of significant structural change, whether divorce, separation, death of a parent, or a new cohabitation arrangement.[18] And while single-parent births are most prevalent among blacks (71 percent) and Hispanics (53 percent), the growth rate is actually strongest among whites, especially working-class whites (29 percent).

In the abstract, I couldn't care less if a kid has one parent, two parents, or three. I know some amazing single parents and have every reason to think their kids will do just fine. But that is anecdotal, and the broader numbers are devastating on the economic and social consequences of single-parent families. It is universal across the developed world that there is a significant correlation between single-parent households and poverty. In the United States, with relatively limited investments in child care and after-school programs, the problem is particularly acute. And it is not only the existence of poverty, but also the stickiness of poverty that affects single-parent households. Single-parent families— and I really mean single-mother households, by and large— have less social mobility than two-parent families; without the multiplying hands of two parents, and without adequate social resources, single parents live constantly on the edge, trying and often failing to juggle jobs, children, illness, and security. There is always going to be a question of causation here, whether single parents create poverty, or poverty (and related factors like incarceration) causes single parents. But whatever the directionality, the relationship between single parentage and social weakness is what the evangelicals predicted decades ago.

Jesus would have understood this. The revolutionary nature of the gospel emanated from his willingness to take on the unspoken tragedies of the day, the vast inequity of society, the failure to take care of the poor, the disposed, and the lost. For Jesus, this was not a failing of policy but a failure of morals and family structure. We have responsibilities to our communities, but those obligations start with stable family structures. That is why Jesus was so clear on divorce: not because of some arbitrary promise to keep family units together until "death do us part," but because of the economic consequences of divorce, which at the time fell almost exclusively on women and children.

I'm curious what Jerry Falwell Sr., were he alive today, would say about all this. Much of the power of the Moral Majority came from an innate sense of devolution, that American society was pulling apart. It originated in a nostalgia for the 1950s, when things were good for the nation—if you conveniently forget segregation, sexism, and a whole lot of other ills that made the time nice for white, Christian men but not so commodious for everyone else. He was full of bile and anger at what America was becoming, but also had a way of capturing the challenge of the country in graspable, even funny, language: "We are developing a socialistic state in these United States as surely as I am standing here right now," Falwell preached in one sermon. "Our giveaway programs, our welfarism at home and abroad, is developing a breed of bums and derelicts who wouldn't work in a pie shop eating the holes out of donuts." And he understood the relationship between moral creed and social success, one reason that he, unlike other fundamentalist leaders, threw himself into the political world.

Many of his beliefs were abominable—and he even repented his own overt racism and hostility to gays (without changing his policy views)—but his belief in a strong family was correct all along. Simply put, there is a clear link between single parenting and poverty. Nearly a third of households headed by single mothers live below the poverty line, compared to just 6 percent of families headed by married couples.[19] And the effects do not end at one generation. More than ever before, demographics are destiny. The consequences of the birth lottery are now greater than at any other time in modern American history.[20] Having a single parent reduces opportunity and the possibility of success for life. Single parenting affects nutrition, school success, job prospects, and incarceration rates; so much is traceable back to that single variable that poverty researchers Isabel Sawhill and Adam Thomas of the Brookings Institution have estimated that child poverty would decline by 20 percent if marriage rates returned to historical norms.

The public discussion about family structure is a great Rorschach test. Conservatives look at the data and see simple math: that two-parent households mean better parenting, higher income, and better child-care arrangements—all the things that logically lead to better results. For them, the rise in single parenthood reflects the loosening of social values and the declining role of the church in setting cultural norms. Their remedy is a return to common values encouraging marriage before procreation and discouraging divorce, and articulating a more central role in society for God and the Christian church.[21] It is not a view that has much instinctive appeal to me, but it does align with other, more sympathetic figures, like Martin Luther King Jr., who once said something quite similar in a Detroit sermon: "[A]ll I am trying to say is that if we are to go forward today, we've got to go back and rediscover some mighty precious values that we've left behind. That's the only way that we would be able to make of our world a better world, and to make of this world what God wants it to be. . . ."

Liberals see the situation rather differently, that the rise in single-parent families reflects the effects of poverty and economic hopelessness. Marriage rates among the college-educated remain near historical norms, but it is among the working class, who face bleak prospects in a knowledge economy, that marriage has declined. Marriage remains for this group socially desirable, but the absence of potential spouses with stable economic situations reduces the incentives to get married.[22] And America has failed to support this increasing number of single mothers. Where single mothers have access to family support networks, the economic results are significantly improved, but where such networks are not available, the absence of social benefits such as paid maternity leave, paid sick leave, and affordable child care means that single parents work less, earn less, and learn less. This is the poverty trap faced by millions of single parents and their children.[23] As so often is the case in such things, there is truth on both sides, and the failure of each side to recognize that speaks to the continuing division in American politics and society.

★　★　★

Evangelical services are different, I quickly find out during my visit to McLean Bible Church, a megachurch run by a celebrity pastor named Lon Solomon. It has a big, sprawling campus and the air of a social club. As I pick my way toward the main auditorium for the Sunday service, I pass a group for couples in midlife, a group for forty-plus singles, a group for parents of high schoolers, the "edge" for millennials, the "rock" for teenagers, the "lox" for middle-aged Jews (just kidding on that one), but that is all prelude to the main event. Solomon is not preaching today, but it doesn't seem to matter much, because there are plenty of other distractions. Services start with fifteen minutes of music. We're not talking choir practice here; there is a full band, and they are rocking hard. Everyone stands and sings along, most shifting awkwardly from side to side as you might do on the sideline of a high school dance, but some are into it, arms raised to the sky, eyes closed, full-throated singing. The sermon itself is part God, part QVC. The homily is unremarkable, my notes are devoid of any mention of it other than its existence, but interjected into the middle of it is a slick video promoting the upcoming Christmas Fair, "with 75 vendors!" and a promo for the new McLean Bible app, which will feed you a new Bible quote every day and will track how many you read and how much time you spend with them: it's a Fitbit for your soul.

The best is saved for last. As the assistant pastor finishes up, the band returns and with it a young woman trailing along an easel, canvas, and paints. As the band plays, she paints, with speed and purpose. We all strain, 2,500 strong, to see the painting, but it is indecipherable, strong blue and black streaks that only vaguely suggest a shape. She keeps painting, faster and faster, and finally, as the music hits its crescendo, she finishes, and flips the canvas upside down, so we can all see that from that angle she has painted an instantly recognizable likeness of Jesus. The crowd goes crazy, me among them. It's just, in the final analysis, a cute parlor trick, painting upside down, but the whole show was so artfully built that it felt like a minor miracle had just occurred. One hour on the dot and the congregation is racing for their cars.

A week later, I'm talking again with Inazu. He counsels me once more to spend time in churches. I tell him, with a hint of pride, that I've already been to McLean Bible. He laughs gently and says, "That's good, Ken, but you also need to go to an Assembly of God church in Springfield, Missouri, if you want to see evangelicals in action." It is a bit deflating, since I have no strong desire to go back to Missouri, but I'm a literalist, and a few days later I'm on Travelocity, looking for flights. I'm initially surprised at the number and convenience of the flights, until I realize that the Springfield airport also serves nearby Branson, the tourist mecca of the Ozarks. I page longingly through its visitors guide, stopping at Barney Fife Fully Loaded, a tribute show to

Andy Griffith's bumbling, somewhat self-delusional, and wildly insecure sidekick. I don't know exactly why I want to see it—*The Andy Griffith Show* went off the air almost fifty years ago and it felt terribly dated even when I watched it in reruns as a boy in the early 1970s—but I really do. There is something, let's face it, appealing about pure kitsch and nostalgia for its own sake, and it doesn't need to hold any larger meaning than that.

But it's too much travel, with all my other trips, and I decide that I need to find an Assembly of God church closer to home, if there is one. Without any real expectations of success, I google away and am stunned to find hundreds of AG churches just in the wider D.C. metropolitan area. I would have never thought that to be the case, and it is yet another rebuke to my ingrained belief that evangelicals are found mostly in the foothills of the Ozarks and the hollers of the Appalachians.

From the hundreds, I home in on Freedom Church in Fredericksburg, Virginia. Pastor Steve is hesitant about my visit but reluctantly relents, and I make my first drive down I-95 to visit the church. I may have been expecting a miniature version of McLean Bible, but that is not what I get. All the same ingredients are there—videos, preachers, arms raised to sky—but the cake tastes a whole lot different. There is none of the choreographed precision of McLean Bible; my first visit lasts a punishing two hours and forty-five minutes. There is a band and singing and a homily that runs as long as Pastor Steve wants it to go.

But what gets me at Freedom Church is that there is always time for fellowship: not the perfunctory "peace be with you" handshakes I have seen at St. Anastasia but a visiting period that feels a little bit like halftime. There are only thirty or thirty-five people in the tiny church and everyone knows everyone. People cluster in small groups, making small talk, catching up with the latest news. There is a respectful curiosity about me, and several people stop by to shake hands, but no one presses me about my clearly unusual presence. When the service ends, everyone lingers around, even though it is a football Sunday and everyone knows that Pastor Steve loves football.

From time to time over the course of the year, I've talked politics with Pastor Steve and some of the other congregants. Like many people I've met in my travels, they care passionately about one or two issues (in this case abortion, most pointedly) and feel that America has lost its moral core. They believe the church, not government, should be the center of society, and that makes them instinctively skeptical of Washington, even though some of them work directly in the orbit of the federal government. At first they all gravitate toward Carson and Cruz, but they willingly vote for Trump because he is a better bet on the issues they care about, as Pastor Steve reminds the congregation just before the election. Because of this, I wasn't surprised to find out after the election that evangelicals voted for Trump in the usual proportions, notwithstanding his obvious moral failings, his string of marriages, and his only passing familiarity with the truth. It was for most of them a practical, not a passionate, vote.

But politics and policy are only the subtext to my visits. Even in this obsessive election year, when Trump and Clinton seem to occupy the molecules of the air we breathe, the stuff of life inside Freedom Church is the care of their little community: the building of their new playground, the prayers for Jeff's gravely ill father, or the fund drive that would finally allow Pastor Steve to work at the church full-time. Our policy positions and political instincts are assuredly different. But I think of Sam Adams and Kevin Palau and try to ignore the two points of divergence in favor of the eight points of agreement. During the course of the year, I find myself nodding my head in agreement as Pastor Steve talks about the importance of community, of helping those who live in the shadows, of concern over violence and hatred toward minorities and immigrants, and in supporting others, in the church and beyond. After the election, Pastor Steve writes to me: "My prayer is that we will still be able to have a friendship that defies the law of politics, positions, and power and be able to accept and appreciate one another in finding common ground in the things of life that matter most." I can't think of a better hope for our nation.

3

THE BASKET OF DEPLORABLES

They got a name for the winners in the world. I want a name
when I lose.

—STEELY DAN, "DEACON BLUES"

S
ix weeks before the New Hampshire primary, I head to
Chantilly, out toward rural Virginia, for a Donald Trump
rally. Trump is already a phenomenon: leading in the polls,
drawing outsize crowds, erupting in outrageous statements,
doing things no political professional would ever contemplate,
and generally dominating coverage and conversation. I want the
Trump experience for myself, before his inevitable grand political
flameout.

After passing through metal detectors and the brief but professional Secret Service pat-down, I join the long line of attendees snaking into a cavernous, hangar-like structure, a building
that doubles as the main livestock barn of the Prince William
County Fairground. If Prince William County is a battleground
between the old, white, rural Virginia of the past and its mul-
tiethnic, more urban future, it is immediately clear that I have
come to a marshaling point for the forces of yesterday: a small
army that is overwhelmingly white and mostly male. As you
might suspect in a crowd of several thousand, clothing is all over

the map, including my bright yellow University of Wyoming sweatshirt, but the fashion tends toward flannel shirts, baseball hats promoting John Deere or similar brands, and a variety of other clothing that suggests most of the attendees drove in from the country rather than out from the city like me.

It is standing room only. I know that phrase connotes a large, overflow crowd, and the crowd here is certainly large, but I use "standing room" in a more literal sense. There are no chairs, and that reflects a certain slapdash nature of the event. None of the niceties of campaign events are observed: no camera-ready backdrop and no place for distinguished guests. There is no provision for heat in a semienclosed building on a chilly winter evening, and we all shift from foot to foot as we wait in excitement and the cold for Trump to appear. And wait. After ninety minutes, the program begins without Trump, with several local elected officials giving welcoming remarks. I couldn't tell you who they all are. No one really seems to care, and I am not taking notes—the press is already deep in disrepute with the Trump campaign and has been confined to a large pen at the back of the barn. I do not want to be marked as a reporter gone rogue.

Finally, Trump appears, and he is greeted with a roar, a reinvigorated energy, and our modern form of prayer: arms extended high, phones aloft, and cameras flashing. Trump's speech is long and meandering, jumping from polls to health-care issues to his new D.C. hotel to *The Apprentice* to the exploding sales for his book *The Art of the Deal*, all without any organizational structure or focus. Some in the audience, who have waited so long, shuffle out the back. I check my watch countless times; it's a weekday night, after all, and a long drive home. Finally, blessedly, Trump winds up his speech and, perhaps with a keen sense of theater, takes questions, starting with a young boy about Nate's age who raises his hand and asks, "What will the wall be made of?"

Trump is delighted, summoning the boy up to the stage, giving him a kiss, and then hoisting him up to the microphone to repeat the question. And then he answers the question with great gusto. It "will be made of concrete, and rebar and have a nice, heavy foundation." Trump goes on to give great detail about height and length and depth, with much more nuance than anything he has provided before. The crowd applauds and begins a loud, rhythmic chant: "Build the wall, build the wall, build the wall!" There is widespread delight, a fair amount of whooping and hollering, and we end the evening on a high note.

I've told that story for a better part of the year now to my liberal friends, and it is always good for at least a snort of derision. For their purposes, the story is about a man, now our president, who has real knowledge and passion for construction but at best only glancing familiarity and interest with the tough issues of government, such as health care, taxes, trade, and defense policy, to name just a few. Lean in with President Trump on the details of high-rise development and I am sure you will get an amazing education; engage him on poverty programs and you will probably come away more stupid than when you went in. My friends lap that up. They smile knowingly at the rubes of Middle America voting against their economic interests, instead betting on the dissembling billionaire who revels in the diversity of the superrich of Manhattan and the super-superrich of Mar-a-Lago.

But there is another side of the story: one of a man who knows his audience, an audience that is equally indifferent to the nuances of policy and just wants a champion who will fight their fight, build their wall, and perhaps restore America to the time when the white working class was more than a punch line in a Stephen Colbert monologue.

Many people have dismissed this election as a rearguard action. Trump won this election because, at least in part, white voters without college degrees went for him by an astonishing 39 points (Mitt Romney, by comparison, won that group by "only" 25 points). It is true that in the future that number will not be sufficient by itself, but demographics move slowly and there are still many decades between now and a majority-minority America. At least for this time around, Democrats ran on the demographics of 2048 and lost on the demographics of 2016.

The list of people caught off guard by Trump's triumph is lengthy: every last member of the mainstream media, pollsters, television pundits, urban dwellers, most of the Democratic Party apparatus, most of the Republican Party apparatus, and apparently anyone named Nate: Nate Silver of the blog FiveThirty-Eight, Nate Cohn of the *New York Times*, and Nate Stern of the bedroom down the hall from me. The list of people who predicted the outcome accurately is far shorter, and includes Allan Lichtman, the American University professor who has accurately forecast every election for the last thirty years,[1] large sections of the Breitbart commentariat, and anyone who has studied the psychology literature on what happens to majority groups when threatened with the loss of status.

The last category is a small number, but it should be much larger, because the psychologists who have studied the shifting political attitudes of white voters in some ways predicted the outcomes here. In 1960, the late Hubert Blalock, then teaching at the University of Michigan, proposed the "power threat theory," the concept that whites would perceive the growth in minority populations as a threat to economic entitlements, political power, and even symbolic, cultural norms such as what does an "All-American" person look like. Blalock argued that whites would respond by creating new social control practices that would ensure their dominant position. The power threat theory has been used, for instance, to both predict and explain developments in the criminal justice system, such as the steep penalties for "black" crimes such as crack cocaine possession and lesser penalties for similar "white" crimes such as powder cocaine possession.

In recent years, researchers have found a more subtle impact among white Americans on the demographic shifts that will make the United States, according to the Census Bureau, a "majority-minority" nation by 2044 (or by 2055, according to the Pew Research Center).[2] In 2014, a research team from Northwestern and New York University conducted a series of experiments where it exposed one randomly selected group of whites to information about the changing racial composition of the United States, and a second group to similar information, but this time related to changes in the Netherlands. The researchers found that the first group, who had been primed with information about how the United States would become a majority-minority nation, exhibited greater pro-white and anti-minority sentiments. "These findings suggest that rather than ushering in a more tolerant future, the increasing diversity of the nation may actually yield more intergroup hostility," the authors wrote. But they didn't stop there: in later, similarly structured experiments, the white Americans who were exposed to stories about the census data expressed greater support for conservative policies and were more likely to describe themselves as "conservatives." The most fascinating insight coming out of this later research was the finding that this group was not only more supportive of conservative policies that relate to changing demographics, such as immigration, but also more conservative on a range of issues wholly unrelated to the topic, such as the environment. It's utterly baffling to me, and similarly baffling to the researchers, but it is a significant data point in understanding not only the 2016 election but the next ten or so presidential elections as well.[3]

Knowing this research, you would expect that some whites

as they move into minority status would increasingly emphasize their group status and their whiteness. When the vast majority of people are white, it doesn't create much of a team identity to think of yourself as white, so people differentiate by thinking of themselves as Jewish, or Italian, or southern, or blue-collar, which creates identity and solidarity. That begins to change when whites are a minority of say 35 percent or 40 percent. We are still decades away from that in reality, but not in perception. Most people already vastly overestimate the numbers of blacks and Hispanics in the country and believe that whites are already in the minority. In 2001, Gallup found that whites making less than $20,000 a year believed on average that blacks make up 42 percent of the population, Hispanics 37 percent, and whites presumably the other 21 percent. They are wildly wrong: the numbers even today are non-Hispanic whites at 62 percent, blacks at 12 percent, Hispanics 17 percent, with Asian Americans at 6 percent, and mixed heritage accounting for the rest. It is an old data point, but likely still true, if not more true today, and it gives a sense of the psychology in which working-class whites increasingly see themselves as marginalized in the public space—and act accordingly. For some that means the most overt and reprehensible racism. It is a sad artifact of this last campaign that you can now find the most odious racism without working too hard: from the Nazi gathering in Washington, to the violent racist posts on the *Daily Stormer*, to the vicious racial trolling of anyone in media (and their families) who opposed Trump.[4]

But in truth, in my travels, I met many people who voted for Donald Trump and for Barack Obama, and while I heard racist notes from time to time, I heard far more about class victimization, that the white working class had been abandoned in favor of special interests and special pleading groups. That also fits with the social science research. In 2011, Michael Norton of

Harvard Business School and Samuel Sommers of Tufts studied the attitudes of whites and blacks on racial discrimination and found that in recent years, whites have begun to perceive that *whites*, not blacks or Hispanics, are the principal victims of racial discrimination. "We suggest that these trends epitomize a more general mindset gaining traction among Whites in contemporary America: the notion that Whites have replaced Blacks as the primary victims of discrimination," they wrote.

Virtually everyone recognizes the tortured history of race in America, but over time, the perceptions of discrimination have shifted. While both whites and blacks perceive a substantial decline in anti-black bias over time (with whites perceiving a more rapid decline), whites, unlike blacks, have detected a significant rise in anti-white bias, so much so that by the mid-1990s, whites believed that anti-white bias had outstripped anti-black bias. This trend has only accelerated into the twenty-first century, and it explains at least in part the very different group reactions to Trump, Black Lives Matter, and even nonrace interest groups like the LGBT community. What one group thinks of as giving needed protection to minorities, others, especially members of the white working class, view as special pleadings that take away time, attention, and funding from their very real problems.

Whites already think of themselves as a minority "in their own country," as it was occasionally phrased to me—a group of people who are called on for wars and college football, but otherwise largely ignored and sidelined in favor of preferred classes. For many whites, diversity and immigration is about a competition for resources, a competition that working-class whites, under the circumstances, cannot really afford to lose. While there is considerable celebration in some quarters of this coming majority-minority country of ours, most people are not jubilant: whites see that there will be more competition without enough jobs to go around (55 percent to 28 percent), increasing discrimination against whites (46 percent to 33 percent), and escalating demands on government services (61 percent to 21 percent) that will invariably degrade what people are already getting. This last piece is particularly important. With fewer good working-class jobs available, working-class whites have increasingly become reliant on government programs like the disability insurance administered by the Social Security Administration, which supported only about 5 million people in 2001 but almost 9 million by 2015. Whites, especially working-class whites, may not be a minority yet, but for all intents and purposes, they think and act like one already.

From the very first time Trump mentioned the wall, in his maiden speech at Trump Tower, it fired up the imagination of a large enough group of people that it eventually propelled him all the way to the presidency. It is not that the wall itself was that important to voters in general or Republicans in particular. In all my conversations with Republicans over the course of the year, I can't remember the wall ever being mentioned spontaneously. Immigration itself has never been a top issue for the vast majority of voters. Election polling consistently reveals immigration as a secondary issue at best, far down from economy and jobs, national security and terrorism, and even health care. A CBS/*New York Times* registered-voter poll conducted just before the election put immigration next to last at 7 percent on a list of top issues, falling well behind the economy (38 percent), terrorism and national security (28 percent), and health care (11 percent). Only the environment, at 2 percent, registered lower for voters. It's not an outlier poll; all these numbers have been largely consistent through dozens of similar polls conducted over the last decade.[5]

Even the wall itself is not particularly popular. A full two-thirds of Americans oppose building a wall along the entire U.S.–

Mexican border and only 7 percent say it should be a top priority of the new president;[6] among Republicans, a wall along the border has solid support (62 percent) but the concept of creating a path to citizenship for illegal immigrants is considerably more popular (76 percent).[7] The wall is important more for its symbolism than for its actual policy value. It stands as a stark, thousand-mile-long barrier to the vision of America represented most colorfully by Barack Obama—multicultural, intellectual, diverse, urban, postindustrial, and progressive—and which is assumed by most Democrats to be the only right vision for the country. But it is not a universally shared vision, and certainly not shared by those who are the minus signs in the equation of the future: white, rural, and less educated. If the wall is a metaphor for anything, it is for a bold stand against this ascendant view of the future and a statement of "not so fast," that this future is as much a cause for concern as it is a source of celebration. This explains why immigration and the Great Wall of Trump have been most popular among older audiences—those ages 45–64 and more dramatically those ages 65 or over—even though immigration poses far less of an economic challenge to those age groups. The answer lies not in the direct economic threat but in their sense that we would be better off as a country in the future if we were more like we were in the past.

If I were to write a song about this year, "I don't recognize this country anymore" would be the refrain, repeated over and over. I had heard it just days before the Trump rally in an Alexandria, Virginia, coffee shop called Killer ESP, from Michael Gerson, the Republican strategist and conservative columnist. Gerson doesn't use the phrase for himself but rather is telling me what he has been consistently hearing from friends and family back home in St. Louis. Unlike the crowds in the Prince William barn, Gerson is rather glum about what is happening to the Republican Party.

He reports to me that the Democrats are amassing a "coalition of the ascendant"—multicultural, educated, bicoastal, urban. He doesn't say it, but he doesn't have to: his party is at risk of becoming the "party of the descendant," the people who are losing out on the economy of tomorrow, the people who are increasingly out of step with policy and cultural tastemakers, the people who shake their fist at change and yell, "Get off my lawn!"

It sounds rather bad for the future of the Republican Party, except that there turns out to be a hell of a lot of people like that. And they believe they're only falling because they've been pushed.

★   ★   ★

In the mid to late 1800s, Martinsville, Virginia, was known as the "plug tobacco capital of the world" and plug tobacco—a variant of chewing tobacco—supported hundreds of local businesses and a robust regional economy. Unfortunately for Martinsville, its success eventually drew the notice of the Duke and Reynolds tobacco concerns, and they swooped in, bought up all the local businesses, and in a burst of anticompetitive exuberance, promptly shut down local operations and fired all the workers. In 1941, DuPont opened a nylon factory in town as part of its war materials strategy. After the war, Martinsville parlayed the nylon factory into a major apparel business, grandly designating itself a global capital for the second time, this time the "sweatshirt capital of the world." But that effort at world domination ended badly as well. Globalization and the trade deals of the 1990s made domestic sweatshirt production economically untenable and the local industry collapsed. Today, Martinsville, like seemingly every other town in America, has proclaimed a goal of becoming a technology and knowledge center. But if my lonely walk through the town center, which has all the vibrancy of a spaghetti western town just before the bad guys roll in, is any judge, its future lies only in being an extended metaphor for the decline of rural, white America.

But what Martinsville has that many other small, fading towns do not is a legendary racetrack. Martinsville Speedway was opened in 1947, held its first NASCAR race in 1948, and was paved only in 1955. Twice a year, the faithful flock to Martinsville, in a parade of trailers and trucks, to see the races that are notorious, or perhaps celebrated, for their "banging." Martinsville is the shortest track in NASCAR and is shaped like a paper clip, which means two straightaways, two tight left turns, lots of hard braking, and more than its share of accidents. Over the years, NASCAR has tried to diversify its heavily white, largely southern fan base, and if the audience at Martinsville is any judge, it has not made it too far from its early days, at least demographics-wise. The occupants of the packed RV campground perched on a hillock above the track are almost uniformly white, generally working class, burdened by a sense of lost opportunity and status, and, if my conversations there are any judge, all in for Donald Trump. That fact explains why NASCAR CEO Brian France, accompanied by several well-known drivers, felt very comfortable becoming an early endorser last February of Donald Trump for president in front of a massive campaign rally in Alabama.

It is not surprising that the people of Martinsville Speedway feel left out of a vision of a multicultural, educated, and urban America. America is getting better educated, more diverse, and less rural every year. That is the America I know and, with all the talk of the knowledge economy and a majority-minority nation, you would be forgiven for thinking that future has already arrived. But it has not. Of the 212 million Americans age twenty-five and older, 140 million of them are non-Hispanic whites. And of that group, nearly two-thirds do not have a college degree, approximately 90 million Americans according to the U.S. Census Bureau.[8] That group is by far the largest group in America, and by virtually every absolute and relative measure—economic, physical, mental, and social—is in complete free fall.

It is a well-known story: the loss of manufacturing jobs to overseas production, the increased automation of industrial production, and the gutting of unions in the private sector have all contributed to a terribly unfavorable economic climate for the working class. But the numbers are still stark and unsettling. The 1970 census counted almost 11 million workers who operated machinery in factories. By 2010, that number had been cut in half, to fewer than 5 million, even though the labor force in 2010 was much larger than forty years before. Over the same period, the number of workers who operated lathes and milling and turning machines declined from 345,000 to a mere 14,000.[9] Some of that was due of course to the offshoring of work, but much had to do with the rise of industrial robots and other labor-saving devices. When Vallourec, a French steel concern, opened up a new $650 million steel plant in Youngstown, Ohio, in 2011, it was a moment of civic rejuvenation, a shot in the arm for a city that had suffered plant closure after plant closure for two generations. Yet, due to automation, the new Vallourec mill generated only about 350 jobs, where it might once have required 5,000, and many of those jobs required advanced training and in some cases even advanced degrees.

The disrupted lives of millions of blue-collar families are for once fairly captured in cold statistics. In October 2016, spurred by the rise of Donald Trump, a firm called Sentier Research looked at the change in economic status for white men with college degrees as compared to white men with only high school degrees. The change in fortune for these two groups over the study period of 1996 to 2014 was extraordinary. It was a good time to have a college degree. Incomes for college graduates in real terms rose 23 percent. Those with only a high school education, on the other hand, saw a reversal of fortune. Income, expressed in 2014 dollars, actually fell 9 percent over that period. It is a shocking number: at a time of broad economic expansion, a huge cross section of the American workforce experienced a Depression-era effect on their income.

Sentier did one other interesting thing: they ran what they called a cohort analysis, following the income of different age groups through the eighteen years of the study. For example, the average twenty-five-year-old white college graduate in 1998 earned $40,487. Over the next eighteen years, as he acquired more experience and more expertise, and as he received promotions and seniorities, his income rose, to $94,252, or by about 132 percent over time. It's a nice progression, and it's perhaps what you would expect over the course of a solid career.

But if you had only a high school education, it is an entirely different picture. Your income in 1996 would have been a step lower, at $32,677. Again, that is roughly what you might expect, a solid and not overwhelming 20 percent differential from a similarly situated person with a college degree. But the real differences emerge only over time. Unlike the college composite, as the high school graduate acquired experience, knowledge, and wisdom, his earnings barely budged. By 2014, the typical high school grad would have been in his midforties and probably close to the top of his earning potential, and yet his income would only be $38,803. Think about it for a moment. In those eighteen years, our newfound high school friend might have acquired a spouse, and kids, and car payments, and perhaps a mortgage. He might have put in two decades of hard physical labor, his body might be breaking down, and his health-care needs might be rising up, and he might be grappling with aging parents and other assorted responsibilities—and he would barely have more money than when he was twenty-five and relatively unencumbered.[10]

It is an enormously bleak picture, and if he had known back in 1996 what he would be facing eighteen years down the road, he might have given some serious thought to just ending it all. And that's exactly what more and more working-class whites are doing. In 2015, two Princeton economists, Anne Case and Angus Deaton (the 2015 Nobel laureate in economics), discovered an unexpected and alarming uptrend in mortality rates among middle-age whites. From 1978 to 1998, the mortality rates among non-Hispanic whites fell by about 2 percent every year. It is what you would expect in a time of substantial medical breakthroughs. But in 1999, that steady trend abruptly reversed and mortality rates started to rise, at about .5 percent per year. It's not that we entered a dark age of medicine. Far from it: statins, genomics, biopharmaceuticals, cures for HIV/AIDS, and advances in vaccines were all widely introduced during this period and, absent other circumstances, should have extended life expectancies across demographics.

This increase in mortality, Case and Deaton concluded, was almost entirely caused by three things that modern medicine can't really solve—chronic liver diseases brought on by excessive and prolonged alcohol consumption; suicide; and drug poisonings—and these problems were only affecting a subset of middle-aged whites, those with only a high school diploma or less.

There has been no similar rise in mortality, outside of war, in modern public health history. And the rise in white mortality was completely out of step with other demographic groups. Mortality rates for Hispanics and blacks continued to fall during the same period, and middle-aged whites in other advanced European countries continued to exhibit improving health outcomes. There is no definitive answer as to why these trends collided together right now for this one single identifiable demographic, but economic decline and anxiety certainly seem to be at the heart of the matter.[11]

The numbers are staggering. Case and Deaton estimated that if the death rates for middle-aged white men had just remained constant at 1998 values, 96,000 deaths would have been avoided from 1999 to 2013, or 7,000 in 2013 alone. Let's pause on this number for a moment and put it in perspective. The number of gun homicides, which is routinely decried as a national tragedy, in this country in 2013 was only modestly higher, at 11,202. And the comparison isn't really complete: the 7,000 figure only relates to a relatively thin slice of the white working class, men between the ages of forty-five and fifty-four. The number would be presumably much higher if the study group were widened further. Case and Deaton further note that if mortality rates had continued to decline at rates experienced between 1979 and 1998, as one might expect with advances in medical sciences, the difference would have been far higher, about 500,000 for the study period. There has been no other public health crisis in the United States in the last half century of similar scale, with the possible exception of the AIDS crisis. It is made further remarkable by the fact that this epidemic—there really is no other word to describe it—has been so badly underreported, and by the fact that these are roughly categorized as "despair deaths." This is the first major outbreak in modern epidemiological history that has no potential answer from medical science.

If you dive deeper into the numbers, you get a clearer, though no less depressing, image of the mental state of white America. In 2014, more than 14,000 middle-aged white people killed themselves, an increase of 43 percent for men and 63 percent for women in that range over the course of the decade.[12] At the same time, opioid deaths continued to rise, from about 8,000 in 1999 to more than 33,000 in 2015. In the latter year heroin overdoses for the first time accounted for more deaths than all gun deaths, an especially surprising fact given that as recently as 2007, gun deaths outnumbered heroin-related deaths by more than five to one. The analogy to guns is an appropriate one. America is awash in drugs, illegal and legal, and like guns, they are widely available to those who want to use and abuse them. When I visited Pikeville, Kentucky, a town devastated by the decline of the coal industry, I quickly spotted several pain clinics, more than you might ordinarily expect to see in a town of fewer than 7,000 people. And when I asked people in town whether it was difficult to obtain opioids, I was met with a snort of derision. You can get a pain prescription in Pikeville and cross over the nearby border to Virginia and get another one, and do exactly the same the next month, without setting off any alarms. And if you don't want to go to all that trouble, it is easy enough, I was assured, to purchase them on the black market around town. Everyone in Pikeville knows someone who has died from opioid or other drug addictions.

With the economic and health decline of the white working class has come the disintegration of their families. Marriage remains an aspiration for most people, but high school–educated young adults continue to adhere to the traditional belief that a young man must have good prospects in the form of a steady job to qualify for marriage. Because dependable blue-collar work is increasingly rare, young adults are in turn increasingly postponing marriage altogether, or seeing marriages disintegrate in the face of economic upheaval. Marriage has declined generally in this country, and remains lowest for blacks, but it has declined the most by far in the white working class. If you look at data from 1980, roughly 86 percent of all whites with a high school degree or less were married. By 2012, the number of married people in the 40–55 age group had declined to about 67 percent, an enormous drop-off fueled by postponed marriages, divorce, and premature death.[13]

But, because cultural norms have shifted so much over the last half century, the men and women of the white working class are not postponing sex and children, and are instead creating substitute family life around short-term relationships. The results of this are a stunning and sharp departure from historical norms. Three-fourths of young mothers who lack a bachelor's degree have had at least one child outside of marriage. As Andrew Cherlin, the leading chronicler of the working-class family, wrote, "A substantial number [of high school–educated women] move on to have children with a second partner, or even a third, creating complex and unstable family lives that are not good for children. The problem of the fall of the working-class family from its midcentury peak, then, is not that the male-breadwinner family has declined—it would eventually have collapsed under its own weight. The problem is that nothing stable has replaced it."[14] As an economic unit, the institution of marriage has become increasingly rare, and even when working-class couples do get married, their marriages remain fragile. While the divorce rate in the United States has declined substantially across most demographics, it has remained steady among white working-class families, at or near historic highs.

At the end of the day, we are left with the grimmest of views: broken communities, broken family structure, high incidence of drug use and depression, and declining job prospects for those without a college education. It seems rather self-evident to say that members of the white working class have—and are entitled to have—a fairly bleak view of the future. America has always prided itself on its perpetual optimism, but we are seeing a long-term secular decline in that optimism among whites. Since the 1980s, researchers for the University of Chicago's General Social

Survey have asked: "The way things are in America, people like me and my family have a good chance of improving our standard of living—agree or disagree?" Thirty years ago, about 70 percent of blacks, Hispanics, and whites agreed, with whites being slightly more optimistic about the future. Since then, Hispanics have remained generally optimistic, with "agree" bouncing between 70 percent and 80 percent, and blacks have largely been the same, with an appreciable uptick during the first term of President Obama. Whites, on the other hand, have seen a steady decline in optimism, which has fallen from its peak in 2000 to under 50 percent today. The absolute numbers are themselves less interesting than their relative positioning, some 25 points lower now than both blacks and Hispanics and some 25 points lower than whites' attitudes just a dozen years ago.[15] Given all that is going on, it could hardly be any other way.

Some perspective is warranted here. By virtually every measure— income, employment, wealth, access to education, marriage rates, and home ownership—working-class whites are still far better off than their equivalent black or Hispanic peers. But that is not the barometer for this group. They measure themselves against previous generations, against their own expectations, against the promise of the American dream, and they find it all wanting. It is the relative decline, the sense of failure, the loss of the opportunities they once had, that fuels the sense that things are unraveling.

If you travel the geographic arc of white-working class decline, it is easy to find stories of people who are being left behind, who have come to see the American dream as a promise to someone else. In Pikeville, I met Walter Dixon, a squat, heavyset former coal miner, now in his thirties. It is hard from a safe distance to understand the promise of the coal mines: the work, especially before automation, was backbreaking and dangerous. But even in the boom-or-bust coal industry, the jobs were relatively secure, definitely high paying, and open to people without a college degree.

Like many I met, Dixon found his first job in the mines with the expectation that he had secured employment for life. And for a number of years, it all went rather well. Dixon started as a scale-house operator making $13.25 an hour, but was quickly elevated to running a coal-washing operation, making $20.25 an hour. That goes a long way in Pikeville, long enough that Dixon could make a good living, and even bypass overtime in favor of spending more time with his wife and infant son. But in September 2013, his employer, the James River Coal Company, abruptly closed four Kentucky coal mines and within hours, Dixon, along with more than 500 other miners and support personnel, was on the street. Along with the job went all semblance of economic certainty. It is one thing to lose a job—many of us have been disfavored with that experience—but another thing to lose a job when your local economy is in free fall. With the exception of a brief interlude when mining resumed, Dixon has been formally unemployed since, living off the underground economy. He has an electrician's skills, but not an electrician's license, so a local electrician has paid him cash under the table for occasional piecework. On the day I met him, he was on his way to interview for a salesman job with Transamerica Insurance. Dixon smiled at me and said, hopefully, "It's the best shot I've had for a long time." Four years ago, the thought of selling insurance into a dwindling marketplace could not have been terribly appealing, but today any stable, respectable job is a potential lifeline for him and his family.

Like everyone else I spoke to in Pikeville, Dixon views the federal government as an oppressive force, the instrument of the coal industry's downfall in Kentucky via clean-coal regulations. The story is similar to Martinsville's, in the sense that economic fates are perceived to be in the hands of distant corporations or indifferent government decision makers. None of the stories are as clean or as neat as the locals would have you believe, but it is much easier to rally against a form of internal colonialism than it is against market forces and economic change. For Dixon, this sense of grievance, of abandonment by those who are supposed to help him, has led him to Donald Trump, not out of any great affection, but out of the belief that he will either "be a great leader or launch World War III." That comment is worth a pause, because that is not a bet I would make on my own behalf or for the country, but when you are on your back in Pikeville, looking up from the bottom of the pyramid, the perspective is quite a bit different.

★　★　★

The story in Youngstown, Ohio, is pretty much the same, except that the economic decline started long ago. The economic struggles of an entire region are typically revealed glacially. Not so in Youngstown. Every person in town dates the miseries of Youngstown to September 19, 1977, known locally as Black Monday, when Youngstown Sheet & Tube abruptly announced the closure of its main steel plant, immediately putting 5,000 people out of work. The closing started a cascade of similar shutdowns; over the next couple of years, U.S. Steel and Republic Steel also shut down local operations, costing the area some 40,000 jobs and about 400 supporting businesses. The closures tore the economic and social innards out of the city; kids went off to school and did not return. The population of Youngstown had actually peaked in the 1950s, at 168,000 people, making it larger at the time than either Kansas City, Missouri; or Phoenix. The current population of 64,000 makes it smaller than Albany,

New York, and Albany, Georgia, and barely bigger than Albany, Oregon.

There is a gallows humor around Youngstown. I drink late into the night at the Royal Oak Bar, which is advertised with a hearse sporting the sign "Ribs to Die For" and is run by two brothers whose language would make a longshoreman blush. The Royal Oak is mostly a working-class bar, typically frequented by people who "shower after work, not before"—but it is not rigorous about it: the bar stool to my left is occupied by the editor of the local newspaper, the *Vindicator*, and the stool to my right is occupied by a retired construction worker and boxing manager named Willie Brandon, who demonstrates the rough-edged friendliness of the place by buying me a drink and promising to take me outside "and fuck me up good" if I don't drink it. I do drink it, with appropriate haste, and it's good, and Willie is an amiable companion for the evening despite his continuing, rather cheerful, threats to beat the tar out of me. The Royal Oak is not an inherently conservative place—one of the owners is named John Fitzgerald Kennedy, which gives you a sense of the politics of his parents, at least—but this year many of its patrons defied the inertia of modern politics and crossed over to vote for Trump. Over and over I was told that this was not because Trump was the best Democrat or the best Republican but because he was neither: he was the "blue-collar billionaire" who spoke like them and cared about the jobs they wanted. In places like the Royal Oak, the dirty words are not "grab them by the pussy," as Donald Trump said to Billy Bush—far worse was said to me that evening—but "retraining" and "NAFTA."

Much of this is a rejection of what the people have been told over and over again, that Youngstown is dead and that there is no future in manufacturing in the United States. America, they so strongly believe, pronounced them dead while they were still awake and their hearts were still beating. They're not convinced it has to be this way. The siren call of Trump would not work if members of the white working class felt represented in the political process. They don't. And more important, they see a political system and cultural elite that shrugs off their very human and real plight. Take, for instance, Kevin Williamson, writing last year in the *National Review*:

> The truth about these dysfunctional, downscale communities is that they deserve to die. Economically, they are negative assets. Morally, they are indefensible. Forget all your cheap theatrical Bruce Springsteen crap. Forget your sanctimony about struggling Rust Belt factory towns and your conspiracy theories about the wily Orientals stealing our jobs. . . . The white American underclass is in thrall to a vicious, selfish culture whose main products are misery and used heroin needles. Donald Trump's speeches make them feel good. So does OxyContin. What they need isn't analgesics, literal or political. They need real opportunity, which means that they need real change, which means that they need U-Haul.

It's a fun screed, as these things go, and to be fair to Williamson, he at least comes from those downscale communities, but it is hard to imagine anyone writing something similar about blacks or gays or women or Latinos or any other identity group within American politics. And Williamson is not alone. Michael Barone, also writing in *National Review*, piled on, somewhat more gently arguing that people should stop playing the victim and abandon Youngstown for Texas, just as their forefathers fled Poland for the opportunity of America. It's a nice economist argument, I suppose, but both Williamson and Barone underweigh the real cost of uprooting families. Barone calls it "a pain." Running out of milk in a snowstorm is a pain. Moving thousands of miles is far more freighted, difficult, and scary to many. And even if the rational decision is to head south on I-65, as many of the more mobile have done, we don't get to ignore the declining status of those left behind.

And that gets us to the heart of the matter. The tastemakers and the opinion elites of both coasts and both parties have embraced a future for the United States that is increasingly urban, multicultural, and powered by a knowledge economy. It is an alluring vision, and one that it is easy for me and Beth and Nate to like, but it is hard for the left-behind to see how they fit into that neat vision. They don't see a place for their rural towns or mining jobs or even for their unabashed patriotism. And in this election, those people have stood "athwart history, yelling Stop, at a time when no one is inclined to do so, or to have much patience with those who so urge it," as William F. Buckley Jr. declared in 1955 at the inception of the *National Review*. In many ways, for all the unbelievable frenzy and hype, for all the crassness and race-baiting and fear-mongering, our political conversation has boiled down to those people sticking up desperately for their jobs, their communities, and their sense of American values.

★ ★ ★

This chapter has been mostly focused on class, but the issue of race is never far behind, and that brings me back to Martinsville, which has had its own difficult relationship with race, most famously in the case of the Martinsville Seven. The case is largely forgotten now, but the facts will still seem unpleasantly familiar. In January 1949, Ruby Stroud Floyd, a white woman, reported to police that she had been raped by thirteen black men as she passed through a poor, black section of town. Seven men were arrested, none with any significant criminal past, and charged with the capital crime of rape. They were tried in six separate cases—twelve jurors per case, seventy-two in all, every one of them white and male. The seven were quickly convicted, and sentenced to death. Their sentence—and a fair amount of doubt about the facts of the case—led to numerous legal and public appeals for clemency. When their appeals were exhausted, the seven men were swiftly executed, making them numbers 46 through 52 in the count of men executed for rape since Virginia implemented the electric chair in 1908. All 52 were black men convicted of raping white women and that fact alone has left a permanent mark on the history of this quiet town.

The people I meet in Martinsville are not of that era of white dominance and would certainly not think they are living in such a time now. They in fact feel like they live in an era of decline and diminished choices. Virtually everyone I meet over two days has some story of economic enfeeblement to tell: they are unemployed or underemployed, or working in jobs that are not the ones they ever imagined for themselves, or living on SSI or some other form of disability. I chat with Dan, a cable company employee from Eden, North Carolina. He is one of the few I meet with a stable job, but he worries for the future for his daughter, who is twenty-six years old and working as a waitress at a local restaurant called the Steak Company. He sees the current economic and political climate as stacked against anyone who is not part of a special protected class. For Dan, blacks, Latinos, women, and gays all receive heightened attention in the American political system, and he sees Trump as a way to "stir the pot" and get adequate attention to his needs. Trump is not a simple decision: like many of the people I speak to, Dan has mixed emotions, thinking Trump unstable and unpredictable—we joke together that this is not the type of person to have his finger on the button, a joke that was not so funny then and seems horrifying now—and I sense that he would be secretly relieved if Trump loses. But for the moment, Trump is his "look at me" statement to get the spotlight on the increasingly poor condition of the white working class. This view is not just an anecdotal one. Many working-class whites had a negative view of Trump—just a week before the election a poll showed that 51 percent of white working-class voters did not believe that Trump had "a sense of decency"—yet they voted overwhelmingly for him because they believed that he was the person most likely to disrupt the status quo, which had served them so poorly in recent years, and to break the rules they have concluded are unfairly stacked against them.[16]

The psychodynamics of bias work on all of us—white, black, brown, young, and old—but it impacts those at the bottom of the economic pyramid most acutely, since they feel the most economic and social vulnerability both in general and from increased competition from newcomers. Research has shown that racial anxiety escalates during economic downturns, suggesting that scarcity environments will lead to increased tensions around resources and competition from outgroups such as immigrants or minorities.[17] We really don't need lab experiments for this. The 2016 election was a Petri dish for the impact of these feelings on voting political behaviors. The state of their economy, as opposed to the economy in general, made white voters more receptive not only to messages around race-laced issues like immigration and crime, but also to conservative appeals in general, a concept that people like President Trump and Steve Bannon, among many others in the Republican Party, could exploit endlessly.

We all have seen the impact of race on modern American politics, but I think Van Jones of CNN was right to call the election of 2016 a "whitewash" and wrong, or at least mostly wrong, to view that in the form of racial animus. There are few things harder in modern life to discuss than race, but of the hundreds of people I talked to during the course of the book, most of whom voted for Trump, the vast majority would be properly offended at being labeled a racist, as many in political life and Democratic circles have done. They work alongside blacks and Hispanics, sit with them in prayer in church pews, mingle at neighborhood events, and in increasing numbers date and marry people of different racial backgrounds.

Williamson can talk all he wants about the ignorance, the passivity, and the victimization culture of the white working class, and maybe that is all true, but whatever the legitimacy of those criticisms, we don't get to shrug off 40 percent of the population without feeling the consequences. History has fallen hard on top of the working class, and the pre-Trump Republicans are as responsible as anyone else for this decline. They have faced all this while the cultural elites on both coasts have told them that their values are wrong, the way they talk is offensive, their religion old-fashioned and oppressive, their hobbies gross and antiquated, and, worst of all, their jobs create too many negative externalities. It is not a pretty picture and it is little wonder that when someone comes along and says, "You've been screwed by those people over there," he will find a receptive and excited audience, even if his words rarely conform to the facts.

4

THE GRAND COAL PARTY

Coal and iron are the kings of the earth, because they make and unmake the kings of the earth.

—ANONYMOUS

We all have a seemingly innate capacity for processing facts in a way that supports our own view of the world, but that capacity may be just a bit higher for conservatives. In his famous essay "Why I Am Not a Conservative," the great Austrian economist Friedrich Hayek pointed to exactly this "propensity to reject well-substantiated new knowledge because [the conservative] dislikes some of the consequences which seem to follow from it" as the most objectionable feature of conservatism. In the same essay, Hayek pointed to the consequences of this failing: "By refusing to face the facts, the conservative only weakens his own position. Frequently the conclusions which rationalist presumption draws from new scientific insights do not at all follow from them."[1] Hayek, in many ways the father of modern conservatism, lamented both the proclivity of conservatives to reject facts that were inconvenient to their own beliefs and the willingness of liberals ("rationalists," in his mid-twentieth-century terminology) to draw false policy prescriptions from those same facts. I cannot think of any other observation that better explains the climate change debate than Hayek's, even though he made it more than a half century ago.

The story of the climate debate—at least my story of the climate debate—begins with the wonderfully named James Mountain Inhofe, now the senior United States senator from Oklahoma. It is one of those fables of political life that few elected officials aspire to be politicians but are instead called to the job through some act of conscience. For Republicans, the political creation myth is often a story of struggle against big government and an indifferent bureaucracy. And so it was for Inhofe. A small businessman and real estate developer, Inhofe jumped into politics out of frustration with the city of Tulsa. According to his own telling, Inhofe proposed to redevelop the Wrightsman Oil Estate, a beautiful historic building that had fallen into disrepair. His plan called for moving an external fire escape from in front of the building to the back, a modest change that nonetheless required a permit from the city engineer. That request was summarily and cavalierly denied, and the appeal process was too long to be useful to a developer saddled with subcontractors and carrying costs. When Inhofe complained about the process, the city engineer shrugged him away: "That's your problem, not mine." In response, Inhofe pledged to run for mayor of Tulsa and, as his first act, fire the city engineer—and, naturally, in his vengeful Jimmy Stewart moment, did precisely that.

The story of a small businessman entering politics to defeat entrenched bureaucrats is a Jungian archetype for Republican politicians, told so often with only slight variation that we can all be a bit skeptical of the legend. But like Jungian myths, the importance of the story is less in its accuracy than in what it represents; in this case Inhofe's view of government as a roadblock to progress. He was not joining government to advance it but to reduce it and get it out of the way of the real doers in our society.

That notion has been the unrelenting theme of Inhofe's career in government. As he climbed the ladder of government, through local government to the U.S. House of Representatives and finally to the U.S. Senate, Inhofe remained a steady and often angry opponent of government bureaucracy, particularly the regulators of the environment, whom he deemed an unreasonable obstacle to business success. Affable in person, Inhofe nonetheless earned a reputation for sharp, and sometimes wildly inappropriate, turns of phrase: while still in the House, Inhofe referred to the Environmental Protection Agency (EPA) and Occupational Safety and Health Administration (OSHA) as a "Gestapo bureaucracy" and the EPA administrator as Tokyo Rose. Inhofe is clearly a man who likes conflict and glories in being seen as the implacable enemy of government and its enablers.

In the past it would have been modestly ironic but today it seems almost inevitable that this foe of government and environmental regulation would find himself chairman of the Senate Committee on the Environment and Public Works, the committee with oversight over the EPA and environmental issues. This job has a substantial bully pulpit, and Inhofe gleefully claimed the role of the key Republican architect on climate change. As we shall see, there are many reasons to be skeptical of solutions for climate change, but Inhofe from the very beginning chose to take the most radical position: that climate change is in fact a "hoax" perpetrated by environmental elites and the United Nations.

Inhofe laid out this argument in his book *The Greatest Hoax: How the Global Warming Conspiracy Threatens Your Future.*[2] The book is an extraordinary undertaking. It's not so much a scientific analysis, but rather a description of a vast global conspiracy to cook the science books on global warming. There has been, to be completely fair, some evidence of science politics and maybe even data manipulation over the years, perhaps not surprising in a sprawling multinational effort spread over a generation. But it is an amazing leap to take from some isolated cases of data irregularities to a vast global warming conspiracy—a silent handshake between science opportunists, environmental elites that profit from eco-scares, Hollywood elites, and mainstream media who are willing dupes of this manipulation. And behind it all, as Inhofe describes it in *The Greatest Hoax*, are the hidden hands of plotters who "want the United Nations to have sovereignty, control of the world's economic and political systems." All very Blofeld.

There are echoes of Trumpism in all this, that the globalists and power brokers of the "Party of Davos" have subverted the nation-state to their own ends. It doesn't seem predetermined that there would be an alliance between those who oppose the environmental movement and those who have rallied to Trump, but there is, and the alliance works at least in part because it fits together into a larger narrative of us against them, the insiders versus the outsiders, and the coastal elites versus the real Americans. There is not a lot of provable fact to this view of the world, but there is considerable emotion, and even a touch of religion. The climate deniers, those who reject even the claim that the earth is getting warmer, are known to cite Genesis 8:22 for that purpose: "As long as the earth remains, there will be springtime and harvest, cold and heat, winter and summer, day and night." This passage comes from the Noah story. After God decimated the earth, drowning everyone but Noah and his family, he declared that he would never again wipe away the human population. But of course, that is no insurance policy against us doing it to ourselves.

For well over a decade, Inhofe has been the object of scorn and derision from the left, so much so that Keith Olbermann of MSNBC once featured Inhofe's entire family, down to the grandchildren, in his nightly feature of "the worst people in the world." It was quite nasty and inappropriate, at least as to the grandchildren, but Inhofe clearly has relished all the attention. Throughout *The Greatest Hoax*, he glories in his notoriety as the only man willing to point out that the environmental movement has no clothes. The most exuberant passages in his book include his being called out at environmental conferences as "[t]he most dangerous man on the planet," Rachel Maddow of MSNBC describing him as a "mountain of indignation," and Dana Milbank of the *Washington Post* referring to him as "the last flat-earther." Most people would recoil from such treatment but Inhofe chases this conflict, racing to Copenhagen for the UN Climate Summit, mainly to assert to the gathered reporters that he would effectively block any enabling legislation in the United States. The resulting press fury is predictable, and Inhofe afterward marvels at his own infamy: "I still find it amazing that they thought me capable of single-handedly destroying the planet."

Many have been astonished by Inhofe's intransigence in the face of mounting scientific evidence, but it is quite easy to understand in context. A mistrust of government intervention, a natural solicitousness toward the energy business, which accounts for a full 20 percent of Oklahoma jobs, and a pugnacious personality all explain an immovable position that was originally rational and now borders on the absurd. When Inhofe first started raising concerns on the issue, some twenty years ago, the available data on climate change was preliminary and cautionary, and it was fair to argue that many were jumping on a popular bandwagon well before the science was cooked. That may have held true for some years, but by now the scientific consensus is quite definitive—that the earth is warming and human activity is the primary cause of this warming (sometimes called "anthropogenic global warming," or even "AGW").[3] Yet Inhofe has not budged an inch, preferring to be, as he likes to say, the "one-man truth squad." In February 2015, Inhofe stood on the Senate floor and dramatically produced a snowball from a Ziploc bag. In a rather unusual procedural moment, he asked for unanimous consent to throw it at Bill Cassidy, Republican of Louisiana, the presiding senator. It calls to mind Jon Stewart's biting description of Inhofe as the man who thinks "global warming is debunked every time he drinks a Slushee and gets a brain freeze. 'If global warming is real, why does my head hurt?'"

To be fair, the tendency to draw larger climate conclusions from local weather events is hardly unique to Republicans and climate deniers. As I write this, some thirty inches of rain has just inundated Louisiana, inflicting a terrible punishment on the low-lying areas of the state. All told, the storm has left eleven dead, thousands of people displaced, and countless homes and businesses ruined. Within hours, the *New York Times* reports breathlessly that "Flooding in the South Looks a Lot like Climate Change,"[4] and global warming celebrities such as Al Gore, Bill McKibben, and Bill Nye link the devastation to global warming. Some reports are careful enough to note the difficulty of associating individual weather events with climate change—we did, after all, have storms before 1975—but the implication is clear: Louisiana and all fossil fuel states, you reap what you sow. In fact, the link between climate change and more intense weather patterns in specific parts of the country is speculative at best,[5] but that has not stopped lots of people from making that connection over and over again.

It is tempting to dismiss Inhofe as a tool of the fossil fuel industry, or just a loon, and I'm not giving up on either of those theories quite yet. But there is some context worth thinking about. Research has shown that the strongest indicator of climate change denial is endorsement of free market economics, the belief that private behaviors are most capable of solving societal problems.[6]

The strongest free marketers have proven to be consistent skeptics on any issue whose resolution might require large-scale government interventions that interfere with market economics and individualized decision making; here the distrust of government intervention is so high that it leads not only to a rejection of intervention as a solution to the problem, but to a sorting of the facts in such a way that the underlying problem does not even exist. It is a little scary what we can convince ourselves of if we are sufficiently motivated, and that explains at least in part the blinders that Inhofe and others wear in the climate change debate.

If the fatal flaw in the conservative mindset is to ignore or dispute inconvenient facts, as Hayek observed, the parallel enthusiasm of progressives is to take these same facts and require vast governmental solutions for them. Just as there is a need to delegitimize the views of people like Inhofe, there is an equally valid need to challenge the other end of the spectrum. The observations of thoughtful conservatives on the climate change policies of the Obama administration have been important in that regard but they have been largely delegitimized by association with the alternative-fact pronouncements of the wingnut wing of the Republican Party. It is a shame, because when you start peeling away at it, you learn that there is far more to the critique than just snowball fights on the Senate floor.

★　★　★

You might think that my story about global warming would start with the meetings of the Intergovernmental Panel on Climate Change, in Switzerland, or in Le Bourget, outside Paris, for the global climate accord negotiations, or maybe, if I am very lucky, on a dwindling patch of paradise called Kiribati in the Central Pacific. All sound like lovely spots for research, but they are not the hand I have been dealt. If you want to understand the Republican perspective on climate change, you need to go to meet the citizens of eastern Kentucky, coal country USA. These are the people who will pay, literally, for our climate change policies, and it is where I am headed.

Highway 23 runs through the Appalachians like a slalom course, gracefully curving right and left through the mountain cuts. I'm slightly obsessed with Highway 23 because it is so beautifully groomed (if I can extend the skiing metaphor further), fast and flawless as it carries me down from Virginia into Kentucky. The roads are wonderfully maintained here, even if the towns and the people are less so, and it signals what the region has always meant to the rest of the country: a direct route from an energy-hungry country into the mines of coal country. As I drive deeper into the mountains, through quaintly named towns like Pound and Cumberland Hazard, the imprint of Big Coal is everywhere. The first town across the Virginia border into Kentucky is little Jenkins, "a city built on coal," which turns out to be a fair judgment for both the town and the entire region.

If you want to understand Appalachia, you have to understand a little about the history of coal, and Jenkins is as good a place to start as any. Most towns grow over time, but Jenkins was hatched essentially fully grown, with the Consolidation Coal Company serving as both mother and father. In the fall of 1911, Consol, as it was genially known, purchased 100,000 acres of coal lands from the Northern Coal & Coke Company and made plans for a major investment in the area. The Lexington & Eastern Railroad was extended into the area to accommodate the planned mines, and Consol broke ground for two towns to be located along the new line: one called McRoberts, in honor of the director of the company, a New York banker; and the other named Jenkins, in honor of George C. Jenkins, a Baltimore banker and another director of the company. The fact that the communities were named after two eastern moneymen who did not live within 400 miles of the area is a tidy summary of the extractive nature of the relationship—the work was done locally but much of the value accrued to companies, like Consol, and its absentee financiers in the East.

To house the hundreds of workers and their families, Consol hastily erected the two towns: roads, houses, schools, medical facilities, everything necessary to serve a burgeoning population. And it owned it all: stores, homes, and theaters. It was said that Consol would bring you into the world, since it owned the only hospital, and would take you into the next one, since it owned the only funeral parlor. Jenkins was the epitome of a company town. When you went to work for Consol, you received a house rent-free. Electricity, sewer, and water all were provided as part of the deal, but you were largely a conscript in the service of Consol. Wages, not surprisingly, were very low, and sometimes paid in company scrip, redeemable only at the company store or theater. But people flocked to Jenkins. The work was dangerous, the life entirely dependent upon Consol, but the economic security, especially compared to the absence of opportunity in by far the poorest region of the country, must have felt marvelous.[7]

By reputation, generally well earned, coal towns were rough places, but the journals of the time give a more nuanced picture of Jenkins. When the people of the town decided they needed a new swimming pool, they didn't petition Consol. The men banded together, turning an old railroad depot into a bathhouse and dance hall. In shifts after work, they dug out a new municipal pool, using materials donated from the community. Befitting the relative financial security of the mineworkers, the town had a prosperous feel, with the local Burdine School hosting a pie-and-box social that raised forty-four dollars for a new school library.[8]

123

Through the long lens of history, it sounds homey and comfortable, and maybe it was, and it certainly provided a touch of middle-class security that was largely unknown in Appalachia outside of the coal business. But it didn't last, because coal has always been a boom-and-bust business. The boom of World War II led inevitably to another bust, and what Mother Consol birthed, Mother Consol could kill off as well. In 1947, Consol announced that it would sell the town: hospital, dance hall, funeral parlor, and everything in between. The great bust of 1947 was followed by other booms, but, like much of Appalachia, Jenkins began a long, slow decline, one that will have no boom on the other side, its glory days just a distant memory.

Jenkins is interesting not just as a glimpse into the bygone days of Appalachia but as a metaphor for life in coal country. The geography and topography of Appalachia have always isolated it from the rest of the country. While most of America developed, the small network of isolated towns and valleys of Appalachia, better known as hollows or hollers, hardly budged. The region remained culturally isolated and shockingly poor for generations. Coal brought good-paying jobs and confederation not only within Appalachia but with the rest of the country. For the first time, Appalachia mattered.

I drive on from Jenkins to Pikeville, the seat of Pike County and the heart of eastern Kentucky coal country. Even in early afternoon, the town is dark, the result of long shadows from the steep Appalachian hills that hem in Pikeville. Write all the metaphors you want about it, but it's just a phenomenally gloomy place. I'm in town to meet with Roger Ford, a local businessman and newspaper columnist. As I wait, I open the local paper, the *Appalachian News-Express*, which only adds to the heavy air. I have arrived, as it turns out, just in time for the turnover of the Big Sandy Power Plant from coal to natural gas.

To anyone who cares about preserving the business of coal, the conversion of Big Sandy has to feel like a sharp punch in the kidney, a painful jab made worse by the fact that it betrays settled rules of the game. The Big Sandy plant, named for the adjacent Big Sandy River, was built by Kentucky Power in 1963 as a coal-powered plant and operated, as you would expect in the middle of coal country, exclusively on coal for more than a half century. The choice to convert to natural gas was not a simple one, or a casual one, here in the middle of economically pressed coal country. Required by new EPA regulations to reduce pollution, Kentucky Power contemplated a $1 billion upgrade to make its coal-processing operations cleaner and compliant with new regulations.[9] After an internal evaluation, Kentucky Power proposed to do just that and pass the considerable costs on to its consumers. That proposal for more expensive power in the middle of recessionary eastern Kentucky was not met with much enthusiasm. Rebuffed by consumers, Kentucky Power looked for an alternative solution, and it found one in natural gas, which is significantly cleaner than coal and, because of fracking, had become significantly less expensive as well. Conversion to natural gas would only cost $50 million—a small fraction of the coal retrofit—and the Big Sandy plant would then be able to rely on a steady supply of relatively cheap natural gas. It was a deal too good to ignore. What began as a matter of pollution and regulation ultimately became a nice business decision for Kentucky Power. In truth, the Obama regulations provided a ready excuse for the utility to do what was already economically attractive, but otherwise politically impossible in the middle of coal country.

When Ford shows up, I ask him about Big Sandy. He eulogizes the plant as a casualty of the War on Coal, but the reality is more nuanced and reflects shifts in the energy economy well beyond the control of the community, and even well beyond government regulation.[10]

Appalachia has a reputation for being clannish and wary of outsiders, but that couldn't be further from the truth in Pikeville. I had called Roger out of the blue just a couple of weeks before and he had immediately offered to spend the day squiring me around Pikeville. When I meet him for breakfast, he is casually dressed but has the air of a man who has the run of town. The waitresses all know him, and virtually every other customer stops to glad-hand with him. All that is befitting a man who was born just down the road and spent the vast majority of his five decades in and around the eastern Kentucky coal business. Today Ford has left coal behind, as has much of the nation, but he has not left behind the dream of a strong local energy economy, now focused on biofuels, and turning local products like beets, sugar, and hemp into energy.

Encouraged by my question about Big Sandy, Ford launches into a story about the Obama administration's War on Coal, which he believes has decimated the Appalachians. "I've seen booms and busts before, but this is different," he tells me. After 9/11, demand for Appalachian coal, the "best in the world," spiked and drove up prices, with metallurgical coal peaking at $275 a ton. But the EPA and U.S. Army Corp of Engineers regulations enacted under the Obama administration quickly undermined the business: air pollutant regulations required expensive new scrubbing equipment on power plants, and water regulations that covered everything from major rivers to small streams on private land hampered the mining efforts themselves.

All of this, Ford tells me, was part of a concerted effort to bankrupt the Appalachian coal business. This view—that the Obama administration was intentionally gunning to get rid of the only industry that mattered to the region—is widely shared.

It might be a conspiracy theory but this one is a conspiracy theory with a solid foundation, since then-senator Barack Obama, while campaigning for president in 2008, declared that his policies would "bankrupt" anyone who would attempt to build a coal-powered plant.[11] As we talk, the restaurant's two waitresses chime in on our conversation. One is a Trump supporter, the other is for Bernie Sanders, but both share a view that Washington has abandoned ordinary working people in favor of very abstract and distant goals around global warming. And it is not just the new regulations, but intentional overenforcement of the law, designed to harass and hamper coal and coal-related companies.

Later in the day, Jesse Salyer, a third-generation miner and local businessman, tells me how the EPA sent "inspectors looking for things to cite. They have been up my ass since the day Obama took office." Whether the specific complaints are entirely true or not, I can't say, but it is a consistent and embittered story across the town: the same coastal elites who have pulled the strings on the town for generations have returned to instruct the town that global warming is more important than coal jobs. It is a terribly difficult pill to swallow.

The decline of coal has caused an economic malaise across eastern Kentucky. Coal production in 2015 was only 28 million tons, down from 45 million tons just four years before. With that decline went jobs; coal jobs in eastern Kentucky dropped 29 percent from 2014 to 2015, and, as the *Lexington Herald-Leader* reported, "[t]here are fewer coal jobs in Kentucky than at any time since reliable records dating to 1927, and probably the fewest in more than a century."[12] And with every lost coal job went transportation, service, and retail jobs as well. Even as the nation collectively recovered from the Great Recession, Pike County plunged downward. In December 2008, just before Obama took office, unemployment stood at 5.8 percent, close to what economists consider full employment, but it has steadily marched higher, standing at 11.6 percent by the fall of 2016.[13] And with coal closures and bankruptcies go pensions, health benefits, and the tax base of the region. In neighboring Letcher County, the loss of tax revenues meant the closure of five senior citizen centers, the reduction of support for community centers, and slashed funding for the sheriff's office.

And with lost income comes lost health. Miners are a bit like professional football players, minus the fame and glorious compensation. Crawling through narrow mine shafts and breathing corrupted air has left many miners with twisted bodies and permanent physical ailments, along with depression, anxiety, and many of the other complexes of economic and social decline. Many have sought relief in alcohol, methamphetamine, and prescription drugs. And on the last part, local clinics have been more than supportive, prescribing oxycodone, methadone, and Xanax at record rates. The flowering of the prescription and addiction culture in Appalachia has been widely reported, and federal regulators have begun to crack down, but, on our tour, Ford was quick to give me the playbook for maximizing my supply of oxycodone. A quick trip to a notorious pain clinic down the street, a drive across the border to Virginia to a similar establishment and I would be the happy owner of some two hundred pills. If I had the patience to wait another month, I would be able to repeat the process without calling the attention of regulators. Not surprisingly, there are plenty of other ways to get pills, too, if I do not want to be so scrupulous about the rules. Kentucky has the second-highest rate of drug overdose deaths in the country (trailing only West Virginia) at 23.7 deaths per thousand, and the rate in Pike County alone is more than twice that figure, at 50.8 per thousand.[14] As Richard Martin reports in his book *Coal Wars*, "[m]ore people died in 2013 from prescription drug overdoses than car accidents, and one out of every three Kentuckians have a family member or close friend who abuses prescription drugs."[15] The term "pillbilly" is not used trivially in Pike County.

Pikeville has always been a bit of a hard place. It was one of the epicenters of the Hatfield–McCoy feud, a fact that some city elders hope somehow to translate into tourism dollars. The names Hatfield and McCoy continue to hold some currency in modern lore but the tale of the feud has lost some of its sharpness over time. Still, in its day, the violence was terrible. The conflict began in 1878 with a dispute over the ownership of a pig, and it led to some twenty years of murder, retribution, and even competing threats of retaliation from the governors of Kentucky and West Virginia. The feud reached its peak on New Year's Night in 1888, when a group from the Hatfield clan attacked the cabin occupied by Randolph McCoy and his family, opening fire on the sleeping family and eventually setting the building on fire. Randolph escaped but several of his children were shot and his wife beaten and nearly killed.

Appalachia has maintained its reputation for lawlessness and violence, and guns seem to be everywhere, but in fact time has rubbed some of the rough edges off the area. The overall crime rate in Appalachia is only about two-thirds the national average and the violent crime rate is only half.[16] Even the Hatfield and McCoy feud itself has been sanitized for modern use. In 1979, in one of the odder moments in television history, the clans reunited for a weeklong contest on *Family Feud*, hosted by Richard Dawson, who in his typical fashion kissed and fondled the women of both clans in a way that might have led to honor killings one hundred years ago and would have certainly led to a social media uproar now, but in the 1970s drew not a complaint. The prize for the winning team was cash—along with a small pig that dozed uncomplainingly in a cage for the week. When the McCoys won the rubber match to win the week, 3–2, the Hatfields "attacked" with an arsenal of dummy weapons, leaving a group of McCoys sprawling in fake death on the stage. We live in a very strange world.

Ford takes me on a slow drive through Pike County, which wears the scars of the coal depression as clear as the aftereffects of any storm. We pass abandoned mining camps, with names like Greasy Creek, Wolfpit, and Marrowbone. We pause briefly in Hellier, where Ford's mother grew up. It's also a mining camp but that label obscures the size and solidity of the place. In its heyday, Hellier had a population of roughly 8,000, with its own theater, stores, and schools. It was universally known as "Helltown" for what was no doubt a generally exuberant and law enforcement–free culture. Today it is a shadow of that, a few run-down trailers, boarded-up public buildings, and a general air of surrender. Ford tells me that most of the population lives on "SSI and meth," which is probably a solid description for wide swaths of Pike County.

It is not surprising that the tale of Obama's War on Coal has found firm purchase in Pike County and in Appalachia. For much of its history, Appalachia has been exploited as part of an internal colonialism that has made outsiders wealthy and left Appalachia sick and destitute. From the first moment Americans spotted wealth in the area, that wealth has been pulled out of the region and transplanted to the banks of New York and the corridors of power in Washington, Baltimore, Richmond, and Philadelphia. By 1810, 93 percent of the land in the area we now know as West Virginia was owned by absentee landlords, and that condition has not changed much over the centuries. In 1974, out-of-state interests still owned two-thirds of all private lands in the state, including most of the valuable coal and timber lands.[17]

West Virginia is by no means unique. In 1979, the Appalachian

Land Ownership Task Force, a patchwork collection of scholars and volunteers, studied land ownership records across eighty Appalachian counties. After two years of chasing paper, they announced that absentee owners owned 43 percent of private lands across the entire region, yet made only shockingly small contributions to the local economy. In three-fourths of the cases, the landowners paid less than 25 cents an acre in property taxes, and in twelve eastern Kentucky counties, the total property tax payment for mineral-bearing land was calculated at only $1,500 in 1979.[18] Let's think about that number for a second. In 1979, coal companies pulled 104.1 million tons of coal out of eastern Kentucky,[19] and for that privilege paid property taxes that would be insufficient to cover the cost of a used Buick. It's an extraordinary breakdown in the normal allocation of resources between business and community.

The profits from coal were enormous but they were rarely reinvested into Appalachia. Instead they padded the fortunes of numerous great eastern families and were poured into the economies and coffers of those families' hometowns. Coal magnates funded great cultural institutions: the Penn-Virginia Coal Company was an important benefactor, for instance, of the Philadelphia Museum of Art. The notion of reinvesting in Appalachia, in contrast, was an entirely foreign concept, not surprising since many of the economic beneficiaries of coal never came to the region. There are no art museums in Pikeville. Instead, the coal barons left behind a legacy of black lung disease, poverty, and drug addiction.[20] All this has led to anger and a sense of abandonment here and in places like West Virginia, Ohio, Louisiana, and Texas and explains much of the resistance to the science and politics of climate change.

★   ★   ★

It is not that all Republicans reject what by now is settled science, that the earth is warming and that human activity is the principal cause of that warming. Over the years, the public, including Republicans, has warmed, if you will, to the notion that climate change is real, consequential, and largely man-made.[21] In Gallup polling, 64 percent of Americans now acknowledge that global warming is real and 65 percent cite human activity as the principal cause of rising temperatures over the last century, a significant increase from 2010, when only 50 percent tabbed humans as the culprits in global warming. While Republicans are still more likely to be climate change skeptics, Gallup found resistance among Republicans to be waning, a finding broadly consistent with other polls. A 2015 University of Michigan/Muhlenberg College poll found fairly dramatic decreases in climate skepticism among Republicans, from 41 percent who doubted global warming in 2014 to just 26 percent in 2015.[22] Most Republicans now recognize that the earth is warming, and a significant minority, about 38 percent, identify humans as the cause of that warming.[23] And even though President Trump has dismissed climate science as a Chinese hoax, some of his relevant cabinet nominees are slightly more sober on the subject, acknowledging the reality of climate warming, if not agreeing with the weight of liberal opinion on the appropriate remedy.

I consider those numbers to be modestly hopeful signs, and they will likely continue to bend toward the settled science on the subject, but, let us not delude ourselves, there is still a long way to go. For decades now, the core Republican message has been a "know-nothing" one: that the science is not settled, that the science is wrong, that the science is a fraud, or some combination of it all. This antiscience, anti-intellectual message has not necessarily been a shared position in all quarters of the Republican Party, but it has shaped what has been politically acceptable for party leaders to say. It has thus forced senior Republicans like Mitch McConnell, John Boehner, Marco Rubio, Bobby Jindal, and Joni Ernst, who in ordinary circumstances might have something useful to say, into dodging questions on whether climate change is real or not with the hollow excuse of "I am not a scientist." That statement, I suppose, is true as a factual matter, but elected representatives by necessity must rely on people with all sorts of unique subject matter expertise: that could be military officers about the conduct of war, or engineers on the state of bridges and water infrastructure, or criminologists and senior police officers on the best ways to reduce crime. If members of Congress can't rely on the expertise of others, they can't do their job—and perhaps shouldn't.

★   ★   ★

I wish these Republican leaders would have been more articulate, because it turns out we need an effective brake on the alarmism surrounding climate change. If you listened to many significant world leaders, you would undoubtedly conclude that climate change posed an immediate, existential threat to humankind. Al Gore likened climate change to "an asteroid colliding with the Earth and wreaking havoc. . . ." President Obama declared in the 2015 State of the Union address that "no challenge—no challenge—poses a greater threat to future generations than climate change." Prince Charles intoned at the Paris Climate Summit, "Humanity faces many threats but none is greater than climate change. In damaging our climate we are becoming the architects of our own destruction."

Not surprisingly, given the rhetoric of these luminaries, climate change often ranks first on the list of the world's worries, though with substantial geographic variability. In 2015, a global poll from the Pew Research Center found climate change to be the issue of greatest worry in an arc of the developing world[24] that runs from Latin America through Africa to much of Asia. Only 19 percent of Chinese were very concerned about global warming, a very low number compared to other nations, but that was still the issue of greatest concern, compared to ISIS or global economic stability or cybersecurity, for instance. The Chinese, if you take this poll seriously, seem to be an unusually calm or perhaps fatalistic people, which makes me like them very much. Americans, on the other hand, are rather worked up about a lot of things. More than twice as many Americans, 42 percent in all, are very concerned about climate change, but that puts it near the bottom of the list of our anxieties, similar in ranking to Western European countries.

But for those in the United States who are very concerned, they have taken to heart the notion that climate change is an existential threat. Google "global warming will kill us all" and you will get some 8.7 million results, with dire warnings from reputable, if highly partisan, figures like Bernie Sanders and Paul Krugman. Media outlets like *Vice* conduct polls asking "How long do we have before global warming kills us all?" and receive answers ranging from hundreds of years to only ten (*Vice* has filed the poll under "global warming" and "apocalypse," so you get a bit of its orientation). And let's not forget Zach, the Democratic National Committee staffer who yelled at his boss, Donna Brazile, for losing the presidential election: "You and your friends will die of old age and I'm going to die from climate change. You and your friends let this happen, which is going to cut forty years off my life expectancy."

This notion of an existential crisis, conveyed by people as different as Prince Charles and Zach, has driven progressive policies on climate and the environment for a number of years now and invited a certain amount of climate hysteria, an entirely warranted reaction if global warming would in fact take forty years off your life span and millions off the human race. But sensible conservatives respond with what Oren Cass of the Manhattan Institute has called "the case for calm,"[25] which goes something like this: (1) liberals have exaggerated the known effects of climate change; (2) because of the liberal impulse to want to "do something," they have proposed policies that have little effect on climate change yet impose costs on those least able to afford them; and (3) they have ignored the most obvious sources of remediation that we have, to our collective detriment.

The problem is that while climatologists agree, biologists and economists don't. Science indisputably supports global warming but does not currently support the conclusions about apocalyptic *outcomes*. Don't get me wrong, you can't read the United Nations' Intergovernmental Panel on Climate Change (IPCC) reports— the state of the art with respect to the scientific consensus— without getting a little sick to the stomach about what we are doing to Mother Earth. It is truly a parade of horribles. But, while climate change poses significant challenges to human systems, they are challenges that are not significantly worse than other problems we face. If you take the core scenario of the IPCC as our benchmark, quite a few very bad things are predicted to happen: the seas will rise, by two feet this century; the global economy will suffer, losing an estimated 3.6 percent of global gross domestic product (GDP) in aggressive scenarios; and farming will suffer, with up to half the world's current agriculture disappearing, to name just a few sobering effects.

Before you run into the street after Zach, sounding the alarm, let us put this in perspective. Losing half of the planet's agricultural production sounds daunting, but that is only .5 percent per year over the course of a century, a rather manageable number when you realize that global agricultural production has advanced by 2.5 percent per year for the last decade, almost all through more efficient production.[26] And while a loss of 2–3 percent off global GDP is also a very big number, trillions of dollars of value most likely, it is certainly manageable in the context of a global economy that is likely to grow more than 670 percent between now and the end of the century.

Under the Dynamic Integrated Climate-Economy (DICE) model, developed at Yale, the cost of climate change "represent[s] the difference between the world being 6.5 times wealthier than in 2015 or 6.7 times wealthier. In the DICE model, moreover, the climate-change-afflicted world of 2105 is already more prosperous than the climate-change-free world of 2100."[27] And because climate change is spread out over almost a century, the economic effect in any one year is almost negligible, with average growth declining from 2.27 percent to 2.22 percent. Math and time have a way of putting things in a rather different light.

The rising of the seas is perhaps the most daunting of the challenges, since it has the potential to uproot entire communities and devastate specific species. It is not the melting polar ice caps that pose a significant twenty-first-century threat—that is a challenge that will likely occur over a millennium or more—but rather the thermal expansion of ocean water as it warms. According to the IPCC, the impact of climate change on human ecosystems would be highly significant, "comparable with land-use change." In other words, the impact on ecosystems would be very substantial, and perhaps devastating in some places, but similar to the impact that humans have already had on the natural world. That is a lot, and perhaps far too much, but it is something we have figured out how to live with at least tolerably well.

Some conservative writers on the topic refer to all this as a "modest risk," perhaps as a way of counterbalancing the perceived alarmism of the other side. It sounds like far more than a modest risk to me, but however you want to categorize it, global warming is not a unique risk, different from other serious problems we need to worry about: overpopulation, global migration, spread of nuclear weapons, or global pandemics, to name just a few. Some of these problems pose even more devastating risks, but we pay far less attention to them. And other current problems, though perhaps less far-reaching, pose significant and solvable dilemmas. Take clean water: at current rates, some 12 million children under the age of five will die from waterborne illnesses between now and midcentury. This is in fact a largely solvable problem—we've known since at least the time of the Romans how to deliver clean water—but there are no war rooms, no international conferences attended by heads of state, no Nobel Prizes to be won. Somewhere along the way, we lost our perspective gene.

The problems of climate change of course get worse if you push out the scenarios and assume higher rates of temperature increase. With a rise of 4 degrees Celsius or more above pre-industrial levels we could face, according to the IPCC, "severe and widespread impacts on unique and threatened systems, substantial species extinction, large risks to global and regional food security, and the combination of high temperatures and humidity compromising normal human activities, including growing food or working outdoors in some areas for parts of the year." It's a big fucking deal, and I don't feel all that calm about it, thank you very much, but even this increase in temperature still does not mean that New York City will be an underwater theme park, nor does it mean that climate change is a greater or more important risk than pandemics or nuclear attacks. Those risks are far more likely to take forty years off Zach's life than climate change.

But if you posit that the problem of global warming is existential, you'd better do something about it, even if the solutions aren't particularly productive. Virtually all the projected growth in carbon over the next fifty years will come from sources outside the United States and Western Europe, so changes to the American energy mix are unlikely to have much of an effect. The various proposals offered by the Obama administration, from the Clean Power Plan to the commitments of the Paris climate agreement, would have virtually no discernible impact. The results, even as projected by the EPA, would reduce global temperatures by less than two-hundredths of a degree, and even if the United States eliminated all of its carbon dioxide emissions, global warming would be only held back by two-tenths of a degree. The math on the subject forced the Obama administration to defend its policies largely on the basis of the need to show leadership to the world.[28] Our persuasive leadership was not strong enough, apparently, to get the nations of Asia and Africa to commit to enforceable goals in connection with the Paris Climate Accords, and understandably so. Many nations need energy development to help provide a decent quality of life to their citizens for the first time—and even need development in order to manage the risks of climate change.

America's leadership on the topic does come with a cost at home, though. Environmental regulations typically form a classic public choice between growth and a better environment, and such is the case here. The Heritage Foundation has estimated that the Paris agreements, if they were to be carried through, would create an aggregate GDP loss between now and 2035 of $2.5 trillion and raise household electricity prices between 13 and 20 percent. Liberals may reasonably think of the Heritage Foundation as the Snidely Whiplash of the think-tank world—I know I do—but that does not mean that they are wrong here. Besides, other, less self-interested, sources have come to similar conclusions. Charles River Associates, a well-known econometric firm, has estimated that cap-and-trade would render energy far more expensive in the United States, almost a $2 trillion tax imposed on the American public each year by 2050. And many of these costs, as they so often do, would fall hardest on those least able to afford them: "the price increases resulting from a carbon cap would be regressive—that is, they would place a relatively greater burden on lower-income households than on higher income households." And that is what chews at me: we all benefit equally from a better environment—or in this case, the less tangible benefit of American leadership on environmental issues—but the real costs are felt in places like Pikeville, where people face a double-barreled hit: loss of jobs and higher energy costs that they can't avoid.

A short stroll from my house is the Adams Morgan neighborhood, best known for its popular bars and restaurants and its occasionally raucous street life, though the volume has moderated a bit as the neighborhood has gentrified and aged. But the politics of Adams Morgan remain resolutely young and progressive, as evidenced by a video that runs from time to time on the blank wall of a nearby apartment building. The video shows what I believe to be the sad impact of climate change. It's a little hard to tell, since brick walls don't make the best movie screens and my long-distance vision has never been particularly good, but I think it ends with a shot of rows of cars swamped by rising tides and a statement exhorting us to "Make Change." It's terribly civic-minded and wonderfully incoherent at the same time. Every time I see the video I wonder what change I'm supposed to make, perhaps other than to move my car to higher ground. I've had that thought several times, and always feel a little pleased at my own cynical cleverness, but as it turns out, and rather to my surprise, I actually have a point. Moving my car to higher ground is an act of adaptation, a very small act, admittedly, but adaptation is the first and highest-order response to a problem—like climate change—

that is going to happen whether we like it or not. Adaptation, resilience, mitigation, and planning are critical strategies, even if they don't solve the underlying problem. And that is because adaptation, unlike the Clean Power Plan, will have a far greater impact on Zach's life than anything else.

If you want to see how adaptation makes a difference, there are few better examples than Bangladesh, a nation that has inherited more than its fair share of misfortune. Space considerations preclude me from presenting the full list of grievances, but if I did, near the top would be geography: Bangladesh sits at the very top of the triangular-shaped head of the Bay of Bengal and much of the country is at sea level. It is a very bad combination. The shallow, narrow point of the bay serves as a funnel for tropical cyclones, and storms gather intensity as their energy is channeled into the narrow water passage leading up to the Bangladeshi shoreline. Because of this topography, about 40 percent of the entire planet's storm surge is recorded in Bangladesh, with tragic results. Cyclones hit the low-lying coast with devastating impact, creating some of the largest natural disasters of the last fifty years. About 750,000 people have died in Bangladesh from cyclones over that time.

If you think global warming would worsen the problem, you are both right and wrong. It is likely that global warming has or will intensify storms in the Bay of Bengal in the future, but the consequence of those storms has markedly decreased over the years. The worst of the cyclones killed 500,000 people in 1970 and another terrible cyclone claimed 140,000 lives in 1991. But since then, the government of Bangladesh has invested heavily in early warning systems, coastal reforestation, infrastructure to move people quickly out of the area, and a series of cyclone shelters. This has driven the annual toll from cyclones down to about 4,000 a year in 2007[29] and just 21 for Cyclone Roanu in 2016.

The rapid decrease in death has little to do with smaller storms and much to do with increased investments in adaptation and infrastructure, all of which require more energy, not less. It is in fact likely that relatively modest adaptation investments in one small region of the world will have already saved more lives than will likely be lost to climate change around the world in the next half century.

Climate change is an example of motivated reasoning on both sides of the equation, from those who seek to discredit the science as a way of minimizing government intervention, to those who exaggerate the risks of global warming in order to justify an agenda that is satisfyingly global in scope and bureaucratic in nature. The risks of the former are obvious. Get it wrong and see New York City become a collection of very wet neighborhoods, as imagined by the designer Jeffrey Lind: the Upper East Tide, Little Venice, Middrown, and Hell's Quicksand. But the risks of the latter are substantial, too: diverting resources from other pressing problems, retarding economic growth to the detriment of those who can least afford it, and, as we will see in the next chapter, ignoring a range of very practical solutions that are irritatingly inconsistent with the progressive narrative.

THE PARTY OF SCIENCE?

When the going gets weird, the weird turn pro.

—HUNTER S. THOMPSON, 1972

I t was trespassing, to be sure, most likely a violation of Kentucky Code Section 511.070, criminal trespass in the second degree, for anyone who is keeping track, but I had come too far to miss sneaking a peek at a 510-foot-long, 51-foot-high replica of Noah's ark. The slogan of the Ark Encounter, which is what this contraption is called, is "bigger than imagination," and I'm not sure it is all that, but it is big, about one and a half times the length of a football field and about half the length of the *Queen Elizabeth 2*. And even from my distant and illegal perch on the workers' parking lot, the ark, sitting incongruously in the middle of an otherwise isolated field in the heart of Grant County, Kentucky, is an astonishing and wonderfully off-kilter sight.

I had convinced myself that my little act of trespass was acceptable not only because no one working at the ark seemed to care a whit about my presence, but also because it was in furtherance of trying to answer a legitimate line of inquiry: why have Republicans turned against science?

It does seem painfully obvious that the Republicans have willingly and energetically assumed the role of the party that hates science, a label that was probably helpful in the Middle Ages and, sadly, not so electorally harmful now. Witness Paul Broun, a former four-term Republican congressman from Georgia, and once a member of the House Committee on Science, Space, and Technology, no less, who told a church gathering in Georgia that evolution, the Big Bang theory, and embryology were "lies straight from the pit of hell,"[1] a claim strikingly similar to the view of Ben Carson, who has on more than one occasion accused Darwin of being the pawn of the devil.[2] Not to be outdone by his own secretary of housing and urban development, President Trump once chalked up the entire global warming "hoax" to a bunch of scientists "just having fun," as if the warning about planetary survival were the result of a late-night binge down at Delta Tau Chi.

It wasn't always the case that the Republicans were the party that routinely challenged the cultural role of science and the role of scientists in public policy formation. In the 1970s, trust in science was higher among conservatives than among liberals or moderates, but over the last four decades, that trust has steeply deteriorated among conservatives, while it has remained largely unchanged among other groups.[3] The drop has been steady, reflecting not an abrupt break but a consistent decline in the reputation of the scientific community among conservatives, and it has been highest among college-educated conservatives. Research has shown that this decline in reputation is largely traceable to the work of party elites around climate change.[4] Republican leaders—both elected officials and lay leaders—have consistently attacked the scientific communities as ideological and issue driven, mostly doing so when the emerging scientific consensus is politically inconvenient to Republican interests. The result has been that faith in science has been reversed, with conservatives now evidencing substantially less trust in science than other parts of the political spectrum. From a leadership role in science and science policy in the 1970s, the Republican Party has in fact moved backward to become the party at odds with the scientific community.

★   ★   ★

Kentucky is a logical place to explore the confluence of science and political ideology, because it is a cultural touchpoint for creationism in America and one of the political epicenters for the fight over climate change. I have long been curious about creationism—the view that God birthed earth in its current form just six thousand years ago—but have largely consigned it to the category of cultural curiosity, dead since the Scopes Monkey Trial in 1925 but not quite fully aware of it. But for a mostly dead perspective, it has a shocking amount of kick. Some 42 percent of all Americans believe in the literal story of Genesis, and this number has remained rock steady for the thirty-five years that Gallop has polled the question, never drifting below 40 percent, never going above 47.[5] Americans are not unique in their skepticism of evolution, but we are among the most intense: in one global study of 34 developed nations, the United States came in next to last, just north of Turkey, in belief in evolution.[6]

Those three and a half decades have seen extraordinary changes in our nation: America has become far more ethnically diverse, better educated, more urban, and more secular. And the last thirty-five years have been a golden age for science in some respects. The Internet has forever changed the availability of information and the movement of ideas. We've uncovered the human genome and invented nanotechnology, decoded DNA and reprogrammed it. We've left our solar system for the first time and seen further back in time than ever before thanks to the Hubble Space Telescope, and we've even figured out that early man mated with Neanderthals, a theory so well developed and apparently

145

enchanting that it was the focus of a successful DreamWorks Animation movie franchise called *The Croods*. And despite all these changes and advances, the march of educational attainment and the spread of information, no one has changed their mind on the issue since Gallup first thought to ask about it in 1982. We are a very stubborn people.

The resilience of creationism is a bit of a mystery, but at least some of it is attributable to an energetic Australian teacher named Ken Ham, who founded the American branch of the creationist advocacy group Answers in Genesis in 1994 and is the modern-day Noah who built the Ark Encounter, or at least hired the workmen to do so. He also built the world's only museum dedicated to creation science, about an hour north of the ark, in Petersburg, Kentucky. The satirist P. J. O'Rourke once compared criticizing evangelicals as akin to "hunting dairy cows with a high-powered rifle and scope." And even though it is easy, or maybe because it is so easy, a few of my colleagues from east coast media outlets have made the pilgrimage to Petersburg to poke fun at it all. It makes for entertaining reading but not much enlightenment. I vowed to give a serious hearing to creationism, not on the truth of it—that is not in the cards for me—but to try to understand its appeal.

The Creation Museum is located, pleasingly enough, on Bullittsburg Church Road. The breadth of the appeal of creationism is immediately graspable in the parking lot. In addition to my heretic-mobile, plated to Washington, D.C., there are cars from Massachusetts, Rhode Island, California, Colorado, and Oregon. But the depth of the museum's appeal is less certain. Despite the large addressable audience for the museum, the parking lot is only sparsely populated on a warm June afternoon. It turns out that this is a common occurrence, as the Creation Museum has not turned out to be a great commercial success. At first it was a big draw, becoming a cultural mecca of sorts for northern Kentucky, but attendance has declined steadily for almost a decade, to barely half of what it was in its first years. Ham and his colleagues at Answers in Genesis have tried many things over the years to stem the decline, adding a zipline, an obstacle course, a mining sluice, and a biblical animal petting zoo. It's all pulled together around a surprisingly agreeable little pond, ringed with purple lilies, but none of it has worked. In a way, it's not terribly surprising: one of the challenges of creationism is that you are stuck with the original story. "Noah, still dead for six thousand years" is not going to bring back repeat customers.

Perhaps because of that, it's rather expensive to enjoy the pleasures of the museum. I grudgingly pay my $30 entrance fee, plus another $8 for the planetarium movie (though I skip forking over an additional $6 to pan a bag of biblical dirt). It's a bit of a business quandary for Answers in Genesis. Belief in creationism is highly correlated with lesser educational attainment, and lack of education is in turn highly correlated with lower income. It's not a small investment to bring a family of four to the museum for the day, even without the zipline, and apparently not enough families are willing to do it more. And surely there is only a limited number of high-horsed wiseasses like me who are willing to shell out money for the privilege of making merry at the expense of the creationists.

I hand over my credit card to the young lady at the ticket booth and ask, "What's the best exhibit here?" She ponders this question for a little too long, making me wonder whether anything is really notable, but then tells me with a hint of pride, "You should check out the Adam and Eve exhibit. I helped make the snake and it's really fantastic." Later, when I reach the exhibit, I have to agree. There is considerable debate among those who care about such things about the serpent in the Adam and Eve story: it is typically depicted in popular art as a snake, often a crafty-looking one. But many have wondered why Eve would trust a snake, of all creatures, since fear of snakes is practically imprinted among humans and other higher-order primates.[7]

One of the theories is that snakes of the early days did not look like the snakes of today. Martin Luther concluded "that before sin the serpent was a most beautiful little animal and most pleasing to man, as little mules, sheep and puppies today." I'd pick a puppy over a snake any day, so I'm with Martin Luther, but that is not the look of the serpent in the museum: it's long, scaly, a deep burnt red, with glowing eyes and a mean tilt to its head that accents a devious face. Nice job by my friend at the front desk, but I wouldn't trust that snake on a dare.

It's not hard to divine, if I can presume to use that word, the logic behind the Creation Museum. In its most rudimentary form, creationism and evolution are offered up as two equal and competing theories, neither of them provable by human observation. Ham would later say to me that all of this is theory anyway and that "none of us were around to see any of this," a rather offhand way of putting into doubt most of human science and, if you want to go there, all historical studies and the deductive works of Sherlock Holmes. It all rests on the notion that man is fallible and scientists perhaps especially so, and a significant amount of space in the museum is dedicated to showcasing the various mistakes of modern science.

And they have a rollicking good time doing it. The world of evolutionary biology has been wrong more than once, including being fooled by forgers and fraud. The most famous case, mentioned prominently at the Creation Museum, is the tale of the Piltdown Man. In 1912, an English amateur archeologist named Charles Dawson, with the support of the lead geologist at the British Museum, announced the finding of skeletal remains of what they claimed was the "missing link" between ape and man. The announcement, made at the august Geological Society of London, was received greedily by the scientific community because it fit perfectly, too perfectly perhaps, into the prevailing view of the development of man. There were some skeptics from the very beginning, and their ranks grew over time as beliefs around human evolution began to shift, but it wasn't until 1953 that new testing methods conclusively established Piltdown Man to be a forgery. Such deceptions are not just a product of a less sophisticated time. In 1999 the National Geographic Society was fooled into displaying bird bones smuggled out of China that it believed to be the missing link between dinosaurs and birds. When the society was forced to confess the next year that it had been fooled by fake fossils, the incident was derided as Piltdown Chicken, another tarnishing episode to evolutionary science. No one is more gleeful at the failures of evolutionary science than creationists, because it plays into a central argument: so who are you going to believe, the infallible word of God as recorded in the Holy Bible, or a bunch of scientists who can't tell the difference between dinosaurs and chickens? It's a seductive approach in some ways, and it is at the heart of the creationism movement.

I've heard variations of this theme many times over the course of this past year. If you accept the Bible as first principle, as a truth before all other truths, then the understanding of evolutionary biology is going to be driven not by the interpretation of the physical facts but by the consistency of the science with your understanding of the Bible. Many find ways to reconcile these differing truths, but if you are of the literalist mindset, it is not so easy to do. But that is the surface, and if you dig further down, there is something larger at work here. When John Inazu told me that evangelicals, especially older ones, are bewildered by the disorienting changes in society, he might as well have gone on to say that they are inclined to find solidity amid uncertainty in biblical truths. Ham himself has been known to specifically encourage that type of thinking: "Many Christians recognize the degeneration that has occurred in society. They see the collapse in Christian ethics and the increase in anti-God philosophies. They are well aware of the increase of lawlessness, homosexuality, pornography, and abortion (and other products of humanistic philosophy), but they are at a loss to know why this is occurring. The reason they are in such a dilemma is that they do not understand the foundational nature of the battle. Creation versus evolution is the bottom line."[8] In this view, creationism is not merely a construct to explain the observed world but a necessary bulwark against the moral relativism and social entropy that are characteristic of our time.

I get that, I really do, and I also recognize that we all choose sides in one fashion or another, that faith in science is a belief system in and of itself. That is not to create an equivalency between science and religion, which could hardly be more dissimilar in origins and approach. However, most of us not specifically talented in science—a group that all my grade school science teachers would say assuredly includes me—have to place a certain amount of faith in the scientific consensus. But it is more than faith in science, it is a belief in the *scientific method*, the process of observation, measurement, and experiment that has defined advanced science since the time of Aristotle. The scientific method is iterative and experimental and by its very nature invites error, but it is also the process that is at the root of advancements that have extended life, taken us into space, and redefined our knowledge of the universe. While I understand the impulse of my fellow museumgoers, I am more than a little hacked off at the likes of Carson and Broun, who owe their medical careers to the knowledge base built on the scientific method but who reject it as the devil's work when they find the results socially uncomfortable.

The social context is a bit of a shame, because as a place to visit, the Creationist Museum is really quite charming. I happily shuttle around the bright, colorful displays, snapping photos of Adam and Eve peacefully coexisting with a dinosaur, a tiger, and a penguin. It is a core belief, fossil records and DNA notwithstanding, that God created man and all the animals simultaneously, and they lived together harmoniously in the Garden of Eden, until they were all cast out after the Fall. The provenance of dinosaurs is a point of fascination within the creationist movement, mostly because it takes incredible mental gymnastics to make them work. Dinosaurs, in their view, were brought by Noah on the ark, which creates all sorts of frightening logistical questions, ranging from sheer weight and balance to the question that every eight-year-old boy (and fifty-two-year-old man, for that matter) wants to know immediately: where did all the poop go? My curiosity on that question is at least temporarily slaked by a handy exhibit on the poop of Noah's ark, and the answer is slate floors, with wood chips below. Once the poop dried, it was shoveled out, for lots and lots of animals (16,000, in estimates made by the Society of People with Too Much Time on Their Hands).[9] That is no small feat, shoveling the poop, dry or not, for thousands of animals, many of them quite productive in that regard—a full-size African elephant reportedly poops up to three hundred pounds a day. Maybe you think life on the ark was idyllic, but think about the eight members of Noah's family, cooped up with 16,000 bored and flatulent animals, feeding and cleaning up after them for almost thirteen months. I'm not exactly sure whom God was punishing and whom he was saving.[10]

You can drive yourself insane trying to make these stories work. To fit their biblically sourced facts, creationists have to maintain that Noah brought only two juvenile dinosaurs on board. Once the ark docked some 4,300 years ago, the dinosaurs quickly branched out into all the various species of the breed—big and small, winged and flat-footed, predatory and vegetarian—with astonishing speed, and then just as quickly died out, from unexplained causes. And even if you ignore carbon dating and the geological fossil records and the evidence more recently found through DNA analysis, you still end up with rather awkward math. Noah traveled with only 8,000 species, but today there are somewhere north of 8.7 million animal species on earth. It is a head scratcher on both sides of the equation: why were so few species created before the Flood, and why did the process of species diversification accelerate so rapidly afterward, to the tune of about a dozen new species every day for 4,000 years? It makes no sense.

I hustle over to the small planetarium just in time to catch the last showing of *Created Cosmos*. The movie turns out to be typical fare, a trip across the boundless distances of space. And the narration is like any other planetarium film, except for the frequent statements that the universe was all the six-day handiwork of God and the occasional potshot at modern science for being unable to explain all the phenomena observed in deep space, as if the failure to answer all the mysteries of the universe negates what we have learned over five hundred years of observational astronomy. As we travel the vast expanse of space, I wonder how the narrator will try to explain how light from the farthest reaches of the universe, billions of light-years away, could have reached earth if the universe is only 6,000 years old. He does, but it is rather unsatisfactory, as he intones that this all has been answered by the great minds of creation science, rattling off some theories I don't quite hear but which sound something like "alternative synchronicity" or "semiarid crapism" or whatever. I've been impressed, if that is the right word, by the efforts of creationists to justify their work and answer questions, but here they seem to be trying to hustle us out the door before we notice the emptiness of the logic. But everyone else seems happy with the show, and I leave amid many smiles and expressions of delight with the film. It reminds me that if you are inclined to take the Bible literally, you will forgive the gaps in the logic—and millions and millions of Americans do.

★   ★   ★

But before Democrats get too smug on this matter: a substantial minority of Democrats, some 33 percent, believe in creationism. This is less than the full 52 percent of Republicans who hold that same view, but enough to force us to recognize that this is mostly about culture, regionalism, and heritage, not just the pull of politics.

There is ample evidence suggesting that when it is convenient to do so, liberals will ignore the scientific consensus just as easily as conservatives do. For decades now, liberal groups have waged wars against genetically modified organisms (GMOs), branding them "Frankenfood" and accusing "Big Food" of poisoning future generations. The range of debate on the left on the topic is rather narrow, best exemplified by Bill Maher, who once asked a guest on his show whether he would rate Monsanto as a 10 ("evil") or an 11 ("fucking evil"). Liberal redoubts such as Boulder County, Colorado, and Sonoma County, California, have banned GMO crops, and GMO denial, if you will, is all the rage in my neighborhood as well. In years past, I would occasionally spy around Mount Pleasant a rather striking car, notable for a roof-mounted model, approximately six feet long, three feet high, of what we think is supposed to be a genetic cross between a tomato and a fish. The tomatofish, we believe, is supposed to be some type of warning against science tampering with the natural order of foods, though frankly, a tomatofish sounds rather delicious to me, maybe paired with a nice California chardonnay. I don't drink a whole lot of wine but I would make an exception here because any wine is in fact a genetically modified organism, one of the thousands of food products that man has developed through crossbreeding over hundreds of years.

Fear of GMOs flies completely in the face of the scientific consensus—a consensus that is as strong or even stronger than the scientific consensus on climate change—that GMOs are perfectly safe. That is the view of the World Health Organization, the National Academy of Sciences, and the American Association for the Advancement of Science (AAAS):

> [T]he science is quite clear: crop improvement by the modern molecular techniques of biotechnology is safe . . . contrary to popular misconceptions, GM crops are the most extensively tested crops ever added to our food supply. There are occasional claims that feeding GM foods to animals causes aberrations ranging from digestive disorders, to sterility, tumors and premature death. Although such claims are often sensationalized and receive a great deal of media attention, none have stood up to rigorous scientific scrutiny. Indeed, a recent review of a dozen well-designed long-term animal feeding studies comparing GM and non-GM potatoes, soy, rice, corn and triticale found that the GM and their non-GM counterparts are nutritionally equivalent.

We pick and choose the science we like, based upon the signals of our peers. As Jamelle Bouie noted in *Slate*, "seventy-three percent of Americans age 18 to 29 accept evolution, but only 39 percent say it's safe to eat genetically modified foods and 61 percent say scientists don't have a clear understanding of genetically modified crops."

You might shrug this off as "better safe than sorry," and many do, but that's not really the case. Real harm is caused by efforts to reduce or eliminate GMOs from the agricultural food supply. GMOs reduce soil damaging tillage, curtail carbon emissions, eliminate the need for some insecticide use, and allow the reduction of the most harmful toxic insecticides in favor of more mild ones. More important, GMOs, which tend to be far more efficiently produced, could play a critical role in expanding the global food supply, an important possibility given that the Food and Agriculture Organization of the United Nations estimates that we will need to grow 70 percent more food by 2050 to meet the demands of a hungry planet. GM crops raise the enticing prospect of growing hardier, efficient crops to feed the rapidly growing populations of Africa, Asia, and other parts of the developing world. And GM crops have, where available, had a substantial impact on farmer income; in India, the introduction of genetically modified cotton had a transformative effect on the nation's 7 million cotton farmers, raising income by as much as 50 percent and reducing the risk that farmers would descend into hunger.[11]

When policy makers and elites attack GMOs and the companies, like Monsanto, that make them, the losers are not the shoppers at Whole Foods, but those who can't afford Whole Foods here in the United States and those in the third world who couldn't even imagine shopping at a Whole Foods.[12] There is real mischief in the work of creationists, but they perhaps pale in comparison to the potential damage done by those who, without scientific foundation, seek to curtail the use of GMOs. All of this may seem a little beside the point, given the topic of this book, but it is to suggest that both parties have a fraught relationship with science and that the current alliance between Democrats and the scientific community operates under a flag of convenience.

★ ★ ★

Somewhere in this world, one might hope, science is a haven from politics. Not here. But in truth, there are limits to scientific analysis anyway; science might tell you the scope and cause of a problem like climate change, but it can't tell you what to do about it. That is the province of policy makers, who generally seem more interested in the temper of their constituents than in the temperature of the planet. Throughout my research on climate, I was struck by what seemed like an absence of practical thinking on how to best address a very real issue. The Obama administration focused on grand gestures, like the Paris accords, and color me unimpressed with the likelihood of successful concerted action from a global community that can't handle far more mundane issues, like rules of passage in the South China Sea, or a standard system of weights and measures, and most of whose domestic initiatives have become bogged down in the federal courts. The Trump policy of just undoing everything the Obama administration wanted to do, including investing in technology and resiliency, seems even less of a recipe for success.

Oddly enough, though, for all the governmental inaction, we're not doing so poorly. In the United States, which has no cap-and-trade policy, and where EPA regulations of carbon emissions have largely been neutralized by litigation, carbon emissions have fallen dramatically, by 12 percent (or 750 million metric tons) between 2005 and 2015. All this has happened even as the economy has expanded, by 15 percent over this period, meaning that on emissions per dollar of GDP basis, carbon emissions are down some 23 percent in a decade. It is a rather remarkable change, and the reason for that change is quite an important story, an implicit refutation of market planning and government intervention.

The first test of market innovation in energy production was a great surprise to virtually everybody, certainly to everyone in government and in the environmental community. For years the discussion of alternatives to coal and oil focused on speculative investments in renewables such as solar and wind—investments that held considerable long-term promise but faced real problems of weather, geography, economics, and even physics. But it captured our imagination nonetheless, so very little attention was paid to traditional though cleaner energies, such as natural gas. In 2008, the International Energy Agency (IEA) projected that U.S. natural gas production would remain flat or decline somewhat through about 2030.[13] The IEA calculated that expected productivity declines in existing fields would be largely offset by a sizable but by no means revolutionary increase in shale oil production. The Natural Resources Defense Council, for one, had projected in 2001 that shale gas production would rise from about 400 billion cubic feet to 800 billion cubic feet in 2010 and onward to a trillion cubic feet by 2020.

But a funny thing happened on the way to 2020: technology innovations in hydraulic fracturing (better known as fracking) and horizontal drilling dramatically changed the American natural gas industry and the country's carbon footprint. When we think of technology breakthroughs, we tend to think of the new and the exotic, and fracking is neither. The first known instance of fracking occurred in 1947 when Floyd Farris of Stanolind Oil & Gas Company (later Amoco) performed an experimental "hydrafrac" in Kansas, using 1,000 gallons of gasoline thickened with napalm, followed by a gel injection to crack open a limestone formation—a horrible-sounding idea presumably first reported by the Widow Farris.[14] But fracking got incrementally and steadily better throughout the 1980s, 1990s, and early 2000s. This progress was marked not by a single great leap forward but by many incremental steps—mostly through trial and error, from a vast field of small companies, in processes, materials, and techniques. The end result of this vast and uncoordinated innovation was a true and still largely unappreciated revolution in natural gas production in the United States. Instead of reaching 1 trillion cubic feet in production in 2020, U.S. natural gas production hit 10 trillion cubic feet in 2012. As Daniel Yergin reported, "Perennial shortage gave way to substantial surplus" and the mix of U.S. energy consumption moved away from relatively dirty fossil fuels, to relatively clean natural gas, with a large and predictable impact on the greenhouse gas profile of the United States.[15] Natural gas use involves roughly half the CO_2 of coal, for example, and the unexpected introduction of roughly 9 trillion cubic feet of relatively cheap, relatively clean energy had an extraordinary effect on the economy and on the American emissions profile. Carbon emissions in the United States have fallen more than 20 percent on a per capita basis, and that is largely due to the expansion of natural gas production. All the time we have been arguing about climate change and government regulation, creating vast subsidies for renewables, and negotiating global treaties that will likely never be enforced, a revolution in production has been going on that is having a larger effect than all the other pieces combined.[16]

Conservatives like to say that the fracking revolution occurred in isolation from government, but that's not entirely true. Federal government subsidies for research and development in areas such as 3-D seismology, diamond drill bits, and horizontal drilling techniques all played a role in the development of the fracking revolution.[17] And having a regulatory regime that provides protection for intellectual property and legal certainty for investors has been critical as well.

The advances in fracking, however, have come over the objections of some environmentalists who claim that it damages drinking waters and land; even if you assume the accuracy of these objections (which you really should not, since even the Obama EPA could not validate them), they would seem rather trivial compared to the safe future of humanity. It makes no coherent sense to be terribly alarmed about the species-threatening nature of climate change, and adamant against fracking, and yet there are many people who fit that description. The same can be said of nuclear energy. The carbon profile of nuclear energy is astonishingly good, on par with wind and hydroelectric power and significantly better than solar; its carbon footprint is mostly created by the fuel emissions of workers' cars and it is astonishing that it is not the apple of the eye of the environmental movement.

Don't get me wrong: nuclear energy can be a horror show, with Chernobyl, Fukushima, and Three Mile Island serving as exhibits A, B, and C—and perhaps the three-eyed fish on *The Simpsons* as exhibit D. And it hardly stops in Springfield. I've long been fascinated by the Hanford facility in Washington State, which for many years was the site of a massive nuclear energy and weapons production plant—and an abject lesson on how to fuck up a local ecosystem. Over a period of almost four decades after World War II, plant operators released, sometimes secretively, some 6.3 trillion liters of liquid waste containing strontium, cesium, plutonium, and a whole lot of other nasty stuff into the Columbia River, causing radiation levels to rise as far as two hundred miles downstream, on the Oregon and Washington coasts. Radioactive materials entered the human food supply through fish and dairy cows, placing an enormous population at elevated risk for cancers and other diseases. And it is not as if the problem has been solved now that the plant has largely been decommissioned. The site still holds a vast array of tanks, some 177 in all, filled with 53 million gallons of highly radioactive waste. No one seems to know what to do with it all. And Hanford is not even the most screwed-up nuclear site in the world. That honor perhaps goes to Sellafield in England; there is so much radioactive material at Sellafield that cleanup is projected to cost £162 billion and last roughly a century.[18]

It is all horrible, unless you compare it to potential extinction of the human species. If you want to propose "deep decarbonization" of the energy sector, then you need nuclear energy, or something quite similar to it, to serve as a fundamental ingredient of the energy mix.[19] And while the story of Hanford is daunting, we have in fact learned an enormous amount about safe operations over seven decades of nuclear power, as you might expect, and the vast majority of sites hum along perfectly nicely. Things could go wrong, for sure, but let's put this in perspective: more people will be killed this morning in the United States in auto accidents than will have been killed in the entire history of the U.S. nuclear industry. Direct deaths are by no means the only measure of the industry, of course, but it gives you some sense of proportion. And that's what progressives seem to lack on the climate change question. If you think the species is at risk, you'd better pursue a fuck-all-of-the-above strategy, even if you pour a lot into figuring out how to make nuclear energy safer. The fact that most (though, to be fair, not all) environmentalists portray climate change as an existential threat and still want to shut down fracking and nuclear power strikes me as the height of irresponsibility. It makes me want to hug a tree and slap an environmentalist at the same time.

The other market-driven change, perhaps even more consequential in the long term, is the potential transformation of the automobile marketplace, with the rise of commercially viable electric cars from Tesla and the astonishing advancement of autonomous vehicles from a wide variety of companies, including Google. The mix of coal, nuclear, fossil fuels, and renewables in power production is important, but so are transportation emissions. Not only do transportation emissions account for 26 percent of U.S. carbon emissions, a big chunk, but the sector is almost entirely driven, at 97 percent, by fossil fuels. That means that major changes in automotive technologies could have an enormous impact on greenhouse gases; if half the U.S. vehicle fleet (cars, trucks, and forklifts) were electrified by 2050—coupled with other shifts away from fossil fuels—American carbon emissions would decline by about 550 metric tons per year, the equivalent of taking 100 million passenger cars off the road.[20] Lots of different things can be done, but saving planet earth means changing how and what we drive.

For many years, the idea of an electric fleet has seemed almost the province of science fiction, something that the Jetsons might have parked in the garage alongside their robot maid, Rosie. The barriers to change included the need not only for substantial advancements in battery technology, but also for a vast charging station infrastructure to support a fleet of electric cars, and the willingness of a critical mass of consumers to jump to electric cars. That last factor should not be casually dismissed, since the automobile has demonstrated a unique design and engineering resiliency over time, and the basic car has changed shockingly little since Karl Benz designed the first internal combustion engine in 1886. Whatever the reason—the American love affair with the car or just the inertia of the car oligopolies[21]—reinventing the car marketplace would be no small feat, and many analysts predicted that would not happen until midcentury at the earliest.

Yet that midcentury moment is already here, and arrived thirty-four years early. That moment occurred on a small stage in Hawthorne, California, in the late afternoon of March 31, 2016, at the design headquarters of electric car company Tesla Motors. Onto that stage strode Elon Musk, dressed in various shades of black and gray, to unveil the new people's car, the Tesla Model 3, affordably priced, comparatively speaking, at $35,000. The unveiling of the Model 3 was widely anticipated, and within days more than 400,000 people had plunked down a $1,000 deposit, without seeing the car and certainly without having any idea when they might receive one. But as Musk told his rapturous audience, this announcement wasn't about a new car, it was about how to "accelerate the world's transition to sustainable transport" and was critical for the "future of the world." There are plenty of corporate CEOs who talk about world-changing ambitions, and it is usually wretched stuff, fodder for memes on corporate self-aggrandizement. But here Musk was right, since the vision, engineering, and marketing prowess of Tesla has seemingly ushered in an entirely new automotive era, one far more friendly to our global carbon profile. Virtually every car manufacturer in the world—from Toyota to Volkswagen to Hyundai—is now chasing Tesla, because they know that if Tesla can create a new market for electric cars, it will change the automotive business forever. As Mike Fox, the executive director of the Gasoline & Automotive Service Dealers of America, a man whose industry entirely depends on pumping more gas into more cars, told the *Wall Street Journal*, if Tesla can deliver on the promise of the Model 3, "gas vehicles are history—it's horse and buggy days."[22]

The rush to electric vehicles is not the only leapfrog innovation in the automotive industry. Advances toward fully autonomous cars, now only a handful of years away from reality, suggest that the entire model of automobile ownership will likely change within a matter of years. Like most things, the vision of a self-driving car is not new; some even have argued that Leonardo da Vinci sketched out a very early version.[23] Its more modern roots trace back to the General Motors Futurama exhibit at the 1939 World's Fair, where the automaker predicted "abundant sunshine, fresh air [and] fine green parkways" upon which self-driving cars could travel. It is a vision that ties automotive innovation with good weather and environmental quality, a surprisingly forward-looking notion in a time before global warming concerns.[24] Progress on autonomous vehicles was sporadic for much of the next sixty years, but it included a team of Carnegie Mellon roboticists taking a self-driving Pontiac across the country in 1995 in the self-styled "No Hands Across America" tour, as well as other experiments by labs and universities around the world. But the goal of autonomous driving really took off with a government intervention, not a mandate or a big spending program but a challenge from the Defense Advanced Research Projects Agency (DARPA) to foster the development of robotic cars. The first Grand Challenge, held in 2004, was hardly a smashing success. DARPA erected a 150-mile course through the Mojave Desert, and an autonomous Humvee from Carnegie Mellon got the farthest, only 7.3 miles before it skidded off a hairpin turn. But only a year later, five teams, led by Stanford's Stanley car, successfully navigated the entire course, and within two more years they were completing ever-more-challenging urban layouts. Spurred by DARPA, the race toward autonomy was on. Today numerous car companies have experimental fleets on the road, and several, including Ford and BMW, have pledged to put autonomous cars in the marketplace by 2021.

The transportation system of tomorrow now looks very different from what we have known for almost one hundred years. And this future has been created mostly by private innovation, though spurred by government investment and encouragement. As we have seen, the original DARPA Grand Challenge, even though it was backed only by a $1 million prize that was never paid, spurred an entire generation of excitement and innovation. Tesla itself would not have been possible without significant government support. In 2015, the *Los Angeles Times* reported that Tesla had received almost $2.4 billion in government subsidies. Those subsidies came from all levels of government and include a $1.29 billion Nevada state incentive for the building of Tesla's giant Gigafactory,[25] $45 million in discounted Department of Energy loans, and $284 million in tax credits for buyers of Tesla Model S sedans. [26] These subsidies have been widely criticized, reflexively as some form of crony capitalism and more thoughtfully for the uncoordinated and inefficient nature of government subsidies. The objections are fair, perhaps, but these subsidies may also prove to have been the difference between success and failure for Tesla. And the product and marketing brilliance of Tesla has in turn been the lynchpin for the development of the electric car market and the changing face of the global transport market.

These dramatic changes—from natural gas production to the advent of the electric car to the looming future of the autonomous vehicle—have not only disrupted a number of industries but also shifted the carbon curve in at least portions of the developed world. None of them happened because of heavy-handed government interventions; they happened because the American marketplace is the strongest innovation lab in the world. It is a lesson, a Republican lesson if you will, about knowing the limitations of government and the relative merits of the private sector.

It is similarly true that state regulation, when implemented, has struggled to achieve its intended purpose, mostly because unpredictable conditions in the real world tend to frustrate fixed regulatory schemes. While the United States has made considerable carbon progress, Germany, in many ways the home of the worldwide green movement, has struggled, despite the aggressive launch of the *Energiewende* ("energy transformation") policy to push renewables (solar and wind) and a heavy reliance on the

European Union's cap-and-trade systems. Germany has had historic success reducing greenhouse emissions. Throughout the 1990s and early 2000s, CO_2 emissions in Germany declined significantly, even as the economy expanded—though much of this had to do with the retirement of East German heavy industry and modernization of the extraordinarily dirty power facilities of the former Soviet bloc.[27] In 2010, Germany adopted the *Energiewende* plan as part of an aggressive move toward a low-carbon future. The plan hinged on the continued growth in renewable power, which now accounts for almost 25 percent of German electrical consumption. But the plan almost immediately ran afoul of the unintended, though perhaps predictable, consequences of environmental decision making. Because of concerns about environment degradation, Germany has long outlawed fracking, and after the Fukushima nuclear disaster in Japan, Chancellor Angela Merkel moved to shut down German nuclear power capacity as well. Those two decisions left a rather large hole in energy capacity, one that couldn't be filled by natural gas or other fossil fuels. Because of the so-called feed-in tariff, which requires distributors to buy renewables at fixed prices before buying power from other sources, German power producers had simply been unable to develop alternative sources, so when the crunch hit, only coal was left standing as a viable alternative, even given the additional financial penalties associated with the cap-and-trade system. As a consequence, CO_2 emissions rose in 2011 and 2012 (even as they fell in the United States), and again by about 10 million metric tons in 2015 (approximately 1.1 percent).[28] The coal renaissance put environmentalists on edge and created a gleeful schadenfreude in places like the editorial pages of the *Wall Street Journal*:

Berlin is scaling back some taxpayer subsidies for green power. But Germans still also pay for the energy revolution

165

when job-creating investment goes to countries with lower power costs, as happened earlier this year when chemical company BASF said it would cut its investments in Germany to one-quarter of its global total from one-third, and when bad incentives skew generation toward dirtier coal instead of cleaner natural gas. None of this is what environmentalists promise voters when they plug the virtues of a low-carbon future. Germany's coal renaissance is a cautionary tale in what happens when you try to substitute green dreams for economic realities.[29]

And it is not likely to get better soon, even though new pollution regulations, designed to shut down older coal plants, went into effect in 2016. The German government, as governments do, has made competing promises: to close the entire nuclear power capacity by 2022 even though nuclear power still amounts to 14 percent of national capacity, to continue to drive down carbon emissions, and to fuel economic growth. Those numbers don't add up, and it is likely that coal, and carbon, will be winners at the end of the day.

The situation in the United States is almost the complete opposite. Ten years ago, coal accounted for 50 percent of electrical use in the United States, while natural gas accounted for 19 percent. In 2015, natural gas overtook coal (with both at roughly 33 percent) as the primary source of energy in this country, for the first time ever. The turnover is extraordinary in its rapidity. In April 2015, the U.S. Energy Information Administration predicted that coal would remain the dominant source of energy for another twenty-five years. It lasted instead for twenty-five *weeks*, with the crossover effectively happening for good in September 2015.[30] And that is all natural markets at work: fracking and shale gas have inverted the pricing marketplace. Spot market prices for natural gas typically hovered between $5.00 and $10.00 per million BTUs during the 2000s, with spikes as high as $18.48 in 2003, but in 2016, as I write this, prices have settled into a range between roughly $1.50 and $3.00 per million BTUs.[31] With that huge drop, driven by increased supply, the shift toward cleaner natural gas has happened more swiftly than any government program could possibly manage. With big changes coming in the automotive markets as well, there are substantial tailwinds in the United States in the fight to reduce carbon emissions, and they have relatively little to do with the policies or nonpolicies of the Obama and Trump administrations.

★   ★   ★

There is a slow but significant shift, one that I suspect will not be reversed, in Americans' attitudes toward climate change. More Americans are worrying about it, if for no other reason than our recent run of record temperatures, and more Americans are attributing the increased temperatures primarily to human activity. Republicans are latecomers to this party but they are grudgingly, ever so creakily, coming around to recognize the scientific consensus. There is even a subtle, though hardly revolutionary, shift in how party leadership talks about it: President Trump's cabinet, unlike him, has generally acknowledged the fact that the earth is getting warmer. I suppose it is progress that the head of the EPA does not think that climate change is a hoax, even if that reduces the potential for more fun snowball fights in the Senate. But it is only so much progress when he continues to try to obscure the scientific consensus on human causation, a smoke screen that most any twelve-year-old with a computer and a reasonable facility with Google can pierce. There is much insight in the conservative critique of climate change, but it is nearly impossible for me to feel enthusiasm for a party whose leadership continues to stick its head into (hot, burning) sand.

I don't feel much more kindly at the end of the day toward progressives, either, who seem to have their own challenges with identifying the scientific consensus, though it is their inclination, as Hayek predicted, to exaggerate it rather than minimize it. Witness Bernie Sanders at the confirmation hearing for Scott Pruitt, when he declared that the "vast majority of scientists are telling us if we do not get our act together and transition our energy sector away from fossil fuels there is a real question of the quality of the planet." This notion of a scientific consensus around *policy* is not an exaggeration; it is an out-and-out fiction. Nevertheless, it begins to build the case that those who dispute the Democrats on policy grounds are somehow climate deniers themselves. The single exchange between Sanders and Pruitt, where one exaggerated the science and the other one disputed it but both obviously got it wrong, is a maddening example of where our politics have gone off the rails. It reflects poorly on everyone.

I don't feel the same, though, about Pikeville, even if the prevailing science in town is just as bad. There is an old axiom known as Miles's law, that "where you stand depends on where you sit." Its origin is in bureaucratic politics, but it might as easily be applied to the micropolitics of our age. If you are sitting in Pikeville, staring down the chute of a rapidly decaying community, you are going to have a very different perspective on the politics of climate change. From Pikeville, the whole debate over climate change looks like nothing more than another chapter in an autobiography that somehow the people of Appalachia did not get to write. Their jobs, their businesses, and their futures were all sacrificed to a policy even the Obama administration describes as largely about leadership, not impact. I'm all for symbolism, but you can't cash it at a bank, you can't feed your family with it, and you can't build hopes for the future around it. I always thought that it was the Democrats who were supposed to stand up for people without power, but it sure doesn't look that way from Pikeville. If there were a place where I started thinking the title of this book should be "Independent Like Me," that place would be Pikeville.

6

THE GREATEST SOCIETY

If you've ever seen the look on somebody's face the day they finally get a job, I've had some experience with this, they look like they could fly. And it's not about the paycheck, it's about respect, it's about looking in the mirror and knowing that you've done something valuable with your day. And if one person could start to feel this way, and then another person, and then another person, soon all these other problems may not seem so impossible. You don't really know how much you can do until you stand up and decide to try.

—KEVIN KLINE, IN *DAVE* (1993)

George McDonald is a rather unusual choice to be the Republican Party's poster child for poverty. He is a lifelong Democrat, and, even worse, a political operative who ran Teddy Kennedy's New York State presidential campaign in 1980. He even once campaigned on the Communist Party ticket to be New York City Council president, though in truth that was mostly to harass the Democratic nominee, Andrew Stein, who was a political nemesis of long standing. McDonald is loud and crass, brilliant and scheming, a New York pol through and through. He is as unlikely to be a model for the Republican approach to poverty as anyone I can think of, but nonetheless, McDonald and his nonprofit, the Doe Fund, have become exactly that.[1]

A story like McDonald's needs a little room to breathe, so let's start at the beginning, which for McDonald was Spring Lake, New Jersey, the "Irish Riviera." It was, by all accounts, a typical childhood: McDonald would begin his day as an altar boy at St. Catherine's Church each morning, and "the nuns would beat the shit out of [him]" at school every afternoon. Not surprisingly, McDonald rebelled against his strict upbringing and moved to New York City to seek the freedoms and pleasures of the big city. When I ask McDonald to date the move, he pauses and says, "I think it was the year *The Graduate* came out," which is handy because it both answers my question (1967, if you care) and gives us a nice celluloid snapshot of McDonald as Benjamin Braddock, the aimless, disconnected title character, played by Dustin Hoffman.

McDonald did not find his first job in plastics, but instead in fashion, at McGregor Fashions on Fifth Avenue, where he worked for fifteen years. Though he stayed for a decade and a half, McDonald considered McGregor to be merely a way station. His focus in those early years was on, in his words not mine, "enjoying the fruits of the sexual revolution." He partied with Joe Namath, and though I have not seen pictures of the time, it is easy enough to imagine the younger McDonald as a prosperous, swaggering libertine of the day. Fashion was not his calling, but it was an easy entrance into a life he was most assuredly enjoying.

New York City, though, was less clearly enjoying life. A number of trends threaded together to turn the city into a dark, dangerous place. The collapse of the garment industry and the city's manufacturing base and white flight in the late 1960s and 1970s ravaged the local economy and its tax base, leading to the near bankruptcy of America's largest city in 1975. At a time when poverty rates overall in the United States were relatively stable, poverty in New York City skyrocketed, from about 15 percent in 1975 to 25 percent in 1982.[2] Crime rose: murders, which numbered only about 631 in 1965, reached almost 1,700 by 1972. Robberies went up almost tenfold, vehicle theft became a cottage industry, and rapes almost tripled, from 1,154 to 3,271.[3] It is hard for me, some fifteen years or so younger than McDonald, to remember the dystopian nature of New York City for a generation of people, but in many ways and by the numbers, the New York City of that era was nasty, brutish, and tall.

The disconnect between the decay of the city and the hedonism of fashion eventually got to be too much for McDonald. He became "tired of stepping over homeless people on the way to two-hundred-dollar lunches" and entered politics, mostly unsuccessfully, and began working with the homeless, with far better results. In the early 1980s, McDonald began collaborating with a young lawyer named Robert Hayes, who founded the Coalition for the Homeless, an advocacy group focused principally on the needs of homeless men who began appearing on the streets of New York for the first time in the 1970s.

At least for storytelling purposes, the link between Hayes and McDonald was an important one, because it exposed two dramatically different philosophies about how to reduce poverty, homelessness, and need in this country. Hayes took the view, one classically associated with modern liberalism, that the best way to solve the challenges of homelessness was to seek an expansion of government rights and support, sometimes through legislation and sometimes through the courts. In 1979 he filed suit against the state of New York in a landmark case called *Callahan v. Carey*, claiming a right, under the New York State Constitution, to shelter for homeless men. The Callahan plaintiffs prevailed, at least in that the city agreed to a consent decree opening a network of shelters around the city for every homeless man (and eventually woman) who met the eligibility criteria. It was a landmark win for the homeless community, though in a sad codicil, Robert Callahan, a homeless man, himself never got to enjoy the fruits of his victory, having died "sleeping rough" on the streets of New York just months before the consent decree went into effect.

The *Callahan* case was a significant milestone for the Coalition for the Homeless, though in some ways it papered over strong divisions on how best to deal with the problems of homelessness and structural poverty in New York City. McDonald himself broke sharply with Hayes over strategy. He had been heavily influenced by his own experiences, passing out sandwiches for seven hundred consecutive nights in Grand Central Terminal, where he was told by a homeless person, "this is a great sandwich, but I really wish I had a room to stay in and a job to pay for it." From these interactions, McDonald began to evolve a theory that focused less on government services and more on the idea of work and opportunity to break the cycle of homelessness, criminal recidivism, and substance abuse.

In 1985, to advance these theories, McDonald and his wife, Harriet Karr-McDonald, opened the Doe Fund, named after a white-haired, diminutive woman who was among the many homeless whom McDonald served in Grand Central. She had died of pneumonia Christmas night at her usual spot and McDonald was called upon to identify the body, which he did, but to his regret he could not supply a name and she ended up as another Jane Doe.

McDonald will tell you now that he started the Doe Fund without any real idea of what he was doing, beyond a desire to test ideas about the transformative value of work. The early strategy, if you want to aggrandize it with that term, of the Doe Fund was to take advantage of any work opportunity McDonald could find. Early on, McDonald was able to latch successfully on to a new city program called "Supportive Work." In the wobbly days of the 1980s, the city of New York had found itself through foreclosure, escheatment, and forfeiture to be the owner of a vast range of run-down properties, often in seedy neighborhoods. The Supportive Work program was a tidy way to provide income opportunities for hard-to-employ immigrants and criminal parolees and also maintain some semblance of maintenance and repair in this property empire. McDonald bought a van, finagled a city contract (he was a politician, after all, and knew how to work the system), and started taking crews out to do Sheetrock work and general repairs on these city-owned properties. Most of the better sites were already locked up, so McDonald, out of necessity, took his crews to the places "where the fucking unions wouldn't go," as he rather colorfully puts it. It was dirty, dangerous work—his vans were target practice, he recalls, on more than one occasion—but it allowed the Doe Fund to grow and the McDonalds to evolve their views on work.

Their theory is at its heart straightforward, based on the core belief that people, whether they are ex-cons or in some way down-and-out, prefer the dignity of work to the paternalism of the government handout. It is not an ideological objection to government largesse or to providing a safety net for those in need, but a question of priorities, the need to invest in allowing people to stand on their own two feet, for everyone's benefit. The Doe Fund focuses almost entirely on a generation of mostly young black men who have been denied access to the wider economy—to the skills necessary to survive and to the experience that gives reassurances to employers. The fund's target is the parole population, in recognition of the extraordinary high unemployment rate of parolees (65.6 percent), the high rates of recidivism, which are a direct function of the lack of opportunity, and the absence of structural support. The New York State prison system releases more than 25,000 people every year, and the city jails set loose an additional 64,000 people every year. Collectively, they are launching an entire city of people into New York every year, and, for many of these parolees, a support infrastructure from family, friends, employers, or government simply does not exist. Many, if not most, in the parole population are, on day one, homeless, jobless, ineligible for public housing due to HUD rules, and otherwise without resources. It is little wonder that so many men—and we are largely talking about men—end up back in jail. The singular goal of the Doe Fund is to break the chain of hopelessness that ties together this cycle of poverty, lack of opportunity, and crime.

In the early 1990s, McDonald bought an old industrial home for the blind and converted it into a transitional facility with seventy rooms. His plan was to house recent parolees in the new facility and train them for work opportunities through the Supportive Work program. But in the early years of the Giuliani administration, the city began to sell off many of its properties, substantially reducing the scope of the Supportive Work program and thus the work (and income) opportunities available to the Doe Fund. It was a bit of a crisis and led McDonald to do what must have seemed very odd at the time. He purchased blue uniforms—windbreakers, pants, shirts, and hats—for a number of men in the program, designed a "Ready, Willing & Able" logo, and sent the group out into the Upper West Side with brooms and instructions to sweep the streets clean. It could have gone very badly, sending a large group of unfamiliar black men into one of the wealthiest neighborhoods in the city, but it worked. Perhaps it was the uniforms, perhaps it was the obvious dedication to work, maybe it was the little American flags that McDonald had sewn onto the shoulder of each windbreaker, or maybe it was that New Yorkers just love clean streets, but the neighborhood embraced the Doe Fund teams that day and many since. The blue men of the Ready, Willing & Able program have long since become a familiar part of the New York cityscape.

Today the Doe Fund has about 680 resident participants in the program at any one time. Participants are referred from the Department of Corrections upon release and are first put through one month of post-incarceration stabilization training. Upon completion of the reentry course, the parolees begin paid work on street cleaning crews. Three months into the transitional work program, activities are broadened to include intensive vocational training in disciplines ranging from pest control, to culinary arts and food handling, to commercial driving. In the final month of what is typically a nine-to-twelve-month period, the focus shifts to independent living and job placement.

There is an element of tough love in the program. The Doe Fund only takes in single men but many of those men have children and child support requirements. Making child support payments is a condition of the program. So is staying drug- and alcohol-free, and drug tests are routinely administered through an in-house testing clinic. It's a rigorous testing program and the punishment for failing a drug test is not expulsion but the denial of work. It's perhaps the most interesting rule of the program. Work has become such a coveted aspect of the Doe Fund that getting a day or more off from it is seen not as a reward but as a punishment.

On the outside, the Doe Fund's Bronx transitional facility, where I interviewed McDonald, is dirty, gray, and institutional. It is gray and institutional on the inside as well, but spotlessly clean. As I tour the building, a middle-aged man launches out from one of the offices and introduces himself. Craig Trotta is a supervisor now at the Doe Fund, and has worked there for nineteen years, but like most of the permanent employees, he came there originally as a customer. Trotta comes from the wrong side of Queens and has the accent and scars to prove it, all of which he is pleased to show me. He grew up running drugs—for the mob, he hints—and wound up getting shot in the face and incarcerated for his troubles. After release he ended up in the Doe Fund program and at first didn't know what to make of the place. But then he "found a guy who was doing great, and I just latched on to him and followed him around asking questions." Even now, after nearly two decades and with a wife and a ten-year-old son, he says it is still a struggle. When Superstorm Sandy wiped out much of his life, Trotta felt the pull of trying to find quick, if not entirely legal, money. But he is a lifer now, a Doe Fund lifer, and the sense of purpose that it provides has brought him through.

Over the years, the McDonalds and the Doe Fund have generated an impressive record of success. The organization has grown to three residential facilities in New York, and the McDonalds have also opened a model program in Philadelphia. They have also demonstrated an unusual and commendable dedication to research and programmatic evaluation. The Doe Fund tracks every program participant for up to three years after graduation, recording employment history, legal or drug problems, wages, education, and any reversions to the criminal justice system. This deep record of data has permitted independent researchers to evaluate the program in detail. They have uniformly concluded that the Doe Fund increases employment opportunity, reduces poverty, and, perhaps most important, keeps people out of jail. A 2010 study by Bruce Western of Harvard concluded that graduates of Ready, Willing & Able are 60 percent less likely to be convicted of a felony within three years. Given that approximately 22,000 men have come through the program over the last two decades, we are talking about a difference in the lives of thousands of men who might otherwise be right back in jail but are instead leading law-abiding, and presumably productive and happier, lives. This evidence of impact is rare in the nonprofit world and convinces me that the Doe Fund is truly onto something worthy.

The program's emphasis on the transformational power of work has made it a bit of a darling of the right. Researchers from the Cato Institute and the American Enterprise Institute have all trotted up to New York for a tour. Various foundations associated with the Koch brothers have been keen on supporting the Doe Fund as part of their overall strategy of reducing the prison population and ultimately reintegrating hundreds of thousands of mostly young black men back into what passes for polite society. When I asked how they felt about being a conservative poster child, Alexander Horwitz, the chief of staff at the Doe Fund, gave me a funny look and said, "Look, I'm Jewish, gay, and liberal," but the money supports the mission. And that's right, money is green, not red or blue, and like foreign affairs, politics should stop at the water's edge when it comes to creating opportunity for the poor and the dispossessed.

★   ★   ★

In 2012, President Obama shared with a group of Democratic donors his view of the heartless society that America would become if Republicans had their way: "If you get sick, you're on your own. If you can't afford college, you're on your own. If you don't like that some corporation is polluting our air or the air that your child breathes, then you're on your own." The president's depiction of callous conservatism may have been a touch patronizing and modestly impolitic, but it was hardly out of step with public opinion. Americans are five times more likely to describe the Republican Party as "not compassionate" than they are to describe it as compassionate, and only about 5 percent of the public describes Republicans as "very compassionate." Conservatives don't do themselves many favors when people like Rush Limbaugh say "the poor in this country are the biggest piglets at the mother pig and her nipples. They're the ones who get all the benefits in this country. They're the ones that are always pandered to." The view that "poor people have it easy because they can get government benefits without doing anything" is a minority view in this country overall, but it is endorsed by fully 80 percent of conservatives. It is a view at odds with the evidence on the matter—the life spans, health, and stress levels all suggest otherwise—and I sure don't see many conservatives rushing into poor neighborhoods for that easy living environment. I know enough about the evidence on individual philanthropy to see a more nuanced picture than these numbers suggest—conservatives give significantly more in money, time, and even blood (donations) for charitable causes. However, I've always pretty much sided with the rest of America when it comes to viewing conservatives as uncaring and uncompassionate.

The fact that conservatives present as cynical sons of bitches does not mean that they are necessarily wrong about policy. The conservative critique of the welfare state begins with a serious indictment: the programs not only do not work to reduce poverty, but they in fact have tended to cement intergenerational poverty, creating a permanent underclass. It's a bold critique but one generally shared by the American public. Fewer than half of Americans think federal government programs have any positive impact on poverty and only 5 percent think that they have a big positive impact. And about one-third of Americans say that government programs have made poverty worse, a view that is most prevalent among conservatives, 47 percent; blue-collar whites, 43 percent; and, interestingly, poor people themselves, 40 percent. It is not the report card that you would wish for, given our collective investment of $22 trillion in fighting poverty over the last half century.

A lot of people, experts and neophytes alike, seem rather certain that our poverty programs have failed, but is that so obviously true? If you consider the official Census Bureau measure of poverty, the picture is grim. When President Lyndon Johnson declared his intention to end "poverty as we know it," the massive economic engine of the midcentury United States was already doing a pretty good job of that. Poverty had already declined from over 30 percent in the postwar years to under 20 percent by 1964, fueled mostly by economic expansion. It was one of the great lessons of the twentieth century, one not lost on President Kennedy, that general economic expansion can "lift all boats" and bring millions of people out of poverty.

The poverty level continued to decline for a few years after the extraordinary legislative burst of activity in 1964 that created the Great Society, though it was most likely the continuing consequence of the economic boom rather than the effects of government programs that were still in their infancy. Poverty rates leveled out in the late 1960s at around 15 percent and since then have undulated slowly, rising a few points in bad times, falling a few points in good. In 2015, the rate stood at 13.5 percent, and if you will allow for a little rounding, the same rate as 1990, 1980, and 1970. Twenty-two trillion is a lot of money to spend to just tread water.

And it is not for lack of trying, or at least for spending. The annual spending on means-tested welfare programs across federal and state governments has substantially increased virtually every year since 1973. After adjusting for inflation (and omitting entitlement programs like Medicare and Social Security), spending has gone from under $200 billion in 1973 to almost $1 trillion today. You would expect spending to increase even in constant dollars because the population has increased substantially, as has the economy, but spending on poverty programs has outstripped most other benchmarks, growing faster than inflation, faster than the economy, and at rates higher than government spending in general, including, for instance, military spending. These are substantial increases, and rather surprisingly, the increases have been steady through Democratic control of the federal government, through Republican control (including during the Reagan administration), and during times of shared control.[4]

And it is not for lack of imagination, either. Administration after administration, Republican and Democrat alike, has launched dozens of new programs to help the poor. The House Budget Committee has identified ninety-two separate federal programs to help lower-income Americans and those programs span virtually every major agency of government, and not just the obvious ones like the Department of Health and Human Services and the Department of Housing and Urban Development but also the Department of the Treasury, the EPA, the Federal Communications Commission, and the Department of the Interior. There is some dispute over the precise number of programs, due to definitional disagreements as to what constitutes a poverty or low-income program and what does not, but let's just stipulate that there are a whole mess of programs spread across a whole mess of federal agencies.

If that were the end of the story, as some conservatives would have it, it would be a pretty damning one, but it is far more complex. Cash income is not the best measure of poverty, because it ignores pretty much the entire War on Poverty, which, contrary to public perception, is not focused primarily on cash payments to poor people but mostly on housing, food vouchers, tax credits, and the like. When you start counting the value of what people consume, rather than the amount of cash they take in, as Columbia University researchers did in 2013 and others have done since, the picture looks considerably different. If you look, for instance, at child poverty on a cash basis, it has actually increased since 1970 and would stand at roughly 20 percent today. But if you measure consumption, and start calculating in noncash benefits that turn into food and health care and education, real child poverty has declined substantially in recent years, from about 15 percent in the late 1970s to under 10 percent today.[5] And if you ask the Columbia team what would have happened without the War on Poverty, they would tell you that poverty in America would be much higher today than it was fifty years ago. In that sense, the War on Poverty looks rather different; because of it, millions of children can eat, go to school, and visit a doctor.

You won't find many conservatives bragging on those numbers, at least in part because their measure of success is not the absolute reduction of poverty but rather the increase in self-sufficiency. It is now almost an accepted part of the conservative canon that federal poverty programs are ineffective and wasteful. Paul Ryan, the Republican bandleader on poverty, has been frequently quoted over the last few years as saying that the War on Poverty "failed miserably" to give "the forgotten fifth of our people opportunity not doles." In this view, fifty years and $22 trillion later—three times the cost of every single American war since the American Revolution—the War on Poverty has failed to lift poor people out of poverty and give them the opportunity and tools to succeed. It is a rather extraordinary challenge, since in many ways the War on Poverty has defined American governance for the last half century and its success or failure is not just an evaluation of a particular program (or programs, in this case) but a rejection of our entire approach to modern scientific governance:

The War on Poverty crippled marriage in low-income communities. As means-tested benefits were expanded, welfare began to serve as a substitute for a husband in the home, eroding marriage among lower-income Americans. In addition, the welfare system actively penalized low-income couples who did marry by eliminating or substantially reducing benefits. As husbands left the home, the need for more welfare to support single mothers increased. The War on Poverty created a destructive feedback loop: Welfare promoted the decline of marriage, which generated the need for more welfare.[6]

And that is perhaps the strongest indictment of our poverty programs. It is much better to live in poverty today than it was fifty years ago—food is more plentiful, calorie counts are higher, medical services are often available—and that is real progress in a society that believes that no one should have to choose daily between feeding themselves or their kids. But poverty is as much a trap as ever. If you are born poor today, you have no better chance of escaping poverty than if you were born in 1964. It is certainly not fair to blame our poverty programs for all of that failure, but it is nonetheless a rather negative bottom line to a half century of government intervention.

If the goal of the Great Society was to create opportunity and greater social mobility, it failed miserably. Despite the massive government interventions developed in the Johnson administration and gradually expanded since, measures of intergenerational economic mobility in the United States have not changed significantly over the last fifty years. If you are born to the bottom 20 percent of the income ladder, your chances of climbing up that ladder are very poor, probably around 9 percent, and that number has not budged in any meaningful way in more than half a century.[7] The "birth lottery" still controls access to education, connections, and resources, and still dictates, in ways that we are loath to admit, ultimate financial success in our economy.

What has changed is income inequality, which has increased substantially over time, meaning that the rungs of that ladder have moved apart. The growth of inequality does not mean that life in the bottom 20 percent has gotten worse; to the contrary, much of the evidence suggests that poverty programs have ameliorated the worst and most fearful aspects of poverty. But we have not come anywhere close to achieving Johnson's vision of an opportunity society. It may be an overstatement but there is still a stinging truth in President Reagan's observation that "we waged a war on poverty, and poverty won."

The sense of all this might be lost at the political conventions, but it has not been lost on the American people. Across the political spectrum, the American people are remarkably skeptical of our government's ability to reduce poverty. We think that poverty programs have failed generally, attribute that to the failure of design (56 percent) rather than the lack of funding (20 percent), and believe that even if government had unlimited funding to attack poverty, it wouldn't have enough knowledge to solve the problem (73 percent). It is unwise in my view to make too much of public opinion on the issue, what with all the vast complexities of poverty programs and with the gross misperceptions of "welfare queens," but it is still hard to shake the perception that the public is onto something here. Not that poverty programs are without important successes—millions of people, including the working poor, would plunge back into real functional poverty without them. But over the course of a half century we have added program after program, budget line after budget line, without getting the transformative impact we should have expected. If LBJ descended back down to earth, if that is the right direction, and saw something approaching ninety major poverty programs and $1 trillion a year in spending, and saw the results that we do have, he might say something to the effect that this is not what he had in mind, though no doubt in substantially more colorful words.

★ ★ ★

Critiquing poverty programs—that's easy. Fixing them is a different matter. I started this chapter with the story of the Doe Fund because it goes to the heart of the conservative case for reforming the American approach to poverty. There is a comprehensive through-line in conservative thinking about the importance and power of work, that work, jobs, and fulfilling responsibilities are an essential ingredient of the human character and of creating purpose in life. And that one of the central purposes of government is to put people to work. It is a Rooseveltian view of governance, and some would argue that the Republicans, especially Trump, are remembering what Democrats once knew: that good jobs come first. When Dave Betras, the head of the Mahoning County Democratic Party in Ohio, recounted to me the defections of working-class voters to Trump in 2016, he blamed it squarely on the "political fucking malpractice of the Clinton Campaign. . . . because they have forgotten how to talk Democratic."

The same holds true with poverty programs, which, Republicans would say, should be transitional programs designed to help people get back to work. Unfortunately, again in their view, the programs have become misaligned, creating a welfare dependency that is a permanent poverty trap. Realigning the programs to support, and require, work is one of the fundamental insights of the Republican approach to poverty relief. The McDonalds would tell you that work is the goal not as a matter of cost reduction or punishment—though God knows there is plenty of racially tinged animus out there toward poor people—but out of a belief that work is what people want and is a pathway to self-respect and personal fulfillment. They may or may not be right as a matter of policy, we will get to that, but they sure are right as a matter of public opinion. Late in 2016, the *Los Angeles Times* and the American Enterprise Institute conducted a wide-ranging survey on public attitudes toward poverty. There are plenty of interesting insights in the poll and some significant disagreements across party lines, but Republicans and Democrats alike agree that poverty programs should be transitional in nature, that they should help people get back on their feet (58 percent) rather than just support people who are poor (38 percent). And respondents agreed by almost a 10:1 margin that welfare recipients should be required to seek work or enter a job training program in exchange for benefits, rather than getting benefits without requiring such an effort in return. Even those in poverty agreed with that by huge margins, 81 percent to 13 percent. It is so rare to find such agreement in polling, especially when work requirements for poverty programs are one of the most fractious policy debates of recent times, and will certainly be a central dividing point for years to come.

While many people still think of "welfare" as being a general term that covers the entire range of federal poverty programs, it refers only to what is now called the Temporary Assistance for Needy Families (TANF) program. TANF is the largest cash assistance program (most programs provide noncash assistance such as food or housing), but it is a relatively small component, perhaps 1.5 percent, of the overall government poverty support structure. TANF still holds an outsize role in the public debate, in part because of who it helps (primarily single mothers), in part because it has been around a long time (more than eighty years under various names), and in part because it has been at the epicenter of the policy struggle over work requirements.

In 1992, President Bill Clinton came to Washington promising to end "welfare as we know it." In that respect, at least, he was well aligned with the Republican Party, and that cross-aisle handshake produced the inelegantly named Personal Responsibility and Work Opportunity Reconciliation Act (PRWORA) in 1996, which reformed welfare to create work incentives and time limits on program participation. PRWORA is often described as a bipartisan piece of legislation, and indeed it passed with support from both sides of the aisle, a necessity in a time of a Democratic president and a Republican Congress. But the bill was highly controversial within the Democratic Party. Two prominent members of Clinton's welfare policy team, Peter Edelman and Mary Jo Bane, resigned in protest, and Senator Daniel Patrick Moynihan, a formidable expert on these topics, predicted that the new five-year time limit on eligibility for federal cash benefits "might put half a million children on the streets of New York in 10 years' time." He went on to predict that "[w]e will wonder where they came from. We will say, 'Why are these children sleeping on grates? Why are they being picked up in the morning frozen?'"

You might think that twenty years of experience would settle some of these questions, but, as with many things in politics, the battle lines have not moved very much over the years. At the very least, the cataclysm that Moynihan predicted did not come true, and the status of single mothers and their children has improved significantly since the passage of welfare reform in 1996. In 1993, when many states began implementing major welfare reform programs under a federal waiver program, child poverty in America stood at roughly 22 percent; for almost a decade, poverty rates fell steadily until they hit 16.2 percent in 2000. The poverty rates jumped back up during the Great Recession but have settled back to a little under 20 percent in 2015. More important, the adjusted measures of child poverty—the calculation of what families with children can actually buy and consume—have fallen steadily in the post–welfare reform era, from 14 percent in 1996 to under 8 percent today.[8] Perhaps most important, this decrease was co-incident with a substantial jump in work among single mothers, which increased by about 15 percent from 1996 to 1999. That number has drifted down somewhat since then but remains a good 10 points higher than in 1996. It is possible that all these things are unrelated, that the increase in work and the decline in poverty had little to do with welfare reform and are perhaps more related to the strong national economy of the period, but that is not where the weight of evidence rests. It is more likely that these all worked together, that work requirements, and the increase in work, combined with other supports like the Earned Income Tax Credit, drove a substantial decrease in child poverty. Welfare reform remains a significant achievement of the Clinton era. It is one of the oddities, though, of our modern politics, one that makes me want to beat my head against the nearest wall, that a large majority of voters philosophically agree with work require-ments, and the evidence tends to support them, but the politics of the day make the Clintons or any other Democratic politician loath to take credit.[9]

The evidence of progress is sufficiently compelling that the opponents of work requirements and welfare reform have shifted the ground a bit. Many of them rather grudgingly concede that the five-year restrictions on receiving TANF did have a modest downward effect on overall poverty, but at too high a price: by depriving millions of single mothers of cash assistance in an un-sympathetic economy, welfare reform had the unintended, but predictable, consequence of deepening extreme poverty. This view was popularized in a book called *$2.00 a Day: Living on Almost Nothing in America,* by the sociologists Kathryn Edin and Luke Shaefer. According to Edin and Shaefer, more than three million children live in extreme poverty, a number that has increased dramatically since the inception of welfare reform. If true, it would be an enormous blow to the case for work requirements. Any plan, even if it reduces overall poverty, that condemns millions of children to lives that are more reflective of third-world poverty is not a plan, one would hope, that even the most doctrinaire of Republicans would support.

However, the case for extreme poverty is somewhat less than the authors, or at least their book title, would have you believe. Their analysis of extreme poverty focuses heavily, and somewhat anecdotally, on the reported cash economy, and tends to gloss over the web of noncash and unreported cash support from the government, from charitable and community organizations, and, perhaps most important, from family. When those supports are factored in, the picture changes dramatically, even according to the authors: "Due to our public spaces, private charities, and in-kind government benefits such as SNAP, this level of destitution is probably extremely rare, if not completely nonexistent here." There are, tragically, families in America that make two dollars a day, and in fact there are even some families that report, at least for some period, no cash income whatsoever.[10] But it is also true that below $20 a day per person, American households tend to consume the same amount, regardless of reported cash income, reflecting the matrix of public and private supports that exist outside the cash assistance system.[11]

It is true that if you focus only on cash income, there are some very troubling trends, though they predate welfare reform. Extreme cash poverty for female-headed households stood under 1 percent in the late 1970s and gradually rose, hitting a peak of 1.5 percent just before the enactment of welfare reform. But after welfare reform, the increase in extreme cash poverty accelerated rapidly, surpassing 2.5 percent during the Great Recession before settling back to around 1.75 percent in the recovery years. By itself, the data may suggest that welfare reform created more extreme poverty, but there are two big caveats. As we just saw, cash income analysis by itself ignores the range of noncash benefits that reduce consumption poverty substantially; equally important, other groups that were not affected by welfare reform saw similar, even greater, increases in extreme cash poverty at the same time. Childless families and the elderly both saw faster rises in extreme poverty, and those changes were not driven by welfare reform, because they were never eligible for welfare in the first place. It seems likely that whatever the merits of welfare reform, work requirements were probably not the root of the problems identified by Edin and Shaefer.

I love statistics, as you may have gleaned in this book, but have found myself becoming a bit of a statistic skeptic in this instance. The problem here is that most poverty analyses rely on self-reported income as part of the census process. It's not that I think that people lie a lot to the census takers, at least not any more than before, but the ever-more-indistinct form of the American household makes understanding the data significantly harder. With more unwed parents come so many more variations on household arrangements. Cohabitating, coparenting, short-term, long-term, serial relationships make it difficult to know who is contributing to household income and even what constitutes the "household." Modern life is really screwing things up for the economists. It is quite possible, in fact, that many households labeled as being in extreme poverty are not counting income, whether cash or otherwise, from cohabitation or from family support or from myriad other relationships that mark modern family-style relations. This doesn't necessarily support the argument of one side or the other, but it does suggest a healthy skepticism toward numbers here.

No doubt, there is more than a little bit of the poverty scold implicit in the Republican love of work requirements—reflecting the view of some in the Republican coalition that poverty relief is not really a no-fault process—but there is also solid evidence to support the belief that government poverty programs need to be fundamentally rethought of as transitional programs, supporting, encouraging, and even pushing people to work. That view is largely consistent with what Americans widely believe and what LBJ apparently intended in launching the War on Poverty: increase self-sufficiency and help recipients lift themselves up beyond the need for public assistance. "Making taxpayers out of taxeaters" was Johnson's stated mission, and it is a mission that we seem to have forgotten over the last half century.

If you spend much time listening to some Republicans, it is hard to avoid the conclusion that there is some not-so-secret, and not-so-attractive, pleasure at the failures of the Great Society programs; Republicans held then and hold now a profound and visceral dislike for the social engineering of these programs and a skepticism that they could and can work very well. The movement to extend work requirements throughout the broader set of means-tested poverty programs, both as a mechanism for reducing poverty and as a means to reduce costs, is a reflection of these views.[12] Despite the sometimes off-putting rhetoric, work requirements are not in and of themselves mean-spirited, as Democrats would have you believe, but they are a form of social engineering not all that different from what the Democrats are accused of from time to time, and social engineering requires considerable thought. If the Doe Fund is a model, then we should acknowledge that it creates its own fashion of economic choreography: work requirements are nested in a whole range of social and skill-based programs. Doe Fund enrollees are paced through substantial job training long before they are exposed to the private marketplace. Absent those types of investments, it is unlikely that the Doe Fund would have had such an important positive effect on employment and recidivism.

It is hard to think of a tougher population to place than ex-cons, but if there is one, it is single mothers who need to balance work with the enormous challenges of single motherhood that eat into time, availability, and attention. The Republican plan, authored by Speaker Ryan under the name "A Better Way," is balanced between work requirements and workforce investments, but in real life, the conservative enthusiasm for work requirements certainly overshadows that for job support. It will be the acid test for conservative leadership in the area to see whether reform is just about cutting costs and whacking poor people with the stick of work requirements or about creating a system of tools and support that give people, especially single mothers, the chance to succeed.[13]

★   ★   ★

If Ryan is the front man on poverty, then an energetic seventy-nine-year-old poverty expert named Bob Woodson is the wizard behind the curtain. When Ryan decided to tackle poverty, he turned to Woodson, the president of the Center for Neighborhood Enterprise and a former MacArthur "genius" grant recipient, to be his policy guru and poverty tour guide. Woodson comes by his expertise honestly: raised in a blue-collar, segregated neighborhood of South Philadelphia, he remembers it as a tough, poor, and stable community, where everything was rationed—"if you had a hole in your shoes, you asked for cardboard, not new shoes"—but families had two parents, a critical factor, as we now know, in the fight against poverty. After high school, Woodson joined the army and went on to study child welfare at the University of Pennsylvania. He eventually began working on housing discrimination and civil rights in West Chester, worked with the Unitarians on poverty programs, and did a turn at the Urban League. Everywhere Woodson went, he told me, he saw waste and abuse, 70 percent of funding going into overhead rather than services to the needy, people feasting at the trough of government largesse.

Woodson was particularly incensed by the Boston busing case, where both white and black families argued against busing and in favor of more investment in community schools. It was only when "outside" civil rights leaders presented their case that the federal judge overseeing the case opted for the busing solution. More than forty years later, that outcome still angers Woodson. From all his many experiences, he has concluded that there are fatal structural design flaws in our poverty system: the destructive pressures that poverty programs place on stable family structures, the financial incentives that empower "race hustlers" and others who drink at the tap of Poverty Inc., and the centralization of decision making in ways that ignore community needs and greater local knowledge. All this has contributed to making our poverty programs a massive, expensive failure, in his view.

When you ask Bob Woodson how to fix this, he just lets it fly: get the federal government and their chosen contractors out of the poverty business; move the money closer to the problem, to communities and community organizations that have greater local knowledge; and give them greater flexibility to solve problems. Get the rule-making power out of Washington, D.C., and move it to Washington State, or to Washington County, Arkansas, or to Washington Township, Indiana. You get the idea. That concept has been the inspiration behind Woodson's organization, the Center for Neighborhood Enterprise, so it was natural that when Paul Ryan wanted to see how poverty programs would work on the local level, he turned to Woodson for guidance. Woodson in turn took Ryan on a poverty tour to see community organizations around the country. That has significantly shaped Republican planning on a new poverty agenda.

I had been curious about that tour, which was how I found myself one morning sitting across from the Reverend Billy Stanfield. I had driven up that morning to Park Heights, a decaying neighborhood in northwest Baltimore. The drive had taken a little longer than planned, since in the last few miles of the journey, I was forced to drive slowly, just to avoid the car-swallowing potholes that littered the streets. The slow progress gave me extra time to survey the neighborhood. Many of the houses are built from formstone, a type of stucco shaped to imitate masonry that is found in east coast cities but is principally associated with Baltimore. The director John Waters once called formstone "the polyester of brick" and in function it is not all that different from aluminum and vinyl siding, but I love it for its sense of place and the unique visual aesthetic it brings to Baltimore. My appreciation for the architectural tour is diminished by the fact that many of the houses are abandoned, sport broken windows and snapped doors, or feature porches that are buckling under the weight of neglect and disillusion.

Stanfield runs the Violence-Free Zone (VFZ) program in Baltimore, one of the projects founded by Woodson and toured by Ryan. VFZ employs school-based mentors, known as youth advisors, who "model and encourage positive behavior among high-risk youth." The staff for the program often come from difficult backgrounds similar to those of the students they mentor, and they provide a range of structured counseling along with informal mediation and monitoring. The program is school focused but it starts with a family meeting so that the family can be an extension of the program and the program can be an extension of the family.

The underlying theory of the Violence-Free Zone program is that if you can improve the behaviors of the most challenging 10 percent of the student population—kids who disrupt classes, harass other students, and consume a huge amount of school and teacher attention—you can have a positive impact on the entire school. It makes sense.

Stanfield is an interesting choice to run the program in Baltimore because he is in some ways off-spec for his job. Unlike most of the target population, Stanfield grew up in a stable two-parent household. He was spotted early as a basketball talent and ended up playing basketball at Cardinal Gibbons High School, then a local Baltimore powerhouse. He became a star at Gibbons, a junior college All-American at Hagerstown, and was under recruitment by Clemson and DePaul, both national basketball powerhouses at the time. But he "made some choices that were not reflective of [his] upbringing but of being stupid." Already a father, he quit school to return to Baltimore, got a job at Domino's, and started using his money to buy marijuana, first for personal consumption and eventually to sell. It turns out that Stanfield was very good at his work, not the pizza work but the drug work, and he gradually parlayed his modest weed business into a city-wide enterprise. Over a period of years, he became, as he has described to me and to others, one of the biggest drug dealers in the city, working with the Colombians on cocaine and the Africans on heroin and making $20,000 to $30,000 a week. It was a financially rewarding but dangerous business, a fact brought home one day when he was confronted in his home by two gunmen wearing monster masks. A brief gunfight broke out, Stanfield's gun jammed, and he ended up on the losing side of the battle, with serious wounds in both his legs, a fact he authenticates by rolling up his pant legs and showing me the scars. People like to show me scars.

Stanfield believes that he survived that firefight only due to the hand of God, but even the hand of God could not push him directly to the path of righteousness. That required the hand of the Drug Enforcement Administration (DEA). From his hospital bed, Stanfield kept his drug empire afloat, but the next year he was arrested and charged, and he ultimately served six years in federal prison. During his time in prison, Stanfield repented, found religion, and became a minister. After release, he found work first at Pepsi, then as an award-winning car salesman (Stanfield is clearly good at sales of any type), and then as a youth minister for a local Baltimore church. There he was spotted by Woodson and tapped to start the Violence-Free Zone program in Baltimore. The program has grown slowly since then, and now operates in five Baltimore schools, with two full-time counselors per school. Stanfield confesses to me that he has found expansion difficult, since it is challenging to identify, recruit, and train staff with the requisite background, commitment, and skills.

We drive together to Patterson High School, one of the VFZ schools. As we arrive, an armed Baltimore school police officer rushes by us, plainly responding to some sort of alarm. It turns out to be a false alarm, but it is a sign of some of the challenges that the school regularly faces. I'm able to catch the tail end of the boys' mentoring session, which takes place on the football bleachers. The VFZ program takes the kids out of regularly scheduled classes for discussion and mentoring sessions, but it is a trade-off that the school is happy to make. As the middle school principal assures me a few minutes later, outside the girls' session, if they didn't have VFZ counseling, "the ninth-grade girls would be smashing each other in the face all fall," disrupting class for everyone.

Patterson likes the program, it seems, and there is some evidence that the Violence-Free Zone makes a difference. In 2007, a team from Baylor University began a three-year "pre and post" evaluation of the VFZ program in Milwaukee. The Baylor team identified a series of key behaviors of students entering VFZ, combed school records for how those students were doing before they entered the program, and then evaluated whether those behaviors improved during the program. They found substantial improvement over a range of factors: the number of incidents (assaults, bullying, chronic disruption of classes) dropped almost in half, suspensions fell precipitously, and even truancy and GPA improved a bit.[14]

But the program says as much about the challenge as it does the solution. VFZ may be a local point of light, but you need a hell of a lot of points of light to melt away poverty. Unfortunately, programs like VFZ find it difficult to scale to meet the myriad challenges of even a moderately large city like Baltimore. After five years, Stanfield has brought the program to only five schools out of 181 Baltimore public schools and those numbers are not likely to change dramatically anytime soon. That's not an argument against VFZ and programs like it, but it does suggest that these types of programs face significant obstacles.

Wherever I went this past year, to think tanks, to churches, to nonprofits, people vigorously assured me that solutions to our problems lay not in Washington but with local churches and community organizations. They may have been right about the former, but no one offered me any explanation or evidence how local organizations could ever expect to be more than a finger in the dike.

It is an article of faith in the conservative community that we could do better by transferring—or block-granting, in the argot of budget experts—federal funds to state and local governments. Yet local governments are hardly exempt from the critique of inefficiency, self-dealing, and chronic stupidity. Stanfield in fact tells me that VFZ lost its city funding for an extended period because the Democratic-controlled city administration didn't like the idea that they were funding a program that was a poster child of the right. It is hardly reassuring stuff. And if you are inclined to believe that Republican control of local government would be a significant improvement over Democratic, let me introduce you to Sam Brownback.

It is an appropriate time now to evaluate Republicans in local government, just because there are so many of them: 31 Republican governors, an equal number of lieutenant governors, and enough Republicans to control 69 out of 99 legislative chambers. There are no doubt good Republican governors (though that question stumped a number of experts when I inquired on the subject), but, as it turns out, it is far easier to identify Republicans who have earned well-deserved reputations for venality or incompetence. Chris Christie and Bobby Jindal jump quickly to mind, but Sam Brownback gets to be the poster child for his willingness to pile-drive his state straight into the ground in the name of conservative principles. In 2010, Brownback, then a U.S. senator known for his genial personality and his strict social conservatism, was elected governor of Kansas on a platform stating that government and taxes had grown out of scale and needed to be significantly downsized. Once elected, with a substantial majority and with a compliant legislature, Brownback got straight to work. He created the Office of the Repealer[15] to cut unnecessary, outdated, or duplicative government regulations, eliminated four state agencies and 2,000 state jobs, cut spending on education by $200 million, eliminated the state's Earned Income Tax Credit, and privatized the delivery of Medicare. But the centerpiece of his program was a reduction in the top level of income tax from 6.5 percent to 3.6 percent and the complete elimination of certain business taxes. Supply-side guru Arthur Laffer called it a "revolution in the cornfields" and the conservative Kansas Policy Institute predicted a business revival, an increase of 33,000 new jobs, growth in personal income of $1.6 billion, and an increase in revenue of $323 million from local sales and property taxes.

Conservatives often praise the concept of local government as the "laboratory of democracy," a term that Justice Louis Brandeis coined in 1932. It is a lovely and memorable phrase, but in all the glorification of the statement, we have conveniently forgotten the relevant case, *New State Ice Co. v. Liebmann*, in which it was first uttered. In that case, Oklahoma had imposed a rule requiring a state license for ice sellers. The Supreme Court struck down the law, arguing that it violated due process. Brandeis dissented on the grounds that states were entitled to experiment with new processes and procedures, ignoring the fact that the Oklahoma ice licensing scheme was—if I may offer my own lovely and memorable phrase—a dumb fucking idea with the singular purpose of stifling competition. Here is the secret of laboratory experiments: many of them blow up.

And that is precisely what happened in Kansas. In the first year of the Brownback experiment, revenues dropped a staggering $687.9 million, equivalent to 11 percent of the entire state budget. The huge revenue shortfalls devastated the state's public sector. Brownback was forced to make even more draconian cuts to education and to health care. More than 1,400 people with disabilities were thrown off Medicare; spending for the state university system was slashed; six school districts ended their school years early due to lack of funding; and across the state, class size increased, teacher resources were cut, and even school janitorial services were partially eliminated in some districts.

Perhaps it would have all been worth the short-term pain if there were a renaissance at the other end, but nothing like that materialized. Brownback promised 100,000 new jobs for Kansas;

as of last count, the total was 700, and personal income growth for the period 2013 to 2015 was an anemic 3.6 percent, well below recent history and good for only forty-first in the country. Even the compliant citizens of Kansas, who somehow managed to re-elect Brownback in 2014, have grown disenchanted. Brownback's approval rating last year fell to 26 percent, the lowest approval rating for a governor in the country.[16] It was a revolution of sorts, but there are losers in revolutions and the losers here were the sick, the disabled, students, and anyone who cares even a bit about school cleanliness.

I recite the sordid governmental history not simply to insult Governor Brownback—though God knows the man deserves to be flogged—but to point out that the Republican obsession with the wonders of local government may not be exactly foolproof. Local governments have had successes, I am sure, but poverty relief is not one of them.

Work requirements were not the only innovation of the Clinton-era welfare reform; as part of PRWORA, government payments were restructured into a "block-grant" program, put-ting the states in charge of setting the rules for cash assistance to poor families. Local control, it was argued, would create greater programmatic flexibility and allow for more innovation in help-ing poor, single mothers find stable jobs. It has not worked out that way: only 8 percent of TANF funding is now spent on work-related supports, and more than a third goes to a grab bag of other services, including after-school programs and college finan-cial aid, that support many families with incomes well above the poverty line. In a state like Kansas, only about 12 percent of fam-ilies with children in poverty receive TANF benefits,[17] meaning that the nation's premier cash-assistance program provides neither cash nor assistance to the vast majority of needy families. It is a bit of a national disgrace and one that seems to have been missed by the Republican Party leadership, who treasure their theory of devolution regardless of what recent history seems to show.

★ ★ ★

I'm sitting across from Arthur Brooks, the thin, bespectacled president of the American Enterprise Institute, and he is just annoying the hell out of me. It is not anything that he is saying. I'm there to interview him, but he is peppering me with questions, so much that I can hardly wedge my own questions into the conversation. It is not a delaying tactic, as best I can tell, but rather reflects his genuine interest in the people he meets, their motivations and needs. Perhaps because Brooks has similarly talked to many people in poverty over the years, he, unlike Rush Limbaugh, doesn't believe that poor people in the United States have it easy. He knows they are trapped by lack of access to resources and education and by a system that discourages work and lasting relationships. The failure of America to help those less fortunate weighs on him, as he believes it is our shared moral imperative to do better. I quite like that about him.

So much of the conservative critique of the welfare state is written in the pinched prose of the Heritage Foundation, an institution that hangs like the Eye of Sauron over Washington. It is not that I necessarily disagree with everything they say—I've cited them favorably in this book—but so much of what they say comes off as mean-spirited and judgmental. That attitude has wormed its way into policy and into the White House, which casually dismisses Meals on Wheels and school food programs as lacking "demonstrable evidence" of effectiveness. The fact that the Trump administration was so wrong on the merits—unlike many other social programs, there is considerable evidentiary support for the value of these programs[18]—suggests that the statement is a pretext to slash away at the support for the weakest and most vulnerable members of society. There is a desperate need in our government for clear-eyed, evidence-based analyses that expose nice-sounding but ineffective programs, but all I can say is that if you are going to take that on, you'd better get your facts right.

Brooks is as conservative as anyone—he is at the very least a fierce advocate for the power of free markets and economic growth to pull people out of poverty, and a skeptic of government programs—but he also has a vision for "conservative social justice," a strong safety net for those who truly need it, investments in education and job creation, and a profound belief in fostering a culture of faith, family, community, and work. I'm not sure that it is the recipe for all that ails us, but at least it is a recipe.

When you talk with Democrats and you talk with Republicans, at least the Arthur Brooks Republicans, you may not find different end goals, but you certainly will have different conversations. For Brooks, the conversation about poverty reduction begins with economic growth. It is a reasonable place to start. The period of greatest poverty reduction in U.S. history was in the two decades before the launch of LBJ's Great Society, when rapid growth reached all segments of society. And that is not just an American story. Around the world, economic growth, often driven by the expansion of free trade and free market regimes, has similarly lifted hundreds of millions of people out of poverty, more than 450 million in China alone over the last three decades. That is far more than any aid or poverty program could ever hope to achieve. It is an alluring picture, one that is not inherently Republican but one that Democrats seem to have largely forgotten. But we also need to acknowledge the structural changes in the American economy that funnel more and more rewards to the top levels of earners. And, it is far from clear the Republican bromides about reducing taxes and streamlining business regulation will either inspire growth or ensure that this growth reaches the lowest economic rungs of our society.

Maybe all this puts me in the "muddled middle," as one of my new conservative friends put it in frustration. He didn't mean it as a compliment, but I don't take it as an insult. On the poverty issue, and many others, I have found insight on both sides, with more than enough sophistry and pigheadedness to go around. It is yet another area where Americans tend to agree with each other and disagree with the doctrinaire approaches of both parties. The majority of Republicans *and* the majority of Democrats think government is doing a poor job of helping people out of poverty,[19] and trust neither party to fix the problem. It is one of the ironies of our age of polarization that voters are excessively loyal, at least with their votes, to their political parties, but just as frequently reject their political philosophies, or even reject the notion that we need a coherent philosophy—an "ism"—driving government. It is why the incoherence of Trumpism, or even the absence of Trumpism, was an electoral virtue for him in 2016. I won't sign up for a presidency about nothing, but I might like a leader who is not so politically rigid that he can find virtue from different points of view. That is the value of the middle, muddled or not.

7

THE PARTY OF THE PRESS

Nobody is going to be taken in [by the devil] if he has a long, red, pointy tail. . . . [H]e will be attractive! He'll be nice and helpful. He'll get a job where he influences a great God-fearing nation . . . [and] he will just bit by little bit lower our standards where they are important.

—ALBERT BROOKS, IN *BROADCAST NEWS*, (1987)

D o you remember Paul Smith, the owner of the Independence Ranch? He may not have shown me how to use a gun or found me a hunting party, but he wasn't entirely inhospitable. Once he had successfully exiled me to my lonely folding chair, he relaxed a bit and permitted our conversation to turn to him. On the surface, Smith is an American success story. Local Texas boy, starts his own software company, makes lots of money, and gives up the rat race to pursue his love of hunting. Lovely stuff. But as our conversation turned to politics, we entered a darker space, a place of conspiracies and secret agendas. Paul told me of his firm belief that the White House and the federal government are under the secret sway of some international cabal. Paul wouldn't name it, somewhat to my annoyance, so I didn't find out if it was the Trilateral Commission, or the New World Order, or Jewish bankers, but it was clearly something nefarious and odious, a powerful manifestation of how authority has been usurped from the people for the benefit of the few. Whatever the nature of the conspiracy whose name must not be spoken, it "owned" not only President Obama, but all the Democratic and Republican presidents who came before him. Paul tells me this matter-of-factly and pleasantly enough, but there is a sharp and heated paranoia at work here. I was curious to know where Paul finds his information, and he demurred on details there as well, offering only that there were "lots of places out there, on You-Tube and Facebook, where you can find all sorts of information." This was many months before fake news became a major source of public conversation, long before Breitbart and InfoWars became household names, and it was one of my first inklings of how many rank-and-file Republicans get their news from somewhere beyond Fox, the *Wall Street Journal*, and Rush Limbaugh.

★   ★   ★

I've spent much of my career in media, so I was curious from the outset to understand the impact that our fractured media world has had on political polarization. I've always styled myself a bit of a media expert, but that expertise has been strictly limited to the mainstream media. I knew from the beginning that I would have to broaden my experiences, which is how I find myself standing with George Washington, lustily singing happy birthday to Charles Koch. To be accurate, it's not just a duet with me and George; there are some eight hundred or so other well-wishers in the room, all of us attendees at the Right Online Conference, the annual gathering of conservative bloggers, social media experts, and various camp followers who form the core of the Republican online army. The singing is a tad bashful (other than me; I'm into it), a fact probably explained by the absence of the birthday boy not only from the conference but from the host city as well. But it turns out, if you are the immensely wealthy financial patron of the conference, they are going to serenade you whether you are within earshot or not.

George Washington, easily recognizable by his full colonial dress, tricorner hat, and presidential demeanor, is entirely another matter. Absent a trip or two to Colonial Williamsburg, I've spent very little time with historical reenactors. Nor have I had much desire to, but here I am, chatting away with the father of our country. No one else takes much notice of him. Maybe it's not so odd to have someone dressed in full colonial regalia at these gatherings, a visual reminder of the lasting authority of our Founding Fathers. But I'm new to this and, I admit it, I think it's more than a tad strange for a grown-up to play dress-up, especially when no one else is.

George, though, is thoroughly enjoying himself, never breaking character during our conversation. When I ask him his name, hoping to get a little about the man behind the president, he fixes me with a gaze suitable for a particularly addled Tory and says, "George Washington, of course." He bends character only once to complain about the portrayal of his friend John Hancock as a bit of a fop in *The Sons of Liberty*, a popular History Channel miniseries on the early revolutionary events leading up to the Boston Tea Party. Hancock is portrayed, at least initially, as a dandy, brought into the conflict only out of mercantile necessity, but George is having none of it. "He fought in the French and Indian Wars, after all," he intones rather presidentially to me. I don't like to think that George Washington might tell a lie, but I do some quick fact checking on my iPhone. I don't find anything to support the claim, but perhaps our first president knows more than the collective wisdom of Wikipedia.

It seems fitting for the commander in chief of the Continental

Army to be lounging around the Right Online Conference, because war imagery is everywhere. Participants at the conference are routinely exhorted to fight the good fight, against liberals, Democrats, and, most of all, the mainstream media. This notion of war against the liberal social media collective is a key part of the story of Right Online: "the battle of ideas is being waged on a digital field, and Right Online uniquely prepares you to take your place at the intersection of new media, technology, digital advocacy, and integrated messaging that is critical for victory."

Media has always played an important role in politics, of course, and in many cases media has operated at the behest of political parties and factions. Many of our early newspapers were created by political groups to spread their message and create additional influence for political leaders. In recent years, and especially in conservative politics, media has become a separate source of power and authority. Talk radio hosts such as Rush Limbaugh and Mark Levin and Fox News hosts such as Sean Hannity have become opinion leaders and kingmakers; figures such as Mike Huckabee and Sarah Palin cross back and forth between electoral politics and media, effectively blurring the lines between the two. All that was prelude to 2016, when the right-wing website Breitbart became the center of a political movement that Donald Trump eventually stumbled upon and then rode all the way to the White House. I didn't know it at the time when I went to Right Online, because it was still in the future, but we would eventually see an inversion of authority, by which media organizations would create the political faction and not the other way around. It still stuns me to think about it.

American political dialogue has always had an angry and deviant voice to it. In recent years, that voice has been heard most distinctly through conservative talk radio, the deep headwaters of modern political partisanship. But radio was always somewhat limited by signal range, dial space, and audience availability. These limitations have disappeared on the Internet, as have the muting factors of advertisers, FCC regulations, and even good taste. That has opened the political space to more voices but also to a welter of discordant, increasingly angry views. And it has worked. The Internet made stars of, and legitimized, a new breed of political provocateur.

Many of the early Internet pioneers styled themselves as revolutionaries fighting the accumulated power of the Democratic establishment. They were the outsiders, who couldn't get in a word edgewise, because "the Complex," the Kafkaesque name bestowed on the establishment by Andrew Breitbart, dominated schools, newspapers, network news, art, music, film, and television and through them controlled the very ideas and information available to society. The Complex were the bullies, insistent on their ideas, their values, their narrative, and willing to punish through public humiliation those, like Justice Clarence Thomas, who took a different view of matters. It was a profoundly paranoid and dystopian view, but for the Breitbarts of the world, the Internet was the chink in the armor, the first opportunity to attack the Complex. This was not meant to be a battle of ideas, but a direct frontal attack focused on the hypocrisy and venality of the leaders of Washington and Hollywood. And like any good revolutionary, Andrew Breitbart was going to use bombs and guerrilla tactics— f-bombs and guerrilla videos in his case.

Say what you will about Breitbart, but he brought an amazing amount of energy to that task. Che Guevara once said that "passion is needed for any great work, and for the revolution, passion and audacity are required in big doses," and Breitbart fit the bill. Starting in 2005, Breitbart launched an interlocking series of websites—Breitbart.com, Big Hollywood, Big Government, and Big Journalism—to take, in his words, the narrative away from the liberal institutions that controlled media and public dialogue. His websites, largely a blogger network from around the country, were threaded together by angry denunciations of government, politicians, journalists, and Democrats, and were fueled not by traditional norms of journalism, but by anger. As the *New Yorker* wittily described it, Breitbart and his fellow bloggers and aggregators were not content providers, but "malcontent providers—giving seething, sneering voice to what he characterizes as a silenced majority."

Breitbart himself would have hardly disagreed with that notion. For him, the angrier, more graphic the description, the better: "I like to call someone a raving cunt every now and then, when it's appropriate, for effect. . . . You cocksucker. I love that type of language." And the angry, confrontational style was not limited to the safe distances of the Internet. In preparation for the Right Online Conference, I watched a video of Breitbart and his henchman Larry O'Connor challenging Max Blumenthal, the liberal blogger, outside the annual CPAC conference. The confrontation, recorded on the video cameras that seemingly followed Breitbart everywhere, is angry, personal, extremely unpleasant, but also rather genuine and honest.

To be fair, though, while this new type of political interaction originally found warmest purchase with the conservative movement, it was hardly limited to one part of the political spectrum. After Breitbart unexpectedly died of a heart attack in 2012, at the age of forty-three, leaving behind a wife and four young children, his death was met with cheers from some quarters. Matt Taibbi, a frequent political dueling partner for Breitbart, wrote a not-so-fond farewell in *Rolling Stone* magazine titled "Death of a Douche," which began: "So Andrew Breitbart is dead. Here's what I have to say to that, and I'm sure Breitbart himself would have respected this reaction. *Good!* Fuck him. I couldn't be happier that he's dead." And indeed Breitbart would have enjoyed this send-off, because it was in effect an homage to the type of angry, personal, and mean-spirited political dialogue that he pioneered in modern American life.

This type of political "dialogue" makes enormous impressions on audiences, who do not hesitate to emulate the language and swagger of their Internet heroes. Within twenty-four hours of Taibbi's article running on rollingstone.com, Breitbart's followers hacked Taibbi's website, published his personal phone number to Twitter, and inundated his phone and email with a montage of threats and insults, many of them directed at his family and sufficiently graphic and vile that I do not want to describe them here (and consider that I just used the words "cunt," "douche," and "fuck" in the previous two paragraphs).

For better or for worse, Breitbart was an innovator, and perhaps his most important innovation was turning the political Internet into a political actor, creating the news. His breakthrough moment in that regard came in August 2009 when he met for the first time a then-unknown video producer named James O'Keefe. At the time, O'Keefe was only twenty-five, tall and thin, and, according to Breitbart, bearing an uncanny resemblance to "Matthew Modine from [the movie] *Vision Quest*, after he sweated himself into the lower weight division for high-school wrestling."[1] He brought to Breitbart a series of secretly recorded conversations with employees of the Association of Community Organizations Now. ACORN at the time was a forty-year-old collective that advocated for the poor and for minorities through efforts around access to adequate housing, voter registration drives, education reform, and the like. Conservatives despised ACORN, claiming it fraudulently registered ineligible voters and misused federal funds. The dislike was rather predictable—ACORN voter registration drives largely targeted poor and minority communities that are

Democratic Party redoubts—but O'Keefe's videos seemed to confirm every charge ever leveled against the group and then some. The videos showed ACORN employees counseling O'Keefe and his collaborator, Hannah Giles, disguised as a prostitute (with O'Keefe her boyfriend), on how to avoid detection for a wide variety of illegal activities, including tax evasion, child prostitution, and human smuggling. They were cringe-worthy videos, and the most astonishing thing was that O'Keefe and Giles had replicated the experiences in four separate ACORN offices (Washington, Baltimore, Philadelphia, and New York), making it virtually impossible to argue that these were isolated or rogue incidents. In a carefully orchestrated campaign, Breitbart released the videos serially over the course of a week, creating what he called with characteristic bluster and overstatement "the Abu Ghraib of the Great Society." Whatever it was, it had its intended effects: within days, the House and the Senate had both voted to defund ACORN, and the organization collapsed shortly thereafter. It was an astonishing takedown of a major organization and it turned Breitbart from an angry political voice into an angry political player.

O'Keefe did not stop there, though ACORN has clearly been the pinnacle of his career. In 2011, three years after I left NPR, O'Keefe secretly recorded a meeting between NPR's chief fundraisers and two O'Keefe associates, masquerading as representatives of a group associated with the Muslim Brotherhood. Shortly after the meeting, O'Keefe released a video that showed Ron Schiller, NPR's vice president for development, criticizing both the Republican Party and all of Christianity, and appearing sympathetic to the spread of sharia law. Subsequent comparison of the edited video with the raw tape of the event revealed a rather different story. Michael Gerson, in his *Washington Post* column, concluded that "O'Keefe did not merely leave a false impression; he manufactured an elaborate, alluring lie." *Time* noted that the video "transposed remarks from a different part of the meeting," and called it "a partisan hit-job."

The tapes had all the hallmarks of O'Keefe's work: selective editing, manipulating the order of events, and jumbling together scenes to create a false impression. The manipulation would become obvious over time, but O'Keefe was able to take advantage of the quick-draw aspect of modern news and social dialogue. By the time critics had the chance to respond to the pieces, the damage was already done. Schiller resigned within twenty-four hours of the video release and his boss (and my successor at NPR), Vivian Schiller (no relation to Ron, and already on shaky ground due to her handling of NPR commentator Juan Williams), resigned almost immediately thereafter.

Over the years, seemingly every single project undertaken by O'Keefe has been criticized by fact checkers for creating a false impression of the real events. O'Keefe is by no means the only person to have ever been accused of selective editing or story bias—that is a daily part of our politically charged atmosphere now—but his work stands as an early example of the slippery nature of facts in the Internet world. In O'Keefe's world, there is no standard of fairness, just the objective to use the video to bludgeon and humiliate his political opponents. Video seems like the most real and verifiable of media, but it can also be twisted by those with the skills to do so. Even in some of his early ACORN videos, O'Keefe switched video cuts so that he was always seen wearing his 1970s Superfly pimp outfit, when in fact he was often wearing a shirt and tie and presenting himself as a law student.[2] O'Keefe's work is certainly an early example of "alternative facts," believed and trusted by those who want to believe and trust but ultimately unreliable and misleading. I don't hold O'Keefe responsible for the Orwellian online world we live in now, but he certainly has his part in inspiring it.

I'm intrigued to find that O'Keefe is a speaker at the Right Online conference and eager to see what he is like in person. I find him autographing his book: *Breakthrough: The Guerrilla War to Expose Fraud and Save Democracy*. I'm pretty confident that his book isn't going to save democracy, but for twenty dollars, it's a modest price to pay to pull him into conversation. Throughout this year, I've been scrupulous in telling everyone I talk to that I am researching a book, but I feel no compunction to disclose that to O'Keefe. I buy the book, and O'Keefe signs it "veritas," perhaps a little too grandly and self-importantly for someone who so gleefully uses deception in all of his work. As it turns out, O'Keefe is not the chatty type. I'm lucky—he less so—that there is no one pressing behind me in line to buy the book, but it is still difficult to get him talking. His guarded, suspicious nature is understandable given that he is in the business of deceiving people. I ask him what he is working on and he tells me that, while as a matter of "policy" he doesn't talk about such things, he is continuing his fight against the government and the powerful. O'Keefe has learned a few hard lessons along the way, mostly around the arrest record he sports for a bungled hidden camera escapade at the offices of Senator Mary Landrieu. He tells me he won't go into federal buildings, because of fear of being prosecuted for "false pretenses," though "politicians go there under false pretenses every day." He puffs up and says that he doesn't understand those who won't offer up their lives, liberty, and sacred fortunes in pursuit of freedom, as he has. Maybe George Washington would think he is noble. I think he is a jackass.

My personal dislike notwithstanding, I snap off a picture with him and text it, without explanation, to Beth. To my surprise, she instantly recognizes O'Keefe. When I ask, she texts back, "People still oppose housing funds with the lame (and inaccurate) excuse that they will be 'slush funds for acorn.' So yeah, I know who that guy is." She's not too happy later that evening to see his book lying around our kitchen, either. But I use it to kill seven flies, a big score in our battle against an ongoing infestation; maybe it makes Beth feel better about the book itself, if not its contents. I start thinking of O'Keefe as "Flyslayer."

Later that evening, I read the chapters in *Breakthrough* about his arrest and conviction. In January 2010, O'Keefe and three colleagues (or coconspirators if you prefer) were arrested after an aborted video sting at the Landrieu offices in a federal building in New Orleans. The underlying purpose of the operation was to expose an alleged, and rather trivial, deception from Landrieu that her office phone lines were inundated with calls, and that was why Tea Party members could not get through to her and her staff. Dressed as telephone repairmen, two of O'Keefe's colleagues planned to engage Landrieu staff in conversation about their phone system and somehow lure them into confessing that the busy lines were just a ruse to avoid constituent callers. O'Keefe, lounging nearby in the office waiting room, was to catch all this surreptitiously on video. None of it made much sense, especially since the fake repairmen couldn't answer the most basic questions about why they were there, where to find the phone closet, and what they would do inside the phone closet without any tools. They were quickly spotted as imposters, U.S. marshals were summoned, and arrests quickly followed.

The media lapped all this up, and the arrests were gleefully splashed across television, the newspapers, and the Internet. O'Keefe was initially charged with a felony attempt to bug Landrieu's phone, but after the media klieg lights dimmed, the U.S. attorney grudgingly agreed with O'Keefe's contention that he never had the intention, or the means or expertise, to bug anyone's phone system. The charges were reduced to entering a federal facility on false pretenses, a misdemeanor that resulted in three years of probation.

Putting aside the strange circumstances and all the strange participants, it is still a very odd prosecution. The federal building in New Orleans, like all federal courthouses, is an open facility, accessible to anyone who can make it through a magnetometer. O'Keefe and team were entitled to enter the facility, however dressed, so it is difficult to understand a prosecution for false pretenses when they didn't need any pretense in the first place. If the case stands for anything, it probably stands for the proposition that it is unwise to screw with anyone named Landrieu in New Orleans, a city where two mayors and one U.S. senator have shared that name. The whole caper may have been foolhardy and incompetent, but I feel some very small and very grudging sympathy for O'Keefe and the criminal label that he now permanently shoulders.

My sympathies don't survive the day or even the whole chapter. It's not the arrest, or the keystone repairmen act that leads up to it, that leaps out at me from the book. Rather, it's how O'Keefe describes the scene and his treatment at the hands of the hated federales. O'Keefe spent exactly *one night* in St. Bernard Parish jail but manages to compare his incarceration to Guantanamo Bay, the Turkish prisons in *Midnight Express*, and the prisons of Kafka. And he drips contempt on the competency, fairness, and intelligence of virtually everyone involved in the case, including the U.S. Marshals Service, the magistrate judge who manages his case (like "Fred Gwynne's judge character in *My Cousin Vinny*, but without the charm or wisdom"), the U.S. district court judge who oversees his case, the parole officers who become his court-appointed babysitters for the next three years, and the press that covers the whole three-ring circus. It's a bit of a theme with O'Keefe, the claims of mistreatment at the hands of his real and imagined enemies, but all of it would be more compelling if he himself weren't in the business of humiliating his targets.

The next day, O'Keefe is the first speaker on a panel to honor the legacy of Andrew Breitbart and it turns out to be a rather odd tribute. When he presents, he revels in the story of people, often low-level staffers, who get caught on his tape. He delights in the humiliations and punishments that befall them, whether it is the public shame or, in some cases, the loss of jobs and livelihood. O'Keefe clearly loves the notoriety that accompanies his stings, bragging that he was once trending along with "Honey Boo Boo Lover" and "Kim Kardashian's Ass" on Facebook, certainly notable company but perhaps not the right sensibility for someone who fashions himself a civic truth-teller. It's an uncomfortable departure from the overall tone of the event. The two days of the Right Online Conference up to that point had been generally upbeat and collegial, but here the mean-spirited thread of the online world peeks through. O'Keefe recounts his victory lap to Louisiana after Mary Landrieu's defeat in 2014, a trip with the single purpose of celebrating her loss. Simply toasting her defeat on Bourbon Street is not O'Keefe's way. While in New Orleans, he breaks from the revelry long enough to ambush Kirstin Alvanitakis, the communications director for the Democratic Party of Louisiana. Alvanitakis had made herself an O'Keefe target because she had inaccurately, along with hundreds of others, described him as a convicted "felon." O'Keefe, camera crew in tow, finds Alvanitakis in her office and a brief, largely one-sided exchange occurs, mostly between O'Keefe and Alvanitakis's fleeing back. The video captures the startled Alvanitakis in a most unflattering pose, face puckered, hair askew. O'Keefe finds the most offensive shot and posts the photo, and it quickly turns into an obnoxious and very popular Internet meme replete with sexually suggestive poses for Alvanitakis. It is no doubt the single greatest point of public humiliation in her life, and O'Keefe plays it in the room for laughs, which he receives from his dutiful audience. Say what you will about Andrew Breitbart, but he always seemed to take on targets who had the means to fight back, whether it was a major political figure like Anthony Weiner or an entire national organization like ACORN. Some of his heirs do not seem so selective. I've been told by those who worked closely with him at the beginning that Breitbart hated "bullies" and that his career was all about the fight against them. In some ways, O'Keefe's presentation is less an homage and more of a repudiation of this part of the Breitbart ethic.

★ ★ ★

The new tone of the Internet may have been created by men like Breitbart and O'Keefe, but none of that would have happened without the culmination of structural trends that began years before. The first major change was a fundamental alteration in the statutory and regulatory schemes that govern broadcast news operations. Beginning in the 1980s, the Congress and the FCC first watered down and then eliminated cross-ownership rules, spawning the creation of broadcast giants such as Clear Channel Communications (now iHeartMedia), which jumped from 43 stations in 1995 to more than 1,200 stations by 2000. At the same time, Congress wiped out the Fairness Doctrine, erasing the requirement of equitable and balanced presentation of controversial public issues. Later and less prominently, but no less relevant here, Congress eliminated in 2000 the "personal attack" and "political editorial" corollaries to the Fairness Doctrine, paving the way for a new onslaught of rough, politicized programming. The result of all these changes pieced together was a new commercially driven news world, the "outrage industry," with key players competing to be the angriest, most mean-spirited, most personal among the group. First in radio and then on cable television, outrage became the prevailing mode of expression rather than an occasional point of emphasis. Keith Olbermann referring to Tea Party protestors as "a bunch of greedy, water carrying corporate-slave hypocrites" became the norm. Radio hosts Mark Levin and Michael Savage used "outrage" speech or behavior at a rate of more than one instance per minute, according to some exhausted and no doubt shell-shocked researchers from Tufts University.

The Fairness Doctrine and other relevant FCC regulations never applied to the Internet in the first place but the cultural change in broadcasting, and resulting shift in public standards, certainly paved the way for the vastly more riotous playing field of the Internet. The opening of the Internet created space not only for the big players in online political commentary—the *Drudge Report*, *Daily Kos*, *Town Hall*, to name a few—but also for every single person in America to participate in public discourse in one way or another. There are now well over 150 million blogs in the world and a new one is launched every half second. Most of those blogs are not political in nature, of course, and many have no appreciable audience, but millions of blogs have pursued, reasonably, it appears, a strategy of increased agitation as a means of gaining attention in a highly competitive and fragmented media environment. In effect, the blogs have flatteringly imitated, and often exceeded, the movement toward "combat journalism," as Michael Goldfarb and Matthew Continetti of the conservative *Daily Beacon* have called it—a group that has taken Tony Blair's description of the media as a "feral beast . . . [that] tore people and reputation to bits" as a compliment and a rallying cry.

And even for those who do not maintain a blog of their own, opportunities to participate in this frenzied public discourse abound—by adding comments on websites and sharing on social media. Not surprisingly, given its spanking-new vintage, the "commentsphere," as it is awkwardly called, is not well understood or deeply studied, but it encompasses a new and enormous participatory element in American political dialogue. Recent content analyses of comment streams have found them equally, and in many cases more, uncivil than the underlying author work being commented upon. I spent a lot of time on the comment board of Breitbart this past year and can personally attest to the proliferation of racist, sexist, and profoundly ignorant comments in digital media. Whenever I read the comments on Breitbart, I learn a whole new vocabulary—"snowflakes," "libtards," "lefttards," "DemoCucks," "cuckservative," to name just a few—that are notable for their sophomoric crudity. The king of the online trolls, Milo Yiannopoulos, laughs it all off as the new culture of the Internet—boys (and it is almost always boys, it seems) having fun—but the comment boards give credence to every charge of racism and anti-Semitism ever leveled against the Breitbarts of the world. It is a shame for many, rather obvious, reasons, but they include the fact that they drown out any reasonable points that the Breitbart team wants to make. In truth, the organization was ahead of the curve in raising issues, sometimes underreported ones, about immigration, trade, and the deteriorating status of the working class in America, but it is virtually impossible to access those arguments underneath the gory race baiting, wild exaggerations, and mean-spiritedness that characterize the Breitbart experience.

There is always a fair amount of sniping back and forth on Breitbart.com on critical issues of the day—do the Jews control the media, how awful is Lena Dunham, or should the members of the NAACP be most properly compared to monkeys, bacteria, or Neanderthals? These are all important questions of the day, mind you,[3] but most of the anger is directed outward, toward people who would not be caught dead on Breitbart. That is typical: studies have shown that more than 85 percent of the uncivil comments on Internet forums are focused not on flaming other participants but are instead directed at individuals or groups of people not involved in the comment stream. Comment boards reinforce the partisan norms of the group and strongly repel (and further alienate and anger) anyone with views contrary to the prevailing group norm. This phenomenon is hardly limited to conservative sites like Breitbart, though. The *New York Times* comment boards may seem like Paris salons by comparison, but they are hardly less of an example of groupthink—Hillary Clinton won New York State by 59–37 percent in 2016 but she still routinely wins the *New York Times* primary 90–10 by my ad hoc count. It is all very nasty and self-serving, and explains some of the partisanship we see today.

Historically, voting preferences in the United States have mirrored racial, religious, and union affiliations—even after controlling for other characteristics, such as income, education, and occupation. Political scientists have come to view political preferences as more akin to "cultural tastes" than anything else, and explain them in connection with group affiliations and the pressure to conform to the larger collective. But over the last four decades, as unions were busted and religious institutions abandoned by the millions, these traditional identity groups have begun to lose their hold in American society and politics.

What has replaced them? Informal "discussion networks," loose associations of like-minded individuals who in the last half decade have organized themselves around social media. These discussion networks operate on unspoken yet powerful rules of social and political influence and of cultural and behavioral norms. Forty years ago, the German political scientist Elisabeth Noelle-Neumann developed a theory that the expression and formation of public opinion results from people's perception of the climate of opinion. Individuals use a "quasi-statistical sense" to determine whether their opinions are popular or unpopular. If they perceive that they share their opinions with the majority, they may be willing to speak out. Alternatively, if they perceive their opinions to be those of the minority, they either keep silent or conform to the majority view. Noelle-Neumann called this the "spiral of silence." In the intervening four decades, it has been widely supported in quantitative research, and it explains lots of different things, including the fact that no one on Hobart Street seems to know who the Republicans might be.

Noelle-Neumann's work was undertaken in the context of mass and offline media, and many have hoped that the emergence of digital and social media would break down the spiral of silence. In this view, the greater anonymity and physical isolation of the Web would reduce the fears of social ostracism, leading to greater political interchange and empowerment and less polarization. It was the great political promise of social media—a new Athenian model of participation.

It did not work out that way. In 2014, the Pew Research Center took the first quantitative look at the "silence spiral" in social media and found that the pressure to conform to public opinion norms was even stronger in social media than in face-to-face interactions. In polling on the Edward Snowden/National Security Agency debate, Pew found that Twitter and Facebook users were far less likely to share their opinions in social media than in face-to-face interactions—half as likely in the case of Facebook users and half again for Twitter users. Most intriguing, the researchers found that significant exposure to social media norms reduced the likelihood of opinion sharing in offline interactions: heavy users of social media are less likely to share their opinions in face-to-face conversations with family, friends, and colleagues, even after holding constant for age and other relevant variables. The social media bubble is even stronger than the geographic bubble, it turns out.

Research has shown that to a certain extent everyone sees a mix of information with some viewpoint diversity coming through their news feed, though people with the strongest ideological beliefs tend to surround themselves with the most like-minded, viewpoint-reinforcing friends. Social media gives users opportunities to not only select their friends, but eventually to deselect their friends based upon ideological views. And social media users do that with surprising frequency. More than a fourth of all Facebook users confess to having blocked or defriended someone based upon a politically oriented post, and this percentage gets higher as we move out along the ideological spectrum. Almost a third of consistent conservatives report blocking or removing social media friends, and almost half of all persons who describe themselves as "consistently liberal" have blocked someone for the social crime of divergent political views. All these numbers predate the 2016 election, and it would be a shock to me if these numbers are not significantly higher now. Social media has thus created two seemingly contradictory trends—it has encouraged reckless, often outlandish, public comments and at the same time has imposed groupthink and uniformity of mind. It is one of the greatest puzzles of our time: our views on issues have not changed much, but the language of how we express them and who we are willing to engage with has changed enormously, and not for the better. If I found a dystopian view of America during this year, it was not in my encounters in Pikeville, or in Texas, or even at Trump rallies, but on my social media feeds and on the comment boards of major media sites. By and large, in face-to-face conversations, people typically try to be thoughtful and respectful and open to others. In social media, they are just mostly assholes. If I didn't love Uber and Wikipedia so much, I'd chuck my phone out the window today.

★   ★   ★

Right-wing media would not exist without left-wing media. Or, more accurately, it would not be so vibrant absent the perception in some quarters that liberals control mainstream media—CNN, the *New York Times*, and the *Washington Post*, for example. I left NPR in 2008, so my views are somewhat dated, but it was always my direct observation that journalists and editors worked hard to be nonpartisan, too hard sometimes, but that view has never been shared by Republicans. During the 2004 elections, 60 percent of Republicans complained of media bias, and in 2016 the figure had risen to 86 percent.[4]

The concerns of Republicans, to be fair, are not without some evidentiary basis. Virtually every survey of major media has indicated that newsrooms are dominated by liberals. For instance, in 2004, a nationwide survey conducted by the Pew Research Center found that 34 percent of national press identified themselves as liberal, as compared to just 7 percent who described themselves as conservative.[5] It is a huge, almost 5:1, ratio, but I suspect even that understates the real situation, as many journalists may be reluctant to be formally seen, even in the context of a poll, as picking sides. When I was at NPR, I never asked people about political affiliation, but it was always clear from conversations where the sympathies of most people lay. From time to time I would urge the NPR newsroom, which was deeply interested in fostering gender and racial diversity, to add political and geographic diversity to the agenda as well. No one ever disagreed with that notion, but no one ever did anything, either.

In truth, I was never overly concerned about the issue. I knew at some level that political orientation could affect story choice and tone, but it was outweighed in my mind by the obsessiveness of the NPR newsroom to show balance and the views of all sides, which brought almost a metronome style to its reporting. And the claims of equivalency with, for instance, Fox News, which featured advocacy personalities like Sean Hannity and Bill O'Reilly, always seemed absurd.

I was wrong. Not in rejecting the moral equivalency between Fox and, for instance, the *New York Times*; that is still the rankest nonsense. But in undervaluing the impact of groupthink on what is covered and what is not, in what a largely liberal newsroom will deem as editorially relevant and what is dismissed as not worthy of airtime. It means you get coverage that is obsessive on mass shootings, but largely absent on the defensive use of guns; it means you dedicate oceans of coverage to the looming apocalypse of climate change and find little room for the concerns of the "lukewarmers" who want to debate the policy implications of it all; it means that the media largely misses (until this year) the hollowing out of the white working class, except when it fits conveniently into the larger narrative of income inequality. We all live in our own bubbles, of course—it is the story of this book—and it is not surprising that the media has its own comfortable bubble like everyone else.

You might think that a growing reputation for bias in the media in the Age of Trump might be the cause for soul-searching and perhaps retrenchment. Not at all. In the run-up to the election, and certainly since, the press has taken on a distinctly hostile position toward President Trump. In one day, just before the election, I counted twenty articles in the *Washington Post* on Trump, each one decidedly negative. Articles attacked his business acuity, his ethics ("How Trump got a personal tax break by defaulting on loans"), his knowledge ("Trump's map of black America needs an update"), and his overall fitness for the job ("A contemptible candidate—and the party to blame for it"). And that was just the front section. Critical articles also appeared in the Metro section, the Style section, and even the Sports section. All this reflects a shared political perspective on Trump, one that is decidedly progressive and coastal, but it also suggests the economics of the situation. In the weeks following the November elections, digital subscriptions at the *New York Times* increased at a pace ten times the normal rate. The paper added 276,000 subscribers in the last quarter of the year, well more than in all of 2015 combined (184,000), and the *Times* expects that growth will continue at twice historical norms.[6] All that additional revenue is very meaningful to hard-pressed news organizations, and no one in media organizations can miss the message: outraged coverage of Trump pays. That means the hostile tones are not likely to go away soon.

I can hardly blame the press for going after the train wreck of the Trump White House and the vainglory and recklessness of the man himself. But the mistrust of Trump has colored the reporting on everything he does, even if they are things that any Republican president would do. The press, for instance, instantly disparaged Scott Pruitt, the administrator of the EPA, as unfit and outside the mainstream, largely because he aggressively challenged Obama-era regulations in his role as attorney general for Oklahoma—under the theory that his challenge to EPA regulations meant that he opposed the clean-air and clean-water mission of the agency. But it is uniformly believed in conservative circles that the EPA under President Obama vastly exceeded its regulatory authority, a view that has been largely supported by the federal courts as well. Any Republican president in 2017, whether a member of the party establishment or not, would have sought to unwind those regulations, but you would not be able to discern that unless you followed conservative media.[7] More and more during the course of the year, I found myself reading the *New York Times* and then retreating to conservative outlets like the *National Review* to get the perspective from the other side. I don't know if it was always this way, but it is the world that Andrew Breitbart saw, and it has certainly come to fruition in the Trump era.

★   ★   ★

It's fair to criticize conservatives for living in a bubble where they think the *New York Times* is as partisan as Truthout.org. However, liberals do the same thing, imagining a kind of mindless uniformity among conservatives, despite the evident proof from 2016 that conservatives come in many varieties. The Republican Party, even as I write this, is riven by rivalries between traditional conservative elements who have long controlled the party and an upstart populist faction with a very different view of the world. It made this whole book significantly more complex, which I liked not at all, and for that I blame Steve Bannon.

When Andrew Breitbart died in 2012, editorial control of the Breitbart enterprise fell to Bannon, his friend and occasional collaborator. In some ways, Bannon was an unlikely choice to be head of such a loud and abrasive organization. A former naval officer and a graduate of Harvard Business School, he had parlayed a keen intellect and a driven personality into a successful career first at Goldman Sachs, where he rose to head its media group, and then at his own firm, Bannon & Company. In 1993, while still running Bannon, he helped negotiate the sale of Castle Rock Entertainment to Ted Turner; as part of his fee, Bannon accepted a small stake in five Castle Rock television shows, including *Seinfeld*, which was just beginning to emerge as a hit. Eventually, with his bank account substantially swollen with proceeds on a show about nothing, Bannon branched out to do something, in his case into conservative filmmaking, producing *The Undefeated* (on Sarah Palin) and *Occupy Unmasked*, and eventually into a collaboration with Andrew Breitbart.

Having grabbed the reins of Breitbart, Bannon began to substantially overhaul its editorial approach. At the time of Andrew Breitbart's death, the site had no core editorial direction beyond attacking "the Complex" for various alleged acts of hypocrisy and venality. At that, Breitbart was very good, as his success with Weiner and ACORN and Shirley Sherrod would attest. But it was still a firecracker site: capable of making loud, startling noises that some people loved and some hated, but in any event, not capable of inflicting any real or lasting damage, except perhaps to the people who were in the direct line of fire. Bannon changed that. He reorganized Breitbart around a series of populist themes: an outsize hatred for the "Party of Davos," the globalists and corporatists, to borrow Bannon's own phraseology, who controlled both political parties; a strong American nationalist ethic that focused on the immigrant threat and on trade deals; a distrust of individualism and the moral dictates of Hollywood and the cultural elites; and a foreign policy view that emphasized the clash of civilizations with Islam. None of that was terribly original, but Bannon had the benefit of a very clear target audience: largely whites who felt alienated from political power and felt economically abandoned at a time when some small group of people was getting immensely wealthy. Under Bannon's direction, articles in Breitbart began to focus on horrible crimes committed by illegal Mexican immigrants, the unfairness of trade deals that enriched Wall Street moneymen at the expense of manufacturing jobs, the overrunning of Europe by Muslim immigrants and refugees, and the moral hypocrisy of Hollywood elites. If you read Breitbart regularly, and I did for much of this year, you would have been inundated with stories of rapes and murders: "Illegal Alien Crime Accounts for over 30% of Murders in Many States," "Illegal Immigrants Accounted for Nearly 37% of Federal Sentences in FY 2014," and "NBC Covers Up Evidence of Immigration Crime

Wave," the last of which is a twofer—both media and immigrants. Much of it is technically accurate but horribly misleading: the 37 percent of federal sentences for instance includes a huge number of illegal immigrants who were, get this, convicted of breaking the immigration laws, and ignores the much lower conviction rate for illegal immigrants in the vastly more important state criminal systems. The Breitbart team knows that of course, but they also know that the stories they are presenting can galvanize millions of Americans who feel scorned by the coastal elites. It is amazing what you can do when you know your audience.

I met Bannon in the summer of 2016, before he was appointed to run the Trump campaign and well before he entered the White House as the chief strategist for the new president. It has been said many times that we should not be "normalizing" Bannon, but my interest in Bannon from the beginning was driven by the fact that what he was doing was in fact terribly normal, in the sense that he and his populist inclinations have numerous American historical antecedents and numerous current European parallels. America invented populism, and we have had many populist moments in American history—from the People's Party of the late nineteenth century to the Ross Perot insurgency one hundred years later. These populist moments typically arise at times of economic and social difficulty and are often warning signs that the existing order is becoming outdated and sclerotic.[8] It is a bit difficult to give a single definition for populism, since there is no common ideology that links together populist movements, but the connective thread is the belief that integrity and authority reside with the common people and that the ruling classes have betrayed this public in the pursuit of their own narrow interests. We have been in a populist moment for some time: the Tea Party and the Occupy movements were both challenges to the permanent power class, though from very different directions, and the successes of both Bernie Sanders and Donald Trump were further proof, if such were needed, of the eroding neoliberal governing consensus.

None of this should be surprising: our current political and economic order has brought immense wealth and power to a relatively small elite, while the status and prospects of the middle and working classes have continued to erode. For two generations, successive governments, of both the Republican and the Democratic varieties, have been either powerless or disinterested in changing any of that. Much of this book has been dedicated to the notion that there is less difference than we think between the political parties. For the true populist, there is no difference at all: both parties, regardless of their minor stylistic differences, serve the current order and have preserved it at the expense of the people. The growing wealth inequities, the failure to hold individuals criminally accountable for the financial meltdown, and the offshoring of jobs as facilitated by NAFTA and China's entrance into the World Trade Organization (WTO) have all served as powerful proof points in this regard.

Since they arise as objections to the existing order, populist movements in the United States are often organized around a series of grievances rather than an obvious coherent philosophy. And the grievances are often presented in the starkest and most incendiary terms, better to fuel the populist movement with the anger of the people. Such it is with Breitbart and Bannon. It's hardly a new strategy. Richard Hofstadter began his famous essay "The Paranoid Style in American Politics" with the observation that "American politics has often been an arena for angry minds." But behind the heated and race-baiting rhetoric is often a serious point, and the case of Bannon, a serious mind.

When I first met him in New York, he described to me how the working class in America are the new Gracchi, the equivalent to the working class of Roman times. It is an obscure reference, or at least I had no idea what he was talking about, but it turned out to have a revealing meaning.[9] The brothers Gracchus, Tiberius and Gaius, were both elected as Roman tribunes during the middle epoch of the Roman Empire. They were reformers who advocated in the Roman Senate for legislation to help the working class, the urban poor, and veterans. Tiberius was elected first in 133 BC and quickly promulgated a plan to help homeless veterans. He proposed to redistribute vast government landholdings for the benefit of the tenant class—a plan not well received by rich landowners who had been acquiring the lands through various secretive and likely illegal means. The landowners, and their allies in the Senate, displayed their displeasure by ambushing Tiberius during a caucus and beating him to death with stools and cudgels.

Nine years later, Gaius was elected tribune; he was, like his brother, a populist, but more persuasive and effective. He successfully revived his brother's land redistribution legislation, and also implemented "corn laws," which provided a monthly food ration for urban dwellers who could not take advantage of the new land opportunities. He was more successful and lasted longer than his brother, but in the end he met a similar fate. Outmaneuvered by powerful Senate interests who successfully ran a candidate who falsely promised even greater benefits for the working class, Gaius and his supporters were harassed by the new tribune. Pursued and without options, Gaius ordered his own slave to stab him to death.

It is a pretty grim story in the end, but it is a window into how Bannon views the conflict between the people and the establishment, one that is deep, wide, and at least politically violent. Most important, it suggests the frame in which the populists view how policies are manipulated to the benefit of elites and to the detriment of the working class. Take, for example, immigration.

Illegal immigration is well-trod ground, and much of Breitbart's editorial focus has been on delegitimizing the presence of illegal immigrants through stories of crime and economic abuse. But Bannon even expressed to me a willingness to shut down *legal* immigration, at least until America has taken care of its own workers first. I'm not sure that this position makes much economic sense. The declining birthrate in America means immigrant labor—skilled and otherwise—provides some of the growth that the country needs, but his view reflects the sentiment that immigration policy has been built without real regard to the interests and views of American workers.

It is not an entirely unreasonable point: the Immigration Act of 1965, better known as the Hart-Celler Act, junked the national origins test that had been the basis of American immigration policy for more than four decades. The change was viewed at the time as a civil rights law that removed the stain of racial and regional bias from our immigration laws, replacing it with the policy of family reunification. At the time, no one expected the law to dramatically change the number of immigrants, but in fact it did exactly that: the last fifty years have seen an extraordinary influx of immigrants into the United States. The foreign-born population has gone from under 10 million in 1970 to more than 43 million in 2015, and the percentage of immigrants in the United States has risen to 13.5 percent, a number not seen since 1910, a time when America was still a vast, lightly populated nation.[10] It is an extraordinary change, made more extraordinary by the fact that it has occurred largely without consideration of whether it has had a positive effect on American workers. Increased immigration certainly has its benefits, especially in a country where the incumbent population is aging, but it is not clear, as Bannon would furiously argue, that it has been good for the Gracchi. As David Frum pointed out in the *Atlantic* in 2015:

[S]even years after the collapse of Lehman Brothers, 1.5 million fewer native-born Americans are working than in November 2007, the peak of the prior economic cycle. Balancing the 1.5 million fewer native-born Americans at work, there are 2 million more immigrants—legal and illegal—working in the United States today than in November 2007. *All* the net new jobs created since November 2007 have gone to immigrants. Meanwhile, millions of native-born Americans, especially men, have abandoned the job market altogether. The percentage of men aged 25 to 54 who are working or looking for work has dropped to the lowest point in recorded history.[11]

In this context, it is understandable why the working class would view immigration with something that encompasses both skepticism and alarm. The fact that the educated elites, whose status and economic positioning are not challenged by increased immigration, have tried to enforce a cultural norm supporting immigration and multiculturalism as an unalloyed good—and that objections to it must come from some latent racism—has not helped matters terribly much. Nor does the fact that indeed some of the objections do come from racism and scapegoating of outgroups.

Much the same could be said about trade with China, another focus for Bannon and the populists. The entrance of China into the WTO in 2001 was hailed by many economists as a remarkable economic opportunity for the United States. Who wouldn't get a little jiggy at the thought of 1.3 billion new consumers? And indeed, open trade with China has been extraordinarily profitable for some American concerns. Take Apple, for instance. It has been able to both sell into the China market and offshore assembly and production to Chinese companies like Foxconn, helping its prof-

its on both ends of the economic equation. But trade has also significantly disrupted certain concentrated sectors of the American
manufacturing sector. In 2016, three well-respected economists,
David Autor of the Massachusetts Institute of Technology, David
Dorn of the University of Zurich, and Gordon Hanson of the
University of California, San Diego, estimated that open trade
with China has cost the United States some 2.4 million manufacturing jobs. The loss of jobs itself was not a surprise—economists
understand that there are winners and losers in trade deals—but
the real revelation was that local labor markets have proven to be
"remarkably slow" to create compensating work for those who
had lost their livelihood. Well over a decade after the first China
shock, the millions of blue-collar workers who lost their jobs have
few suitable opportunities for replacement work. For Bannon, this
is another example of how the system has been rigged in favor of
economic elites. The notion that capitalism has moral dimensions
beyond profit maximization has been lost at places like Apple. As
he summed it up to me, it is not Apple, the symbol of American
ingenuity, but "fucking Apple, making iPhones with slave labor."
Bannon's endgame is nothing less than changing the rules of the
game to redistribute the economic and political benefits to the
working class. The brothers Gracchus would have been proud.

It may sound as if I am sympathetic to Bannon, and, at the risk
of losing my invitation to my reunions at Yale Law and Haverford,
I will admit to that. It is surprising to me that in modern America
no political party in America represents the working class anymore. The Democratic Party, the historic political partner to labor, has long since abdicated that role, in favor of representing an
unwieldy coalition of urban elites, racial minorities, and social
interest groups. Even Vice President Joe Biden, in his postelection
recap, acknowledged as much: "my party did not talk what it
always stood for, and that is how to maintain a burgeoning mid-

dle class. And the truth of the matter is, you didn't hear a single solitary sentence in the last campaign about that guy working on the assembly making $60,000 a year, and the wife making $32,000 as a hostess in a restaurant . . . and they've got two kids, and they can't make it. . . ." It is to the shame of the Democrats that they have lost their voice on the matter, though it is rather ironic that it is the Republicans, the ones who sabotaged many worker protections in the first place, who found an appealing tone for the moment.

My secret sympathies have limits. Populist movements have often had a racist and exclusionary tinge, though they don't have to. Even Marine Le Pen, head of the National Front in France, has purged some of the most racist elements from her party, going so far as to kick her father, Jean-Marie, out of the party in 2015 for his anti-Semitic comments. That move may have been entirely cynical, but at least she knew she had to make it. Not so with Bannon, or with Trump for that matter. The fact that they have only halfheartedly repudiated the racists who have aligned enthusiastically with the movement is one thing, but the unmistakable strategy on Breitbart and in the Trump campaign to vilify minorities and play to the worst instincts of the mob is another. It may be a winning strategy this time around, but I suspect it will ultimately fracture the GOP.

Getting outside my liberal bubble, I found plenty to admire about conservative thinking: the notion of a moral order in a time of social uncertainty, skepticism about the effectiveness of government at a time when the stories of bureaucratic intrusion and ineffectiveness are becoming more and more obvious, faith in the power of the individual in a free society. However, it is also impossible to ignore the fact that the Republican Party has become half political party, half political carnival. Grandiosity, recklessness, vengefulness, and contempt for the facts is not unique to

Trump in American presidential history, much as we would like to ignore Lyndon Johnson and Andrew Jackson in that regard, but the rise of Trump reflects the fact that the Republican Party, at least for now, has become not a party of ideas but a party of grievances. That would be fine if the Republicans had any prospects for resolving those grievances, but the early days of this administration strongly suggest otherwise. That would be a matter for notice in ordinary times, but with Republicans controlling the White House, both houses of Congress, and most statehouses, it should be a source of worry for everyone, Democrats and Republicans alike.

8

THE END AND THE BEGINNING

We are not enemies, but friends. We must not be enemies. Though passion may have strained, it must not break our bonds of affection.

—ABRAHAM LINCOLN, FIRST INAUGURAL ADDRESS, MARCH 4, 1861

This year has changed me. It has altered my opinion on some key issues, as you have seen, and taught me about the complexity of others, even when it didn't ultimately change my mind. But all that is secondary to the fact that this year was a remedial course in the "bonds of affection" that Lincoln spoke of so eloquently a century and a half ago. It has been a hard lesson. We have all convinced ourselves of the inerrancy of our own political views. And we have also convinced ourselves not only that the other side is wrong, but that their wrongfulness comes from a place of greed or poor morals or rank stupidity. If the year has taught me anything, it is that none of us has a monopoly on the right ideas and none of us has a superior claim on values, commitment to our communities, and the desire to make our nation a better place. I didn't learn that lesson on Hobart Street or from Fox or MSNBC, but from Pete Wehner and Pastor Steve and Scott Winship and Roger Ford. I wish everyone could have that experience.

One might hope to find an assumption of good faith inside a functioning democracy, but if we ever had that, it has been badly misplaced. Here is what Democrats, according to a "word cloud" that summarized data from a *Washington Post*/Kaiser Family Foundation poll in 2012, think of Republicans. In that poll, Democrats were asked to pick one word to describe Republicans, and Republicans were asked the same of Democrats. Democrats gravitated to words like "disgusting," "greedy," "crazy," "selfish," and "bastards." Twelve of the top fourteen words are negative, often spectacularly so ("conservative," a neutral word, was high in the ranking, as, somewhat surprisingly, was "good" in a solitary glimmer of bipartisan promise).

Out of fairness, I will tell you that the Republican word cloud for Democrats was similar. Seventeen of the top eighteen words listed by Republicans were negative and most gravitate toward challenging the intelligence of Democrats, among them— "clueless," "liars," "spineless," "idiots," and the ever-popular "suck." In all candor, my personal word cloud at the beginning of this journey would have been similar to the Democratic one. I was wrong.

The thing that has troubled me the most over the last year is not the demagoguery from our politicians, though I don't like that very much, but the demonization of ordinary citizens who hold contrary political views. It happens all the time, but I found one public example particularly jarring. Three weeks after the 2016 election, a freshman at New York University named K. N. Pineda, roughly twelve weeks into her college experience, wrote an op-ed in the *New York Times* explaining her support for Donald Trump. Pineda, like many voters, had not followed the election particularly closely,[1] and, as she recounted, was more preoccupied with her Italian vocabulary lessons than with the details of the presidential election—so much that she had apparently not even voted. But if she had, she so informed her new readership, she would have voted for Donald Trump, because she felt "strongly that as a country we needed to focus on domestic issues, and for me, the Republicans were more prepared to do that."[2]

The electoral preferences of one disengaged college student may seem like pretty thin gruel for the *Times*, even in this era of news dilution. But there is a reason that the editors chose to give Pineda valuable editorial real estate. On election night, Pineda had confided to her college roommate that she, along with at least 62.2 million other Americans, was siding with Trump. That disclosure led to a huge fight. The roommate stormed off and ultimately wrote her own story for the *Times*, laying bare her anger and sense of betrayal that her new roommate had supported Donald Trump. For reasons that will forever escape me, the *Times* printed that story, with depressingly predictable results. Pineda was turned into a social castoff: heckled around campus and labeled on Facebook as "racist," "sexist," and "xenophobic," "white without a conscious [*sic*]," a "misogynist," a "bigot," and a "barbarian."

It was ugly and terribly unfair to aim these insults at a young person, barely old enough to vote, and about whom we know virtually nothing other than that she has a modest preference for the Republican candidate for president.

It is a comment on our times, one that is deeply disheartening to me. But if the responses were limited to NYU or to college campuses generally, I might be willing to chalk it up to an expected if not entirely laudable lack of perspective and grace in our youth, or the groupthink of American college campuses. But it wasn't. If you read the comment section of the *Times* on Pineda's essay, you will find that her story apparently drew the condemnation of the entire Upper West Side as well. I am, I say with no pride whatsoever, a connoisseur of comment boards, having spent more time than I care to remember on Breitbart and similar sites over the course of the last year. I will grant the readers of the *New York Times* a significant advantage in terms of spelling, sentence construction, and quality of language, but they break about even in terms of their willingness to abuse anyone who might have a different point of view. I couldn't make it through the entire comment stream—there were almost one thousand comments at the time—but I pulled a random sampling of some 150 comments and what popped in descriptions of Pineda were words like "fascist," "racist," "ignorant," "bigot," "naïve," "misogynist," and "deplorable"—all of which bear an uncomfortable similarity to the harsh judgment of the college crowd.

I need to stop reading comment boards, but I can't seem to help myself. A few weeks later, I spy another story in the *Times*, on this occasion in the Ethicist column. A husband had written in, asking for advice on how to deal with his wife of thirty years, who had become a "nearly fanatical" Trump supporter, increasingly angry at the "whining liberals" and "sore losers" on the other side. The Ethicist encouraged the husband to speak up and share his own views openly (the Ethicist must be single). The readers, on the other hand, were rather more fulsome in their advice. Many proposed divorce, which came as no real surprise to me, but just as many, apparently in all seriousness, suggested that the wife might need mental health counseling or an examination for Alzheimer's disease. That was startling. Some people are now associating support for Trump, or at least loud support for Trump, with mental illness. It made me wonder how they would react if I described a family member who was angered by the Trump presidency and frequently railed against the perfidy and ignorance of the other side. I know how I would react. I would say, "Hello, Nate, how was your day at school?"

Of all the things that have aggrieved me this year—and God

knows there are many—the one that constantly soared to the top of the list is our astonishing intolerance of the views of others, the certainty that our tribe is right and the other side is wrong. If we can't believe that the other side includes people of good faith, or we can't respectfully disagree with one another, then our democracy is at risk. This is what polarization, our isolation from the other side, has brought to us. I'm not concerned about the political leaders or the polemicists: go ahead, punch Richard Spencer in the head, chain yourself to the door of a Milo Yiannopoulos event, wear a Steve Bannon mask to scare the kids at Halloween, and I will still give you a Snickers bar, fun size of course. But let us give a break to those who voted for the other side out of hope, or fear, or desperation, or dislike of Hillary Clinton. It worries me enormously when we demonize a college freshman simply because she has chosen to voice an opinion so modestly supportive of the other side.

Things can go greatly wrong when our politics become so alienated, when we are willing to vote for the worst of our own side above anyone from the other side. In 1971, a Polish-born, English social psychologist named Henri Tajfel conducted a series of studies to try to understand why people adhere so strongly to groups and join so willingly and enthusiastically in group conflict. It was a question that was long at the forefront of postwar social science, as the academic community struggled with the mighty "how could it have happened?" questions of Hitler's Germany. It was a matter deeply personal to Tajfel, whose family was liquidated at Auschwitz and who only escaped a similar fate through the irony that he, as a Jew, was forced to leave Poland for France before the war to have any chance at an appropriate academic opportunity.

The test subjects for Tajfel were sixty-four boys, all either fourteen or fifteen years of age. The boys were sorted into separate groups on the flimsiest of criteria. In one experiment, the boys were shown a page full of dots and asked to estimate the number of dots. They were then randomly distributed into groups called overestimators and underestimators. Once assigned to a group, each boy was given "money" and instructed that he had to distribute the money in one of two different manners: he could either distribute the maximum to everyone, or he could give his own group less than the maximum and the outgroup even less than that.

Tajfel, quite rationally, expected that the boys would choose to maximize the greater good, if for no other reason than that the group assignments were entirely random, inconsequential, and abstract. He was wrong. Time and time again, the boys favored their own "team," even if that action reduced both the overall and their own group reward. As Tajfel noted, "it is the winning that seems more important to them." The Tajfel experiment has been retested often in the last forty some years and these tests have consistently revealed tremendous power in group identity, no matter how trivial and ephemeral, and the tremendous appeal of having your team win.

At one level, the insight is not revelatory; most of us know that we like to win. But it is not just the ephemeral sense of victory that we like; the Tajfel experiments and subsequent inquiries demonstrate that the social construct of teams shapes a great many of our interactions and turns them into a matter of identity and personal success. One experiment, conducted in the 1980s, found that study participants sorted into entirely random groups immediately associated positive values with their own group and negative values with the other group. This notion that we are better than you—smarter, faster, prettier, cleaner, whatever—is an instant identity mechanism in humans and gives people meaning and a sense of place in a difficult, sometimes painful world.

Group labels, even randomly assigned ones, are powerful because being part of a group provides validation and context for us and helps explain how we fit into an increasingly complicated and rootless society.[3]

Tajfel's research is even more relevant to us today than it was a half century ago. As other sources of identity become less salient—religion and unions, for instance, have become far less important—political labels provide an enhanced meaning and we thus see less and less in common with the other side. Politics in this way becomes more about winning and defeating others and less about finding common solutions. It has made us far too forgiving of the excesses of our own side—whether that be the terrible racism that has latched on to the caboose of the Trump train or the absurd viewpoint-intolerance seen most prominently on college campuses—and enormously hostile to even the best of the other side. None of this is helpful to a functioning democracy. The fact that Tajfel's research arose in the context of Nazi Germany should be a sobering reminder for us all. I am not going to equate the minor scuffles (initiated by both sides) at Trump rallies with Kristallnacht, and our institutions are still plainly stronger than Weimar Germany. But the regular demagoguery of outgroups by President Trump and the vicious anger over minor political differences have some echoes of the past, and it all scares the hell out of me.

Team spirit obscures how much we agree in this country, the fact that we are playing "between the forty-five-yard lines," as the conservative philosopher Yuval Levin put it to me. Don't get me wrong. I met a few people this year who weren't even playing on the same ball field as the rest of us. Spend enough time on Breitbart or at the monthly meetings of the Northern Virginia Tea Party and you will find enough off-axis characters to remind us that the "paranoid style" is alive and kicking in American politics.[4]

But they were corner cases, far outnumbered by those who were interested in serious conversation. I interviewed hundreds of different people over the course of my research for this book. Some were academics and think tankers from places like the American Enterprise Institute, the Cato Institute, and the Manhattan Institute; some were institutional leaders of the right; but most were just people I met along the way, at Trump rallies, at the NASCAR races in Martinsville, Virginia, or at the Golden Dawn Restaurant in Youngstown, Ohio. We often had little in common, if you measure it by background or education or religion, but I almost never had difficulty finding common ground, even on the most tendentious of topics.

It may be easy to dismiss this as one man's quixotic journey, but it is all over the data. Take a dive into the research on abortion, a divisive issue if ever there was one, and follow the attitudes of Americans over time. Abortion is a particularly useful issue, because it has been around for generations (*Roe v. Wade* was decided in 1973), public attitudes have been meticulously tracked over that entire period, and the two major parties have taken increasingly adverse and extreme positions on the issue in recent years. The pro-life lobby, for instance, triumphantly proclaimed the 2016 Republican platform as the most "pro-life, pro-family ever"[5] as it continued the party's long-standing tradition of supporting a Human Rights Amendment to the Constitution, which would effectually outlaw all abortions in this country. And it didn't stop there this time around: the Platform Committee added specific language targeting funding for Planned Parenthood, supporting the elimination of the use of fetal tissues in research, and decrying the subsidization of any health-care coverage that includes abortion and related services. It's hard-core stuff. The Democratic Party, on the other hand, has veered far to the left on abortion. Where once the party focused on making abortions "safe, legal and rare," and recognized it as a "difficult issue," the 2016 platform, as the party bragged in its own press release, "goes further than previous Democratic platforms on women's reproductive rights," by not only arguing for governmental funding of abortion services at home (now barred by the Hyde Amendment) but also by advocating for funding abortion services around the world.

The Democratic and Republican parties have clearly polarized on the abortion issue over the last twenty years, but, intriguingly, Democrats and Republicans have not. Gallup has been tracking Americans' views on abortion for forty years and what is fascinating is how little our views have changed over time and how moderate most people tend to be on abortion. If you ask Americans whether they are for unrestricted access to abortion (essentially the Democratic Party position), are against abortion under any circumstances (essentially the Republican Party position), or favor abortion that is legal under some circumstances, by far the largest group of Americans select the last choice, the number never leaving the tight range of 48 percent to 55 percent.[6]

And that moderation continues to be true if you peer into the data on a party level. Working with a different data set, this time the American National Election Studies (ANES), one of the largest and best studies of American public opinion, you will find that only 1 in 5 Republicans and 1 in 13 Democrats believe that abortion should never be legal under any circumstance. On the opposite end of the spectrum, nearly 60 percent of Democrats and 30 percent of Republicans believe that a woman should always be able to obtain an abortion "as a matter of personal choice." The views of Democrats and Republicans on this issue are hardly uniform, and the 30 percent gap on the "personal choice" issue is certainly real and material, but the overlaps are far more significant than the political parties themselves would lead you to believe. And if you push even a little deeper into the subject, past the bumper sticker identification, as Stanford researchers Morris Fiorina and Jon Krosnick have done, you will find enormous pockets of agreement. Instead of relying on familiar, perhaps overly familiar, formulas like pro-life or pro-choice, Fiorina and Krosnick asked seven questions, each built around a specific real-life challenge, for instance, if a woman were considering an abortion because she did not like the sex of the child, or if the woman were going to die absent the abortion, or if an abortion were under consideration for purely financial circumstances. In each of those cases, the views of Americans from both parties start to converge: 80 percent of Democrats and 70 percent of Republicans speak in favor of abortions where the life of the mother is at stake, and 90 percent of Democrats and 95 percent of Republicans say that abortion should not be legal if the mother does not approve of the gender of the child. And having an abortion for financial reasons has less than a majority support among members of both parties. Fiorina and Krosnick looked even closer at the 57 percent of Democrats who responded that abortion should "always be legal," and they found when pressed, many of them changed their minds about specific situations. Among these "always legal" Democrats, 65 percent subsequently responded that abortion should *not* be legal if the woman dislikes the sex of the child and 23 percent would not support legal abortion in situations of financial hardship. We have been conditioned to think of the world as falling into pro-life and pro-choice camps, and the parties as neatly lining up behind those positions, but the vast majority of Americans don't have tidy views, and in fact participate in a strong cross-party consensus that the issue is complicated, there is truth on both sides, and the right answer is really a balancing of equities.[7] This has not changed much over the years, even as both political parties themselves have staked out more aggressive positions.

Of course there are issues that change significantly, sometimes toward consensus, as in the case of gay rights, and sometimes toward genuine conflict, but in the grand scheme of things, Americans' views of issues tend to be surprisingly moderate and stable over time—even amid all the insanity of 2016. It is just impossible to divine that from the white-hot rhetoric of politicians, the hatefulness of Internet trolls, and the strident pack-journalism of today's press.

Our current politics are extraordinarily ugly, but I haven't given up, because I now know for sure that comity, if not agreement, is only a bubble-busting trip away. That is from my own travels but also from social science. In 2012, Samara Klar, a newly minted assistant professor of political science at the University of Arizona, set out to explore reverse polarization. Aware of more than forty years of social science experimentation that makes clear how frightfully easy it is to get people to divide into rival tribes on the flimsiest of circumstances and differences, Klar hypothesized that social cues may work in both directions. She determined to explore if it is as easy to break down partisan walls as it is to build them in the first place.

To test her hypothesis, she gathered 379 Northwestern University undergraduate students, all of whom identified themselves as political partisans—some weak and some strong. At the beginning of the experiment, all participants were presented brief explainers on two divisive issues—energy policy and health-care policy—describing the Republican and the Democratic positions in equal measures. Participants were then divided into three types of groups: homogeneous groups composed of only partisans from one political party, heterogeneous groups composed of a mix of Republicans and Democrats, and a control group in which participants were not put into any social settings. The first two types of groups were brought together for *only five minutes* and asked to discuss their reactions to the readings. Participants were told nothing about their fellow participants, instructed not to share political affiliations, and told they could comment as much or as little as their comfort level dictated.

The results were extraordinary. After five minutes of conversation, even strong partisans made meaningful ideological concessions to the other side. Democrats became, for instance, more open to drilling for oil and downgraded the attractiveness of alternative fuels. Strong partisans in the heterogeneous group became more open in their thinking than the weak partisans who were part of the homogeneous group or even those weak partisans who were part of the nonsocial control group. And lest anyone think the influences were purely transitory, Klar followed the "downstream" effects of the experiment and found that members of the heterogeneous group continued to express significant preference for diverse political perspectives into the future. In less time than it takes to boil an egg, strongly held partisan views were eroded, and, in some cases, substantially so. In this increasingly discordant and nasty world, where we hurl insults and invectives at each other, mostly from the safe distance of the Internet, Klar's research opens a little window of hope, that if we spend a little time we each other, if we venture outside our bubbles, we might see things a little differently.

I don't mean to be saccharine on the subject. We live in a terribly nasty and conspiratorial time, a period of extraordinary self-righteousness and insularity. It is a time when *The Wilkow Majority*, a popular conservative radio show, can trumpet its tagline—"We are right. They are wrong. That's the end of the story"—four times an hour without any sense of irony or self-awareness. There are far too many people like Andrew Wilkow who reject even the possibility of civil discourse and our bonds of communal affection. And yet I cling to the belief that if the readers of the *New York Times* would spend a little time with the other side—if they had a cup of coffee with K. N. Pineda—they might see her in a new light. If Pineda and her roommate can make up—and they did, despite the very nasty public spat—so can our country.

★   ★   ★

This book is ultimately not about who is right and who is wrong. It is about the belief that no one has a monopoly on wisdom and that we would all be far better off doing a little less finger-pointing and a little more listening to the other side. The truest thing I heard all year was from the columnist Emma Roller, who wrote that "[t]he strongest bias in American politics is not a liberal bias or a conservative bias; it is a confirmation bias, or the urge to believe only things that confirm what you already believe to be true." And that bias is growing stronger as we are finding more ways to ensure that our media, our neighborhoods, our friends, and somehow even our families are entirely congenial to our own views. As the political scientist Lilliana Mason has noted, we used to feel obligated to avoid politics at dinner parties lest we open up an uncomfortable conversation. Now we don't have to be so careful because everyone in our own circles thinks like us.

The impulse toward insulation in our society is strong, so great that some people have dreamed of entire cities of like-minded souls. In 2008, a fellow by the name of Jason Ebacher, an enthusiastic acolyte of the libertarian congressman Ron Paul, purchased fifty acres of land outside of Dell City, Texas, to create the new gated community of Paulville. The town was solely for "100 percent Ron Paul supporters and or people who live by the ideals of freedom and liberty" and presumably shared an aversion to things like taxes and regulations and zoning and perhaps even stoplights. You might laugh Paulville off as a silly idea, but it was to be a perfection of our politically insular world, where no one need be troubled by interacting with people of different views. Paulville is a metaphor for the fact that we live in a world where we have virtually unlimited access to information from all different points of views, and yet we are more and more intent on shrinking our informational horizons.

Paulville is not for me, not because of a disdain for libertarians or Texas, but because this year has taught me the joy of both Vox and the *National Review*, of Sunday football and Sunday church, and of hunting for food in Whole Foods and hunting for pigs in Texas. I love Hobart Street—our neighbors are lovely, there are endless numbers of charming toddlers, and our peripatetic doves, Doug and Ginger, are returning to their occasional roost on the pillars supporting our porch—but I need a bit of Fords Branch, Kentucky, from time to time as well. We all do, because we all need to get outside our red or blue bubbles when we can. The opportunities seem less and less frequent these days, I will admit, but it is not a lost cause. Despite the glories of the Texas scrub desert, Ebacher could find no takers for Paulville. There is still hope for us yet.

ACKNOWLEDGMENTS

loved every minute of researching this book and hated every second of writing it. I did most of my research away from home and most of the writing at home, so Nate and Beth received the full dose of my grumpiness. I won't claim they were uniformly cheery through this whole process—this is a work of nonfiction, after all—but they managed somehow to get me through to the end. I'm not sure I would have made it without them.

I am lucky to have worked with two of the best editors in the business: Adam Bellow, who first saw promise in my book concept, and then Eric Nelson, who picked up the project and worked tirelessly to bring the book across the finish line. And I wouldn't have ended up at HarperCollins without the amazing efforts of my agent, Gillian MacKenzie.

So many people gave generously of their time to educate me on the issues covered in this book. I should start with Pete Wehner, who gave me multiple tutorials and showed me early on how a conservative can be smart, perceptive, compassionate, and skeptical all at the same time. The Republican Party would be better off if more of the leadership were like Pete. A ton of people at the American Enterprise Institute were helpful, starting with Arthur Brooks, Marc Thiessen, Robert Doar, Ben Zycher, and Ryan Streeter, to name just a few. Many other experts around D.C. and around the country served as my faculty advisors on many of the issues covered in this book. Oren Cass, Scott Winship,

John Lott, Lilliana Mason, Dave Nuckols, and John Inazu were all kind enough to educate me.

Wherever I went this year, people too numerous to mention were generous with their time, but in particular I am grateful for my various regional tour guides: Roger Ford in Pikeville, Kentucky; Todd Franko in Youngstown, Ohio; and Pastor Steve Weber in church. Matt Shulman generously introduced me to NASCAR racing, though he forgot to warn me about the need for earplugs.

Many people were kind enough to read portions of the book. Ted Rybeck, Ellen Brodsky, John Inazu, Oren Cass, and Ulrich Boser all offered sage advice, and all the mistakes in the book can be 100 percent blamed on them. I'm responsible for the good stuff.

Luke Peterson took me out on my first shooting adventure, and the fact that he pretended not to notice how terrible a shot I am makes me like him very much.

I spent a fair amount of this past year with the Northern Virginia Tea Party and, sadly, all my material on the Tea Party ended up on the cutting-room floor, but I do want to thank Ron Wilcox, among others, for explaining the Tea Party philosophy to me. Leaving out the Tea Party is one big regret I have about the book (so far), because the Tea Partiers whom I met are an obsessive and loopy cast of characters, practically stepping out of the pages of *A Confederacy of Dunces*. Next book, perhaps.

Finally, I want to thank my brother, Michael Stern. He had almost nothing to do with this book, but he did supply the title of my last one, *With Charity for All*, and I forgot to acknowledge him there, which he has not let me forget. So thanks, Michael. Better late than never.

NOTES

INTRODUCTION

1. Laura Vozzella and Emily Guskin, "In Virginia, a State of Political Separation: Most Clinton Voters Don't Know Any Trump Voters, and Vice Versa," *Washington Post,* September 14, 2016, https://www.washingtonpost.com/local/virginia-politics/in-virginia-a-state-of-political-separation-most-clinton-voters-dont-know-any-trump-voters-and-vice-versa/2016/09/14/f617a2b8–75e8–11e6-b786–19d0cb1ed06c_story.html?utm_term=.4b5d35ed2d97.

2. In 2004, hardly a moment of postpartisan harmony, only about 14 percent of Democrats and 15 percent of Republicans answered in the affirmative; by 2014, that number had ballooned to 27 percent of all Democrats and a full 36 percent of Republicans who believed the opposing party was undermining the health of our democracy.

3. Pew Research Center, "Partisanship and Political Animosity in 2016," June 22, 2016, http://www.people-press.org/2016/06/22/partisanship-and-political-animosity-in-2016/.

4. In the survey, respondents were asked to express their relative warmth to their own party and to the opposing party, on a scale of 1 to 100, with 100 being the most favorable and 1 serving as the chilliest possible view. Over the past forty years, the rating for the opposing party has declined steadily, from a fairly neutral 47 when the survey started to a much colder 30 in recent years. The ANES data is summarized in "Feelings about Partisans and the Parties," Pew Research Center, June 22, 2016, http://www.people-press.org/2016/06/22/1-feelings-about-partisans-and-the-parties/.

5. In 2008, the average rating of Catholics by Protestants was 66, of "Big Business" by Democrats 51, of "gay men and lesbians (that is, homosexuals)" by Republicans 42, and of "people on welfare" by Republicans 50.

6. This number was particularly high, about 50 percent, among Republicans.

7. Shanto Iyengar and Sean Westwood, "Fear and Loathing Across Party Lines: New Evidence of Group Polarization," *American Journal of Political Science* 59, no 3 (July 2015), https://pcl.stanford.edu/research/2015/iyengar-ajps-group-polarization.pdf. For a good, general discussion of the research, see Ezra Klein and Alvin Chang, "Political Identity Is Fair Game for Hatred: How Republicans and Democrats Discriminate," *Vox*, December 7, 2015, http://www.vox.com/2015/12/7/9790764/partisan-discrimination.

8. George Bishop, Alfred Tuchfarber, and Robert Oldendick, "Opinions on Fictitious Issues: The Pressure to Answer Survey Questions," *Public Opinion Quarterly* 50 (1986), http://poq.oxfordjournals.org/content/50/2/240.

9. Mark Blumenthal, "Beware: Survey Questions About Fictitious Issues Still Get Answers," *Huffington Post*, April 12, 2013, http://www.huffingtonpost.com/2013/04/11/survey-questions-fiction_n_2994363.html.

10. "The 2016 EdNext Poll, Including 10-Year Trends in Public Opinion," *EducationNext* (Winter 2016), http://educationnext.org/the-2016-ednext-poll-including-10-year-trends-in-public-opinion/. Full poll results at http://educationnext.org/files/2016ednextpoll.pdf.

11. "Kentuckians on Everything You Can Think Of," Public Policy Polling, June 29, 2015, http://www.publicpolicypolling.com/main/kentucky/.

12. Ariel Edwards-Levy, "Republicans Like Obama's Ideas Better When They Think They're Donald Trump's," *Huffington Post*, September 4, 2015, http://www.huffingtonpost.com/entry/donald-trump-republicans-democrats-poll_us_55e5fbb8e4b0c818f6196a82.

13. Albert Hastorf and Hadley Cantril, "Case Reports. They Saw a Game: A Case Study," http://www2.psych.ubc.ca/~schaller/Psyc590Readings /Hastorf1954.pdf.

14. Craig Gilbert, "Democratic, Republican Voters Worlds Apart in Divided Wisconsin," *Milwaukee Journal Sentinel,* May 3, 2014, http:// archive.jsonline.com/news/statepolitics/democratic-republican -voters-worlds-apart-in-divided-wisconsin-b99249564z1–255883361 .html.

15. Gregor Aisch, Adam Pearce, and Karen Yourish, "The Divide Between Red and Blue America Grew Even Deeper in 2016," *New York Times,* November 10, 2016, http://www.nytimes.com/interactive/2016/11/10 /us/politics/red-blue-divide-grew-stronger-in-2016.html.

16. Morris Florina, "Americans Are Not More Polarized," *Washington Post,* June 23, 2014, https://www.washingtonpost.com/news/monkey-cage /wp/2014/06/23/americans-have-not-become-more-politically -polarized/. Lilianna Mason, a professor of political science at the University of Maryland, studied voters of similar policy views but sorted into different parties, and found an intensity, anger, and drive for victory wholly unrelated to the policy differences at stake. "All of the political arguments over Obamacare, taxes, and abortion (but also minimum wages and background checks) are built on a base of automatic and primal feelings that compel us to believe and demand that our group is the best, regardless of the content of the discussion. A partisan prefers his or her own team partly for rational, policy-based reasons, but also for primal, involuntary, self-defense reasons. These latter reasons are not petty, they are very natural protective mechanisms. Unfortunately, this can cause unreasonable behavior and an oversized emphasis on our goal of victory." Lilianna Mason, "Why Victory Trumps the Greater Good in American Politics," http://eprints.lse.ac.uk/61206/1 /blogs.lse.ac.uk-Why%20Victory%20Trumps%20the%20 Greater%20Good%20in%20American%20Politics.pdf.

CHAPTER 1: THE FELLOWSHIP OF THE PIG

1. U.S. Department of Justice, Bureau of Justice Statistics, "Key Facts at a Glance," http://www.bjs.gov/glance_redirect.cfm.

2. Richard Florida, "The Geography of U.S. Gun Violence," *CityLab* (from *The Atlantic*), December 14, 2012, http://www.citylab.com /crime/2012/12/geography-us-gun-violence/4171/.

3. It is difficult to track the origins of guns used in murders, because murder weapons are frequently not recovered or otherwise reported. Surveys of convicted criminals have indicated that more than 90 percent or more of murder weapons are obtained illegally or through informal channels, though these surveys may not be the most accurate or the most comprehensive. Among the most-cited efforts: In a Cook County, Illinois, jail survey of 70 inmates who had used firearms in the commission of crimes, only 2 said they had bought the guns at gun stores. Also, a 2004 federal government survey of inmates who used guns in the commission of crimes reported that 40 percent of inmates obtained their weapons from the black market or theft, and another 37 percent had gotten them from a friend or family member. Only 11 percent reported buying the guns at gun stores, flea markets, or gun shows. Michael Planty and Jennifer Truman, "Firearm Violence, 1993–2011," U.S. Department of Justice, Bureau of Justice Statistics, May 2013, https://www.bjs.gov/content/pub/pdf/fv9311.pdf. See generally Jon Greenberg, "MSNBC's Joe Scarborough: Tiny Fraction of Crimes Committed with Legal Guns," PunditFact, October 5, 2015, http:// www.politifact.com/punditfact/statements/2015/oct/05/joe-scarbor ough/msnbcs-joe-scarborough-tiny-fraction-crimes-commit/.

4. John Lott Jr., *The War on Guns: Arming Yourself Against Gun Control Lies* (Washington, D.C.: Regnery, 2016), loc. 2067.

5. "U.S. Murders by Weapon Type," Quandl, https://www.quandl.com /data/FBI/WEAPONS11-US-Murders-by-Weapon-Type (compiling 2013 and 2014 FBI databases on murder weapons and crime data).

6. Christopher Koper, Daniel Woods, and Jeffrey Roth, "An Updated Assessment of the Federal Assault Weapons Ban: Impacts on Gun Markets and Gun Violence, 1994–2003," report to the National Institute of Justice, U.S. Department of Justice, June 2004, https://www.ncjrs.gov /pdffiles1/nij/grants/204431.pdf.

7. Lott, *The War on Guns*, loc. 2519; Caroline Wolf Harlow, "Firearm Use by Offenders," U.S. Department of Justice, Bureau of Crime Statistics, November 2001, https://www.bjs.gov/index.cfm?ty=pbdetail &iid=940.

8. Brian Freskos, "Up to 600,000 Guns are Stolen Each Year in the U.S.—That's One Every Minute," *Guardian*, September 21, 2016, https://www.theguardian.com/us-news/2016/sep/21/gun-theft-us -firearm-survey.

9. Barack Obama, remarks at a town hall, Benedict College, Columbia, SC, March 6, 2015, quoted in Glenn Kessler, "Obama's Odd Series of Exaggerated Gun Claims," *Washington Post*, March 12, 2015, https:// www.washingtonpost.com/news/fact-checker/wp/2015/03/12 /obamas-odd-series-of-exaggerated-gun-claims/?utm_term =.8c28149e878d.

10. Helena Bachmann, "The Swiss Difference: The Gun Culture That Works," *Time*, December 12, 2012, http://world.time.com/2012/12/20 /the-swiss-difference-a-gun-culture-that-works/.

11. "Mortality Statistics: Every Cause of Death in England and Wales, Visualised," *The Guardian*, October 28, 2011, https://www.theguardian .com/news/datablog/2011/oct/28/mortality-statistics-causes-death -england-wales-2010.

12. While the NRA is frequently derided as a tool of the gun industry, its effectiveness comes not as a result of corporate largesse but from its ability to mobilize its 3+ million members. NRA members pay annual dues and make small-dollar contributions that average $35, while corporate donations typically make up only 2–3 percent of the NRA's $300 million a year budget. The big individual and institutional

money lies on the other side of the issue, where Michael Bloomberg has pledged more than $50 million of his individual fortune to fund Everytown for Gun Safety and has funneled millions of dollars into local races, including Virginia state senate races and the Milwaukee sheriff's office race. These facts do belie the narrative widely shared in liberal circles that the NRA is a big-money tool of gun manufacturers. For example, the *New York Times* in 2016 endorsed "voter initiatives on gun safety, as citizen movements try to circumvent the gun lobby's intimidation of state legislators." Like it or not, and many probably will not, the real people's movement around guns lies with the NRA, not with gun control advocates. That does not mean that the majority of people, or even the majority of NRA members, side with the organization's implacable stances on every gun issue, but it does mean that the intense interests—the people who care about guns more than any other issue—reside with gun owners and the NRA right now.

13. Elise Viebeck, "Michael Needham Was Stoking Fears in Republicans Long Before Donald Trump," *Washington Post*, March 8, 2016, https://www.washingtonpost.com/news/powerpost/wp/2016/03/08/michael-needham-was-terrorizing-republicans-long-before-donald-trump/?utm_term=.bead050d3f54.

14. Jed Kolko, "Normal America Is Not a Small Town of White People," *FiveThirtyEight*, April 28, 2016, http://fivethirtyeight.com/features/normal-america-is-not-a-small-town-of-white-people/; Jim Vandehei, "Bring on a Third Party Candidate," *Wall Street Journal*, April 25, 2016, http://www.wsj.com/articles/bring-on-a-third-party-candidate-1461624062.

15. "Gun Ownership Statistics & Demographics," *Statistic Brain*, http://www.statisticbrain.com/gun-ownership-statistics-demographics/.

16. Christopher Ingraham, "Just Three Percent of Adults Own Half of America's Guns," *Washington Post*, September 19, 2016, https://www.washingtonpost.com/news/wonk/wp/2016/09/19/just-three-percent-of-adults-own-half-of-americas-guns/?utm_term=.8ffa27ebe156.

17. In 1992, Gary Kleck and Marc Gertz, criminologists at Florida State University, set out to find the extent of defensive gun use in the United States. They designed a random phone survey of 5,000 adults, asking them if they had used a firearm in self-defense in the past year and, if so, for what reason and to what effect. From these interviews, they reported 66 verified uses of guns for self-defense and extrapolated that there are somewhere between 1 and 2.5 million self-defense uses in the United States each year. Gary Kleck and Marc Gertz, "Armed Resistance to Crime: The Prevalence and Nature of Self-Defense with a Gun," *Journal of Criminal Law and Criminology* 86, no. 1 (Fall 1995), https://pdfs .semanticscholar.org/91da/afbf92d021f06426764e800a4e639a1c1116 .pdf. This number was somewhat higher than other private surveys and significantly higher than the National Crime Victimization Survey (NCVS), which estimated the number as falling between 68,000 and 82,000 each year, a significant number in and of itself. Groups like the NRA and Gun Owners of America and politicians like Rick Santorum adore the Kleck and Gertz findings and have for the last twenty-five years used their research as a fundamental argument in favor of gun rights: "In fact, there are millions of lives that are saved in America every year, or millions of instances like that where gun owners have prevented crimes and stopped things from happening because of having guns at the scene." The work of Kleck and Gertz has been subject to withering attacks from the gun control lobby. That all started with David Hemenway, a professor of public health at Harvard, who derided Kleck and Gertz for faulty survey design and lack of independent controls. The Department of Justice reports about 450,000 crimes committed with guns each year, so to accept Kleck and Gertz's analysis, you would have to believe that far more crimes are deterred with guns than are committed with them. It's not even remotely plausible, yet gun advocates cite the study as if it were conclusively proven fact.

18. Matthew Watkins, "The Armed Civilian Who Helped Stop UT's Tower Sniper 50 Years Ago," *Texas Tribune*, July 26, 2016, https://apps

.texastribune.org/guns-on-campus/allen-crum-helped-stop-ut-tower
-shooter-charles-whitman/.

19. John R. Lott and David Mustard, "Crime, Deterrence, and Right-to-Carry Concealed Handguns," *Journal of Legal Studies* 26, no. 1 (1997): 1–68.

20. Abhay Aneja, John Donohue, and Alexandria Zhang, "The Impact of Right to Carry Laws and the NRC Report: The Latest Lessons for the Empirical Evaluation of Law and Policy," NBER Working Paper No. 18294, National Bureau of Economic Research, August 2012, http://www.nber.org/papers/w18294.

21. Ian Ayres and John Donohue, "Shooting Down the More Guns, Less Crime Hypothesis," *Stanford Law Review* 55, no. 4 (2003): 1193–1312.

22. "Firearms and Violence: A Critical Review," National Academies Press, 2004, https://www.nap.edu/read/10881/chapter/2#7.

23. "Opinions on Gun Policy and the 2016 Campaign," Pew Research Center, August 26, 2016, http://www.people-press.org/2016/08/26/opinions-on-gun-policy-and-the-2016-campaign/.

24. Sharon LaFraniere and Emily Palmer, "What 130 of the Worst Shootings Say About Guns in America," *New York Times*, October 21, 2016, https://www.nytimes.com/2016/10/22/us/shootings-gun-violence.html?_r=0.

25. In 2015, 65 percent of all Republicans opined that the federal government posed an immediate threat, while only 32 percent of Democrats agreed with the statement. Frank Newport, "Half in U.S. Continue to Say Gov't Is an Immediate Threat," Gallup, http://www.gallup.com/poll/185720/half-continue-say-gov-immediate-threat.aspx?utm_source=alert&utm_medium=email&utm_content=morelink&utm_campaign=syndication.

26. "65% See Gun Rights as Protection Against Tyranny," Rasmussen Reports, January 18, 2013, http://www.rasmussenreports.com/public_content/politics/current_events/gun_control/65_see_gun_rights_as_protection_against_tyranny.

27. Charlton Heston, "The Second Amendment America's First Freedom" (speech), transcript, September 11, 1997, Rights of the People, http://www.rightsofthepeople.com/features/articles/the_second_amendment_americas_first_freedom.php.

28. Mallory Simon and Ray Sanchez, "U.S. Gun Violence: The Story in Graphics," CNN, December 4, 2015, http://www.cnn.com/2015/12/04/us/gun-violence-graphics/.

29. Christopher Ingraham, "There Are Now More Guns Than People in the United States," *Washington Post,* October 5, 2015, https://www.washingtonpost.com/news/wonk/wp/2015/10/05/guns-in-the-united-states-one-for-every-man-woman-and-child-and-then-some/?utm_term=.ce419dbdd56f.

30. D'vera Cohn, Paul Taylor, Mark Hugo Lopez, Catherine Gallagher, Kim Parker, and Kevin Maass, "Gun Homicide Rate Down 49% Since 1993; Public Unaware," Pew Research Center, May 7, 2013, http://www.pewsocialtrends.org/2013/05/07/gun-homicide-rate-down-49-since-1993-peak-public-unaware/.

31. Mark Perry, "Chart of the Day: More Guns, Less Gun Violence between 1993 and 2013," American Enterprise Institute, December 4, 2015, www.aei.org.

32. Cohn, Taylor, op. cit.

33. Lott, *The War on Guns*, loc. 314.

CHAPTER 2: THE PARTY OF GOD

1. "America's Changing Religious Landscape," Pew Research Center, May 12, 2015, http.//www.pewforum.org/2015/05/12/Americas-changing-religious-landscape/. Estimating the evangelical population is more difficult than it might seem; there are many different evangelical denominations, and thousands and thousands of independent evangelical churches, and no single oversight authority that could possibly be responsible for a census. There is even debate over the appropriate

definition of "evangelical," so there is ample room for disagreement on the numbers. That being said, a number of pollsters have taken on the issue, largely relying on self-reporting from poll respondents. If you triangulate the various estimates and accept the inherent imprecision of this exercise, the estimates typically fall into the 80–90 million range. However you count, it is a lot.

2. Michael Lipka, "U.S. Religious Groups and Their Political Leanings," Pew Research Center, February 23, 2016, http://www.pewresearch .org/fact-tanl/2016/02/23/u-s-religious-groups-and-their-political -leanings/. Pew estimates that minorities (Asians and Hispanics) now account for about 24 percent of the evangelical population. African American evangelicals are categorized separately.

3. "America's Changing Religious Landscape," Pew Research Center, May 12, 2015, http://www.pewforum.org/2015/05/12/americas-changing -religious-landscape/.

4. Glen Chapman, "Flight to Kolokoso," International Ministries, January 5, 2015, http://www.internationalministries.org/read/56927.

5. During my travels, evangelicals frequently expressed to me their concern that the media's fascination with Westboro Baptist Church was unfairly tarnishing the broader evangelical community. It's a fair enough complaint, though I have always thought of Westboro Baptist as tarnishing the entire human race. The Southern Poverty Law Center calls Westboro Baptist "arguably the most obnoxious and rabid hate group in America," and it is easy to see why. The group, essentially the extended family of its founder, Fred Phelps, has made it its mission to use pickets and protests against those who are committing sin, and since their view of sin is horribly wide, Westboro pickets a lot, about six times a day and more frequently on Sundays. Since the congregation numbers only about forty people, each picket is rather thinly attended, but they make up for numbers with both volume and an uncanny knack for offending as many people as humanly possible. WBC has protested at the funerals of soldiers killed in Iraq, at the funeral of a nine-year-old girl killed

in the Gabby Giffords shooting, and at the U.S. Holocaust Memorial Museum in Washington, D.C. They also achieved additional attention for a press release celebrating the Sichuan earthquake that killed an estimated 70,000 people and praying for "many more earthquakes to kill many more thousands of impudent and ungrateful Chinese." All of these protests defy humanity, but some also defy logic, such as the time Westboro Baptist picketed an appliance store. The store's crime? Selling Swedish-made vacuum cleaners at a time when Sweden was unsuccessfully prosecuting Pastor Ake Green for hate speech.

6. "Some Major Dates in Oregon LGBTQ History," Gay and Lesbian Archives of the Pacific Northwest, July 14, 2014, http://www.glapn.org/6013OregonAntiGayMeasures.html.

7. Scott Lively, one of the cofounders of the OCA and of the Abiding Truth Ministries, is still a leader in the global anti–gay rights movement, and is currently (and involuntarily) involved in groundbreaking litigation under the Alien Torts Act. As of this writing, a Massachusetts court is considering a lawsuit against Lively by the Sexual Minorities Uganda Group (SMUG) for his alleged encouragement of the Uganda government's repression of gay rights, up to and including the killing of gay activist David Kato. Sarah Kilbourne, "Will Hate Go to Trial? Following the Case Against Anti-Gay Extremist Scott Lively," *Huffington Post*, December 6, 2016, http://www.huffingtonpost.com/sarah-s-kilborne/will-hate-go-to-trial-fol_b_13136066.html.

8. "Religion in Everyday Life," Pew Research Center, April 12, 2016, http://www.pewforum.org/2016/04/12/religion-in-everyday-life/. The Pew study reported that 45 percent of highly religious individuals (as defined by people who pray daily and attend formal religious services at least once a week) had volunteered in the past week, as compared to only 28 percent of not highly religious people. Lest you think that this volunteerism is focused only on religious activities, highly religious people are also more inclined to help the poor, either through volunteering or donating of goods and services, by 65 percent to 41 percent, according

to the Pew survey. Highly religious people, incidentally, are also more likely to be satisfied with family life and generally more happy with the way things are going in life.

9. Vanderbilt also exempts glee clubs, which is hard to understand, and honor societies, which have the benefit of being at least a superficially sensible exemption.

10. Tish Harrison Warren, "The Wrong Kind of Christian," *Christianity Today*, August 27, 2014, http://www.christianitytoday.com/ct/2014 /september/wrong-kind-of-christian-vanderbilt-university.html.

11. Brandon Ambrosino, "Being Gay at Jerry Falwell's University," *Atlantic*, April 4, 2013, http://www.theatlantic.com/sexes/archive/2013/04 /being-gay-at-jerry-falwells-university/274578/. In his *Atlantic* article, Ambrosino described telling a professor that he struggled with same-sex feelings: "She got up from her chair, and rushed over to me. I braced myself for the lecture I was going to receive, for the insults she would hurl, for the ridicule I would endure. I knew how Christians were, and how they clung to their beliefs about homosexuals and Sodom and Gomorrah, and how disgusted they were by gay people. The tears fell more freely now because I really liked this teacher, and now I ruined our relationship. 'I love you,' she said. I stopped crying for a second and looked up at her. Here was this conservative, pro-life, pro-marriage woman who taught lectures like 'The Biblical Basis for Studying Literature,' and here she was kneeling down on the floor next me, rubbing my back, and going against every stereotype I'd held about Bible-believing, right-leaning, gun-slinging Christians."

12. Julie Zauzmer, "Parting of Ways, Over Gays, among Texas Baptists," *Washington Post*, November 19, 2016.

13. Kevin Roose, *The Unlikely Disciple: A Sinner's Semester at America's Holiest University*, (New York: Grand Central Publishing, 2010).

14. James V. Brownson, *Bible, Gender, Sexuality: Reframing the Church's Debate on Same-Sex Relationships* (Grand Rapids, MI: Eerdmans, 2013).

15. "Changing Attitudes on Gay Marriage," Pew Research Center, May 12, 2016, http://www.pewforum.org/2016/05/12/changing-attitudes-on-gay-marriage/.

16. Brandon Hatmaker's Facebook page, accessed November 2, 2016, https://www.facebook.com/brandon.hatmaker.12/posts/66167782 0673474.

17. Karen Kornbluh, "Why Are So Many Single-Parent Families in Poverty?," *Atlantic*, November 12, 2012, http://www.theatlantic.com/sexes/archive/2012/11/why-are-so-many-single-parent-families-in-poverty/265078/.

18. "The American Family Today," Pew Research Center, December 17, 2015, http://www.pewsocialtrends.org/2015/12/17/1-the-american-family-today/.

19. Emily Badger, "The Relationship Between Single Mothers and Poverty Is Not as Simple as It Seems," *Washington Post*, April 10, 2014, https://www.washingtonpost.com/news/wonk/wp/2014/04/10/the-relationship-between-single-mothers-and-poverty-is-not-as-simple-as-it-seems/.

20. Raj Chetty, Nathaniel Hendren, Patrick Kline, Emmanuel Saez, and Nicholas Turner, "Is the United States Still a Land of Opportunity? Recent Trends in Intergenerational Mobility," NBER Working Paper No. 19844, National Bureau of Economic Research, January 2014, http://scholar.harvard.edu/files/hendren/files/trends_in_intergenerational_mobility_pdf.pdf.

21. Plenty of people, mostly liberals, it would seem, have gleefully charged hypocrisy on this topic since divorce rates, it is reported, are very high for evangelicals. Michelle Goldberg, "Is Conservative Christianity Bad for Marriage?" *Nation*, February 10, 2014, https://www.thenation.com/article/conservative-christianity-bad-marriage/. It is true in fact that counties with high shares of conservative Protestants have elevated divorce rates, but in-depth analysis of the data has indicated that the divorce problem is principally driven by nominal Protestants, people

who label themselves as evangelical Protestants but who rarely attend church. Charles Stokes, "Findings on Red and Blue Divorce Are Not Exactly Black and White," Institute for Family Studies, January 22, 2014, https://ifstudies.org/blog/findings-on-red-and-blue-divorce-are-not-exactly-black-and-white/.

22. Kevin Hartnett, "When Having Babies Beats Marriage," *Harvard Magazine*, July–August 2012, http://harvardmagazine.com/2012/07/when-having-babies-beats-marriage.

23. Aparna Mathur, Had Fu, and Peter Hansen, "The Mysterious and Alarming Rise of Single Parenthood in America," *Atlantic*, September 3, 2013, http://www.theatlantic.com/business/archive/2013/09/the-mysterious-and-alarming-rise-of-single-parenthood-in-america/279203/.; http://thefederalist.com/2015/10/07/the-conservative-case-for-criminal-justice-reform/.

CHAPTER 3: THE BASKET OF DEPLORABLES

1. Peter Stevenson, "Trump Is Headed for a Win, Says Professor Who Has Predicted 30 Years of Presidential Outcomes Correctly," *Washington Post*, September 23, 2016, https://www.washingtonpost.com/news/the-fix/wp/2016/09/23/trump-is-headed-for-a-win-says-professor-whos-predicted-30-years-of-presidential-outcomes-correctly/?utm_term=.3019e9d32792.

2. D'vera Cohn, "It's Official: Minority Babies Are the Majority Among the Nation's Infants, But Only Just," Pew Research Center, June 23, 2016, http://www.pewresearch.org/fact-tank/2016/06/23/its-official-minority-babies-are-the-majority-among-the-nations-infants-but-only-just/.

3. Maureen Craig and Jennifer Richeson, "On the Precipice of a 'Majority-Minority' America: Perceived Status Threat From the Racial Demographic Shift Affects White Americans' Political Ideology," Association for Psychological Sciences, 2014, http://groups.psych.northwestern.edu/spcl/documents/Craig_RichesonPS_updatedversion.pdf. For a good

general (and easily readable) discussion of the topic, see Amy Drew, Scott Sleek, and Anna Mikulak, "When the Majority Becomes the Minority," Association for Psychological Sciences, March 31, 2016, http://www .psychologicalscience.org/observer/when-the-majority-becomes-the -minority#.WCrrsE0m6M9.

4. David French, "The Price I Paid for Opposing Trump," *National Review Online*, October 21, 2016, http://www.nationalreview.com /article/441319/donald-trump-alt-right-internet-abuse-never-trump -movement; Andrew Anglin, "David French: I Saw Images of My Daughter's Face in Gas Chambers, with a Smiling Trump in a Nazi Uniform," *Daily Stormer*, October 22, 2016, http://www.dailystormer.com/david -french-i-saw-images-of-my-daughters-face-in-gas-chambers-with-a -smiling-trump-in-a-nazi-uniform/.

5. "Problems and Priorities," Pollingreport.com, accessed April 22, 2017, http://www.pollingreport.com/prioriti.htm.

6. Susan Page, "Poll: President Trump Has Not Made Progress in Uniting USA," *USA Today*, December 21, 2016, http://www.usatoday.com /story/news/politics/2016/12/21/poll-donald-trump-progress-uniting -usa/95667510/. The border wall does have its fans. Ann Coulter's 100-day agenda for President Trump consisted of "Day 1: Start building the Wall. Day 2: Continue building the Wall. . . . Day 50: Continue building the Wall. . . . Day 100: Report to American people about progress of wall. Keep building the Wall." Ann Coulter, "President Trump's First 100 Days," anncoulter.com, November 9, 2016, http:// www.anncoulter.com/columns/2016–11–09.html.

7. Jeffrey Jones, "More Republicans Favor Path to Citizenship Over Wall," Gallup, July 20, 2016, http://www.gallup.com/poll/193817 /republicans-favor-path-citizenship-wall.aspx.

8. Camille Ryan and Kurt Bauman, "Educational Attainment in the United States: 2015," Department of Commerce, Census Bureau, March 2016, http://www.census.gov/content/dam/Census/library /publications/2016/demo/p20–578.pdf.

9. Andrew Cherlin, *Labor's Love Lost: The Rise and Fall of the Working-Class Family in America* (New York: Russell Sage Foundation, 2014).

10. John Coder and Gordon Green, "Comparing Earnings of White Males by Education for Selected Age Cohorts," Sentier Research, October 2016, http://www.sentierresearch.com/StatBriefs/Sentier_Income_Trends _WorkingClassWages_1996to2014_Brief_10_05_16.pdf.

11. Anne Case and Augus Deaton, "Rising Morbidity and Mortality in Midlife Among White Non-Hispanic Americans in the 21st Century," http://www.pnas.org/content/112/49/15078.full.pdf. Similarly situated working-class whites in Europe, who face many of the same economic pressures as their contemporaries in the United States, have not resorted in the same way to drugs, alcohol, and suicide. Case and Deaton speculated that this may be because of a stronger social safety net in Europe and the continuing strength of defined-benefit retirement plans, which potentially reduce economic anxiety among even those most at risk of losing jobs and status.

12. "U.S. Suicide Rate Surges, Especially Among White People," BBC News, April 22, 2016, http://www.bbc.com/news/world-us-canada-36116166.

13. Report on the Future of Children from Princeton-Brookings, "Marriage and Child Well-Being Revisited," Fall 2015, http://www.princeton .edu/futureofchildren/publications/docs/Fulll%20Journal%20 Marriage%20Revisited.pdf.

14. Cherlin, *Labor's Love Lost*, loc. 261.

15. Trevor Thompson and Jennifer Benz, "The Public Mood: White Malaise but Optimism Among Blacks, Hispanics," Associated Press–NORC Center for Public Affairs Research, 2013, http://www.apnorc .org/PDFs/Public%20Mood/AP-NORC_PublicMoodWhiteMalaise ButOptimismAmongBlacksandHispanics.pdf

16. David Paul Kuhn, "Sorry, Liberals, Bigotry Didn't Elect Donald Trump," *New York Times*, December 26, 2016, http://www.nytimes .com/2016/12/26/opinion/sorry-liberals-bigotry-didnt-elect-donald -trump.html?mwrsm=Email&_r=0.

17. A. R. Krosch and D. M. Amodio, "Economic Scarcity Alters the Perception of Race," *Proceedings of the National Academy of Sciences* 111 (2014): 9079–84.

CHAPTER 4: THE GRAND COAL PARTY

1. F. A. Hayek, "Why I Am Not a Conservative," in *The Constitution of Liberty* (Chicago: University of Chicago Press, 1960).

2. James Inhofe, *The Greatest Hoax: How the Global Warming Conspiracy Threatens Your Future* (New York: WND Books, 2012).

3. There are numerous surveys of scientists and of relevant peer-reviewed articles, and they all tend to circle around the finding that 97 percent of all scientists agree on AGW. It is not quite that, though it is close. One of the largest surveys, often relied upon for the 97 percent figure, found that about 66 percent of all relevant papers expressed no opinion on AGW but of those that did, 97 percent of the papers explicitly or implicitly endorsed AGW and only about 1.9 percent rejected AGW. John Cook, Dana Nuccitelli, Sarah A. Green, Mark Richardson, Barbel Winkler, Rob Painting, Robert Way, Peter Jacobs, and Andrew Skuce, "Quantifying the Consensus on Anthropogenic Global Warming in the Scientific Literature," *Environmental Research Letters* 8 (2013), http://iopscience.iop.org/article/10.1088/1748–9326/8/2/024024/pdf.

4. Jonah Engel Bromwich, "Flooding in the South Looks a Lot Like Climate Change," *New York Times*, August 16, 2016, https://www.nytimes.com/2016/08/17/us/climate-change-louisiana.html?_r=0.

5. The paper, from the *Journal of Climate*, is titled "The Resolution Dependence of Contiguous U.S. Precipitation Extremes in Response to CO_2 Forcing," by Karin van der Wiel et al., November 2016, http://journals.ametsoc.org/doi/abs/10.1175/JCLI-D-16–0307.1. Here's the relevant line from the abstract: "Finally, the observed record and historical model experiments were used to investigate changes in the recent past. In part because of large intrinsic variability, no evidence was found for changes

in extreme precipitation attributable to climate change in the available observed record."

6. Stephen Lewandowsky, Klaus Oberauer, and Gilles Gignac, "NASA Faked the Moon Landing—Therefore (Climate) Science Is a Hoax," *Psychological Science* 24, no. 5 (2013), http://journals.sagepub.com/doi /abs/10.1177/0956797612457686.

7. "They Built a Town," in *The History of Jenkins, Kentucky* (Jenkins, KY: Jenkins Area Jaycees, 1973), http://penelope.uchicago.edu/Thayer/E /Gazetteer/Places/America/United_States/Kentucky/Letcher/Jenkins /_Texts/HJK/C*.html#A.

8. The pie-and-box social was an Ozarks tradition, and apparently traveled well to other parts of the American South. It typically was a fund-raising device for a worthy cause, often the local one-room school, but it was an important social and courtship ritual. Each eligible girl in the community would bake a pie for an anonymous raffle. Whoever won the bidding for the pie would get not only the pie but the chance to share it with the young woman. "A girl who was of courting age and not seriously attached to any boy, would go to great lengths to make sure that her offering could not be identified prematurely. The sporting blood of the boys of the community was naturally aroused by such a challenge, and the order of business of the day of the 'supper' was to associate boxes and pies with their owners before the auction." Robert Gilmore, *Ozark Baptizing, Hangings, and Other Diversions: Theatrical Folkways of Rural Missouri, 1885–1910* (Norman: University of Oklahoma Press, 1984), 103–4, http://penelope.uchicago.edu/Thayer/E /Gazetteer/Places/America/United_States/Kentucky/Letcher/Jenkins /_Texts/HJK/J*.html.

9. Eric Lipton, "Even in Coal Country, the Fight for an Industry," *New York Times*, May 29, 2012, http://www.nytimes.com/2012/05/30/business /energy-environment/even-in-kentucky-coal-industry-is-under-siege .html?_r=0.

10. Eric Lipton, "AEP Backs Down on Coal Plant Retrofit," *New York*

Times, May 30, 2012, http://green.blogs.nytimes.com/2012/05/30/aep
-backs-down-on-coal-plant-retrofit/.

11. Erica Martinson, "Uttered in 2008, Still Haunting Obama," *Politico*,
April 5, 2012, http://www.politico.com/story/2012/04/uttered-in-2008
-still-haunting-obama-in-2012-074892.

12. Bill Estep, "Coal Jobs Fall Sharply in Eastern and Eastern [*sic*] and
Western Kentucky in 2015," *Lexington Herald-Leader*, February 3, 2016,
http://www.kentucky.com/news/state/article57684253.html#story
link=cpy.

13. "Unemployment Rate in Pike County, KY," Federal Reserve Bank of
St. Louis, last modified April 5, 2017, https://fred.stlouisfed.org/series
/KYPIKE0URN.

14. National data at http://www.cdc.gov/drugoverdose/data/statedeaths
.html; Pike County data at http://odcp.ky.gov/Pages/Overdose-Fatality
-Report.aspx.

15. Richard Martin, *Coal Wars: The Future of Energy and the Fate of the
Planet* (New York: St. Martin's Press, 2015), 41.

16. Kevin Williamson, "The White Ghetto," *National Review*, January 9,
2014, http://www.nationalreview.com/article/367903/white-ghetto
-kevin-d-williamson.

17. Ben Franklin, "Appalachian Regional Study Finds Absentee Ownership of 43% of Land," *New York Times,* April 5, 1981, http://www
.nytimes.com/1981/04/05/us/appalachian-regional-study-finds-absentee
-ownership-of-43-of-land.html.

18. Ibid.

19. Kentucky Coal Council and the Kentucky Coal Association, "Kentucky
Coal Facts 2003–04 Guide," http://energy.ky.gov/Coal%20Facts%20
Library/Kentucky%20Coal%20Facts%20-%208th%20Edition%20
(2003-2004).pdf.

20. Matthew Mosk and Randy Kreider, "Amid Controversy, Johns Hopkins
Quietly Drops Black Lung Program," ABC News, September 30, 2015,
http://abcnews.go.com/US/amid-controversy-johns-hopkins-quietly

-drops-black-lung/story?id=34161753. Black lung is a crippling illness whose very existence was denied by the coal companies for decades. Dr. Paul Wheeler, who led the black lung unit at the Johns Hopkins School of Medicine, found not a single case of severe black lung in the more than 1,500 cases he reviewed between 2000 and the closure of his unit in 2015. Dr. Wheeler, who was paid by the coal companies for each x-ray, testified in court that the last time he recalled finding a case of severe black lung, a finding that would automatically qualify a miner for benefits under a special federal program, was in "the 1970s or the early '80s."

21. Lydia Saad and Jeffrey Jones, "U.S. Concern About Global Warming at Eight-Year High," Gallup, March 16, 2016, http://www.gallup.com /poll/190010/concern-global-warming-eight-year-high.aspx.

22. "Acceptance of Global Warming Among Americans Reaches Highest Level Since 2008," National Surveys on Energy and Environment, October 2015, http://closup.umich.edu/files/ieep-nsee-2015-fall-climate -belief.pdf.

23. Cary Funk and Brian Kennedy, "The Politics of Climate," Pew Research Center, October 4, 2016, http://www.pewinternet.org/2016/10/04/the -politics-of-climate/.

24. Jill Carle, "Climate Change Seen as Top Global Threat," Pew Research Center, July 14, 2015, http://www.pewglobal.org/2015/07/14/climate -change-seen-as-top-global-threat/.

25. Oren Cass, "The Problem with Climate Catastrophizing: The Case for Calm," *Foreign Affairs,* March 21, 2017, https://www.foreignaffairs .com/articles/2017–03–21/problem-climate-catastrophizing.

26. Keith Fuglie and Nicholas Rada, "Growth in Global Agriculture Productivity: An Update," USDA Economic Research Service, November 18, 2013, https://www.ers.usda.gov/amber-waves/2013/november/growth -in-global-agricultural-productivity-an-update/.

27. Cass, "The Problem with Climate Catastrophizing."

28. Marc Morano, "No Climate Impact: EPA Chief Says the Benefit of Climate Regs Is to Show Domestic Leadership," Climate Depot, March 23,

2016, http://www.climatedepot.com/2016/03/23/no-climate-impact
-epa-chief-says-the-benefit-of-climate-regs-is-to-show-domestic
-leadership/.

29. Ubydul Haque, Masahiro Hashizume, Korine N. Kolivras, Hans Over-
gaard, Bivash Das, and Taro Yamamoto, "Reduced Death Rates from
Cyclones in Bangladesh: What More Needs to be Done?," *Bulletin of
the World Health Organization*, (February 1, 2012), https://www.ncbi
.nlm.nih.gov/pmc/articles/PMC3302549/.

CHAPTER 5: THE PARTY OF SCIENCE?

1. Matt Williams, "Republican Congressman Paul Broun Dismisses
Evolution and Other Theories," *Guardian*, October 6, 2012, https://
www.theguardian.com/world/2012/oct/06/republican-congressman
-paul-broun-evolution-video.

2. Darwin did get a small measure of revenge against Broun at least. At
the urging of libertarian talk show host Neil Boortz, more than four
thousand people cast write-in votes for Darwin in the 2012 congressional race. The tally was not nearly enough to make Darwin the winner
of the election but it was by far the best showing for a long-dead English
naturalist in many a year.

3. Gordon Gauchat, "Politicization of Science in the Public Sphere,"
American Sociological Review 77, no. 2 (2012), http://journals.sagepub
.com/doi/abs/10.1177/0003122412438225.

4. R. J. Brulle, J. Carmichael, and J. C. Jenkins, "Shifting Public Opinion on Climate Change: An Empirical Assessment of Factors Influenc-
ing Concern over Climate Change in the U.S.," *Climatic Change* 114
(2012): 169–88.

5. "Evolution, Creationism, Intelligent Design," Gallup, http://www.gallup
.com/poll/21814/evolution-creationism-intelligent-design.aspx.

6. J. D. Miller, E. C. Scott, and S. Okamot, "Science Communication:
Public Acceptance of Evolution," *Science* 313 (2006): 765–66.

7. See Lynne Isbell, *The Fruit, the Tree, and the Serpent* (Cambridge, MA: Harvard University Press, 2011). Recent experiments on monkeys have demonstrated the innate nature of this fear, developed as a way of avoiding the dangers that snakes pose. Biologists from the University of California, Davis; the University of Toyoma, in Japan; and the Primate Center at the University of Brasilia in Brazil tested for fear of snakes in monkeys born in captivity. These monkeys had no exposure to snakes and thus no learned fear of them. Despite the lack of familiarity and context, the monkeys responded more strongly and more quickly to snakes than to other stimuli. http://www.smh.com.au/technology /sci-tech/monkey-brains-help-explain-our-fear-of-snakes-20131028–2wcsf.

8. Ken Ham, *The Lie: Evolution* (Green Forest, AR: Master Books, 1987), 184.

9. Jonathan Sarfati, "How Did All the Animals Fit on Noah's Ark?," creation.com, http://creation.com/how-did-all-the-animals-fit-on-noahs -ark. There is considerable disagreement on the number of animals that Noah was commanded to bring on board the ark, with skeptics pointing out the impossibility of fitting only the various animals, big and small, into one boat, no matter how large. Creationists, on the other hand, have gone to great lengths to imagine how the various animals could fit into the ark, starting with the idea that Noah was only required to have two of each "kind," a higher order of taxonomy than "species." And they have calculated that many of the animals would be juveniles, so that the average size of the animal would be little more than a small rat and only 11 percent of the animals would be larger than a sheep. Truly, some people have way too much time on their hands.

10. My new favorite website is the San Francisco Zoo, which has a page for the "Scoop on Poop." Some fun facts: Once a week a sloth will climb down from his tree, carefully dig a hole, and poop. The rest of the week, he holds it in. Also, some animals use poop to attract mates, though the site is frustratingly sparse on how they do that. http://www.sfzoo.org /announcements/the-scoop-on-poop-opening-day.

11. Ramez Naam, "Why GMOs Matter—Especially for the Developing World," Grist, January 22, 2014, http://grist.org/food/why-gmos-do-matter-and-even-more-to-the-developing-world/.

12. GMOs are also an interesting example of intense interests. Public opinion on GMOs is not in fact deeply divided by party, as Republican and Democratic views more or less match. http://www.pewinternet.org/2015/07/01/chapter-6-public-opinion-about-food/ But, as with most issues, there are somewhere between 10 percent and 15 percent of the population who are strong advocates on that particular issue. In the case of GMOs, it is observably the liberals in the "against" camp who have identified GMOs as an intense interest.

13. Jim Manzi and Peter Wehner, "Conservatives and Climate Change," *National Affairs,* Summer 2015, https://www.nationalaffairs.com/publications/detail/conservatives-and-climate-change.

14. John Golden and Hannah Wiseman, "The Fracking Revolution: Shale Gas as a Case Study in Innovation Policy," *Emory Law Journal* 64, no. 4 (2014–15), http://law.emory.edu/elj/content/volume-64/issue-4/articles/fracking-revolution-study-innovation-policy.html.

15. See U.S Energy Information Administration, U.S. Department of Energy, *Natural Gas 1998: Issues and Trends* No. DOE/EIA-0560(98) (1999): 52–53, 53 fig. 22, http://www.eia.gov/pub/oil_gas/natural_gas/analysis_publications/natural_gas_1998_issues_trends/pdf/it98.pdf (comparing emissions of nitrogen oxides, sulfur dioxide, particulates, carbon monoxide, and hydrocarbons from natural gas and coal and noting much lower emissions from natural gas).

16. Stephen Moore, "How Fracking Has Reduced Greenhouse Gases," *RealClearPolitics*, April 16, 2016, http://www.realclearpolitics.com/articles/2016/04/16/how_fracking_has_reduced_greenhouse_gases_130303.html#disqus_thread.

17. Manzi and Wehner, "Conservatives and Climate Change."

18. James Tempterton, "Inside Sellafield: How the UK's Most Dangerous Nuclear Site Is Cleaning Up Its Act," *Wired*, December 22, 2016,

http://www.wired.co.uk/article/inside-sellafield-nuclear-waste-decom
missioning.

19. Jesse Jenkins and Samuel Thermstrom, "Deep Decarbonization of
the Electric Power Sector: Insights from Recent Literature," Energy
Innovation Reform Project, March 2017, http://innovationreform.org
/wp-content/uploads/2017/03/EIRP-Deep-Decarb-Lit-Review-Jenkins
-Thernstrom-March-2017.pdf.

20. Steve Scanzillo, "How Much Can Electric Cars Impact Climate Change?
New Report Says a Lot," *San Gabriel Valley Tribune*, September 29, 2015,
http://www.sgvtribune.com/environment-and-nature/20150929/how
-much-can-electric-cars-impact-climate-change-new-report-says-a-lot.
Electric vehicles generate almost no carbon directly but the production
of the electricity used to power those vehicles does. But even "dirty" electricity for electrical vehicles is more carbon-friendly than virtually any
fossil-fuel car though the carbon footprint of electrical vehicles gets much
better as the underlying electrical generation shifts to natural gas, nuclear, or renewables. This estimate of a low-carbon future also assumes
major structural changes in electricity production and consumption.
"The study's lower GHG scenario also figures a cheaper cost of natural
gas, closure of higher-polluting coal plants and increasing the number of
clean-fuel plants such as those run on wind, solar and geothermal power
for generating electricity, as well as a price penalty on higher-carbon fuels.
The base calculation, without the carbon penalty, will reduce 430 metric
tons in 2050 or the equivalent of 80 million passenger cars."

21. "Behind the Curve: Have U.S. Automakers Built the Wrong Cars at
the Wrong Time—Again?," *Knowledge@Wharton* (July 9, 2008),
http://knowledge.wharton.upenn.edu/article/behind-the-curve-have
-u-s-automakers-built-the-wrong-cars-at-the-wrong-time-again/.

22. Christopher Mims, "Electric Cars Will Be Here Sooner than You
Expect," *Wall Street Journal*, August 29, 2016, B1, https://www
.wsj.com/articles/why-electric-cars-will-be-here-sooner-than-you-think
-1472402674.

23. Tom Vanderbilt, "The Real Da Vinci Code," *Wired*, November 1, 2004, http://www.wired.com/2004/11/davinci/.

24. Tom Vanderbilt, "Autonomous Cars Through the Ages," *Wired*, February 6, 2012, http://www.wired.com/2012/02/autonomous-vehicle-history/.

25. Gigafactory 1 is Tesla's battery fabrication facility, which opened in July 2016, outside Reno, Nevada. It is reported to be the world's second-largest building by usable space and the world's largest building by physical space.

26. Jerry Hirsch, "Three Companies, $4.9 Billion in Government Support," *Los Angeles Times*, May 30, 2015, http://www.latimes.com/local/la-fi-hy-musk-subsidies-box-20150530-story.html.

27. Soren Amelang and Kerstine Appunn, "German CO_2 Emissions Rise in 2015 Despite Renewables Surge," Clean Energy Wire, December 21, 2015, https://www.cleanenergywire.org/news/german-co2-emissions-rise-2015-despite-renewables-surge.

28. Ibid.

29. "Germany's Coal Binge," *Wall Street Journal*, September 24, 2014, http://www.wsj.com/articles/germanys-coal-binge-1411599265.

30. Scott DiSavino, "Natural Gas Likely Overtook Coal as Top U.S. Power Source in 2015," Reuters, January 20, 2016, http://www.reuters.com/article/us-usa-natgas-coal-idUSKCN0UY2LT.

31. U.S. Energy Information Administration, Henry Hub Natural Gas Spot Price, https://www.eia.gov/dnav/ng/hist/rngwhhdd.htm.

CHAPTER 6: THE GREATEST SOCIETY

1. I first came across McDonald's story in a book by Arthur Brooks called *The Conservative Heart: How to Build a Fairer, Happier and More Prosperous America* (New York: HarperCollins, 2015).

2. "Poverty Rates Since 1975: United States and New York City," http://www.nyc.gov/html/ceo/downloads/pdf/chart_1.pdf.

3. Robert Langan and Matthew Durose, "The Remarkable Drop in Crime in New York City," U.S. Department of Justice, Bureau of Justice Statistics, October 21, 2004, http://www3.istat.it/istat/eventi/2003/perunasocieta/relazioni/Langan_rel.pdf.

4. A very high percentage of means-tested spending, 52 percent in fiscal 2011, goes to health care for the poor. Much of the increased spending in this area reflects rising health-care costs and longer life spans—rather than any greater commitment to poverty alleviation—and some of the increased spending goes to "seniors who had middle-class incomes for much of their working lives but whose long-term care needs now exceed their ability to pay for that care." Testimony of Robert Greenstein, President of the Center on Budget and Policy Priorities, Before the Human Resources Subcommittee of the House Committee on Ways and Means, November 3, 2015. But even setting aside the 448 percent growth in means-tested health spending from 1989 to 2008, the 196 percent growth in spending on cash, food, and housing for the poor has still been substantial, more than Social Security, education, or defense over that same period of time. Testimony of Robert Rector, Senior Research Fellow at the Heritage Foundation, Before the Human Resources Subcommittee of the House Committee on Ways and Means, April 5, 2011, http://www2.heritage.org/research/testimony/2012/06/welfare-state-69-means-tested-programs-and-940-billion-in-annual-spending#_ftnref4.

5. Scott Winship, "Poverty After Welfare Reform," Manhattan Institute, August 22, 2016, https://www.manhattan-institute.org/html/poverty-after-welfare-reform.html.

6. Robert Rector and Rachael Sheffield, "The War on Poverty After 50 Years," Heritage Foundation, September 15, 2014, http://www.heritage.org/research/reports/2014/09/the-war-on-poverty-after-50-years.

7. Raj Chetty, Nathaniel Hendren, Patrick Kline, Emmanuel Saez, and Nicholas Turner, "Is the United States Still a Land of Opportunity? Recent Trends in Intergenerational Mobility," NBER Working Paper

No. 19844, National Bureau of Economic Research, 2014, http://www.
rajchetty.com/chettyfiles/mobility_trends.pdf.

8. Winship, "Poverty After Welfare Reform."

9. Scott Winship, "Was Welfare Reform a Success?," Manhattan Institute, 2016, http://www.manhattan-institute.org/sites/default/files/IB-SW-0616.pdf.

10. Laurence Chandy and Cory Smith, "How Poor Are America's Poorest? U.S. $2 a Day Poverty in a Global Context," Global Views Policy Paper 2014–03, Brookings Institution, August 24, 2014, https://www.brookings.edu/research/how-poor-are-americas-poorest-u-s-2-a-day-poverty-in-a-global-context.

11. Winship, "Poverty After Welfare Reform," 24.

12. Richard Rector and Jennifer Marshall, "The Unfinished Work of Welfare Reform," Heritage Foundation, January 22, 2013, http://www.heritage.org/research/reports/2013/01/the-unfinished-work-of-welfare-reform.

13. Ladonna Pavetti, "Work Requirements Don't Cut Poverty, Evidence Shows," Center for Budget and Policy Priorities, June 7, 2016, http://www.cbpp.org/research/poverty-and-inequality/work-requirements-dont-cut-poverty-evidence-shows.

14. Bryon Johnson and William Wubbenhorst, "Multi-State Mentoring Research: The Center for Neighborhood Enterprise's Violence Free Zone (VFZ) Initiative," March 30, 2015, http://www.baylorisr.org/wp-content/uploads/ISR_VFZCaseStudy-FINAL-02172015-web.pdf.4. It is no small thing for a program like this to have such promising data, since it is notoriously hard for a single program to affect education outcomes, but the data is not quite as conclusive as Woodson and others would have you believe. The problem with pre- and post-evaluations is that you can never know for sure whether the progress was due to the program or to other factors—you need a randomized control test for that. It is not uncommon, even for other promising mentoring programs, to show positive results in a pre- or

post-evaluation that disappear under the scrutiny of a more rigorous evaluation.

15. To my great disappointment, there appears to be no person who has the singular job title of "The Repealer." According to its website, the Office of the Repealer has no "staff, budget, or office space." The staff of the Kansas secretary of state supports the functions of the Office of the Repealer, which effectively makes Kris Kobach the Grim Repealer of Kansas. It is a fitting title to hang on Kobach since he seems to reflect the same type of foolishness that got Brownback elected. Kobach waged his initial campaign for secretary of state in 2010 on the largely nonexistent issue of voter fraud, with a specific emphasis on the fear of having noncitizens casting votes. Kobach didn't get his first conviction for illegal voting by a noncitizen until 2017, and even that case was only accidentally uncovered after the voter accepted the chance to register at his naturalization ceremony and it was discovered that he had already voted a number of times. For that he was convicted and sentenced to three months of unsupervised probation and fined $5,000. Kobach's utter lack of success in uncovering voter fraud did not stop President Trump from naming him to be a cochair of a new national commission to investigate voter fraud and voter suppression.

16. Eric Levitz, "The Republican Party Must Answer for What It Did to Kansas and Louisiana," *New York*, March 18, 2016, http://nymag.com/daily/intelligencer/2016/03/gop-must-answer-for-what-it-did-to-kansas.html.

17. "Chart Book: TANF at 20," Center on Budget and Policy Priorities, August 5, 2016.

18. Anthony Campbell, Alice Godfryd, David Buys, and Julie Locher, "Does Participation in Home-Delivered Meals Programs Improve Outcomes for Older Adults: Results of a Systematic Review," https://www.ncbi.nlm.nih.gov/pmc/articles/PMC4480596/; D. F. Jyoti, E. A. Frongillo, and S. J. Jones, "Food Insecurity Affects School Children's Academic Performance, Weight Gain, and Social Skills," *Journal of*

Nutrition 135, no. 12 (December 2005), https://www.ncbi.nlm.nih .gov/pubmed/16317128. See also Aaron Carroll, "The Costs Can be Debated, but Meals on Wheels Gets Results," *New York Times*, March 17, 2017, https://www.nytimes.com/2017/03/17/upshot/the-cost-can -be-debated-but-meals-on-wheels-gets-results.html.

19. "Beyond Distrust: How Americans View Their Government," Pew Research Center, November 23, 2015, http://www.people-press.org/2015 /11/23/beyond-distrust-how-americans-view-their-government/.

CHAPTER 7: THE PARTY OF THE PRESS

1. Andrew Breitbart, *Righteous Indignation: Excuse Me While I Save the World!* (New York: Grand Central, 2011), loc. 2175.

2. Bethania Palma, "Progressive Group Claims to 'Sting' Sting Video Maker James O'Keefe," Snopes.com, January 25, 2017, http://www .snopes.com/2017/01/18/dueling-stings/.

3. Ian Hanchett, "NAACP CEO: Trump's View on Race Somewhere Between Cro-Magnon and Neanderthal," *Breitbart*, February 16, 2017, http://www.breitbart.com/video/2017/02/16/naacp-ceo-trumps -views-on-race-somewhere-between-cro-magnon-and-neanderthal /#disqus_thread.

4. Gary Gates, "Majority of U.S. Voters Think Media Favors Clinton," Gallup, November 3, 2016, http://www.gallup.com/poll/197090 /majority-voters-think-media-favors-clinton.aspx.

5. "Bottom-Line Pressures Now Hurting Coverage, Say Journalists," Pew Research Center, May 23, 2004, http://www.people-press.org /2004/05/23/iv-values-and-the-press/.

6. Matthew Belvedere and Michael Newberg, "New York Times' Subscription Soars Tenfold, Adding 132,000, After Trump's Win," CNBC, November 29, 2016, http://www.cnbc.com/2016/11/29/new -york-times-subscriptions-soar-tenfold-after-donald-trump-wins -presidency.html. President Trump has repeatedly described the *New*

York Times as "failing," but he is unintentionally playing a significant role in the financial resurgence of the newspaper. It is hard from the outside to estimate a lifetime value of a new subscriber, but, just based on annual digital revenues, each subscriber would be worth $200 at the very least, meaning that the "Trump subscribers" are worth $55 million of free-cash-flow value to the New York Times Company every year. Frédéric Filloux, "The NYTimes Could Be Worth $19bn Instead of $2bn," Monday Note, February 15, 2015, https://mondaynote.com/the-nytimes-could-be-worth-19bn-instead-of-2bn-8ab635bc6262#.xo3dblz6o.

7. See, for instance, a six-part *Los Angeles Times* editorial series called "The Problem with Trump," which furiously criticized President Trump's dangerous policies on climate, immigration, military spending, and education and then admitted that these "policies are, for the most part, variations on classic Republican positions (many of which would have been undertaken by a President Ted Cruz or a President Marco Rubio)." "Our Dishonest President," editorial, *Los Angeles Times,* April 2, 2017, http://www.latimes.com/projects/la-ed-our-dishonest-president/.

8. John B. Judis, *The Populist Explosion: How the Great Recession Transformed American and European Politics* (New York: Columbia Global Reports, 2016).

9. I first chronicled my interactions with Bannon in a series of articles for *Vanity Fair's Hive*: Ken Stern, "Exclusive: Stephen Bannon, Trump's New C.E.O. Hints at His Master Plan," *Hive,* August 17, 2016, http://www.vanityfair.com/news/2016/08/breitbart-stephen-bannon-donald-trump-master-plan; Ken Stern, "What Steve Bannon Really Thinks," *Hive,* March 3, 2017, http://www.vanityfair.com/news/2017/03/what-steve-bannon-really-thinks.

10. "U.S. Immigration Policy and Share Over Time, 1850–Present," Migration Policy Institute, http://www.migrationpolicy.org/programs/data-hub/charts/immigrant-population-over-time.

11. David Frum, "Does Immigration Harm Working Americans?," *Atlantic*, January 5, 2015, https://www.theatlantic.com/business/archive/2015/01/does-immigration-harm-working-americans/384060/.

CHAPTER 8: THE END AND THE BEGINNING

1. Justin McCarthy, "Three in 10 Americans Follow Election Very Closely," Gallup, January 25, 2016, http://www.gallup.com/poll/188825/three-americans-say-follow-election-closely.aspx.
2. K. N. Pineda, "Divisions in My Dorm Room," *New York Times,* November 28, 2016 https://www.nytimes.com/2016/11/28/opinion/divisions-in-my-dorm-room.html?_r=0; Romaissaa Benzizoune, "I'm Muslim but My Roommate Supports Trump," *New York Times,* November 11, 2016, https://www.nytimes.com/2016/11/12/opinion/im-muslim-but-my-roommate-supports-trump.html.
3. Henri Tajfel, "Experiments in Intergroup Discrimination," *Scientific American* 223 (1970), 96–102.
4. Richard Hofstadter, "The Paranoid Style in American History," *Harper's Magazine*, November 1964, http://harpers.org/archive/1964/11/the-paranoid-style-in-american-politics/?single=1.
5. Ben Johnson, "2016 Republican Platform Hailed as Most Pro-Life, Pro-Family Ever," *Life Site News*, July 20, 2016, https://www.lifesitenews.com/news/2016-republican-party-platform-the-most-pro-life-ever.
6. "Abortion," Gallup, accessed April 23, 2017, http://www.gallup.com/poll/1576/abortion.aspx.
7. For a good and easily accessible discussion of Fiorina and Krosnick's research, see Lynn Vavreck, "Candidates Fight over Abortion, but Public Has Surprising Level of Harmony," *New York Times*, May 6, 2015.

INDEX

Abiding Truth Ministries, 263n7
abortion, 16, 57, 58, 68, 73, 244–48
Adams, Sam, 60, 62–65, 67, 68, 87
affirmative action, 10
Affordable Care Act (Obamacare), 10, 255n16
Alvanitakis, Kirstin, 217–18
Ambrosino, Brandon, 264n11
American Baptist International Ministries, 59
American Enterprise Institute, 19, 179, 187, 202, 244
American family, 80–84, 104, 105
    defining "household" and, 191
    federal programs and, 183–84, 193
    single-parent families, 80–82, 83, 84, 188
American National Election Studies (ANES), 6, 245, 253n4
Andy Griffith Show, The (TV show), 85–86
Answers in Genesis, 146, 147
Appalachia, 122–24, 127–31
Appalachian Land Ownership Task Force, 130–31
Appalachian News-Express, 124
Apple, 233–34
Ark Encounter, Ky., 143, 146, 274n9
Assault Weapons Ban, 26, 42, 43
Assembly of God, Springfield, Mo., 85
Association of Community Organizations Now (ACORN), 211–12, 213, 215, 218, 228
automobile industry, 160–63, 276n20
Autor, David, 234

Bacon, Kevin, 57
Baltimore, Md., 195
    Patterson High School, 197–99
    VFZ program, 195–98, 279n14
Bane, Mary Jo, 188
Bannon, Steve, 113, 227–34, 241, 282n9
Baptist General Convention of Texas, 79
Baptist University in Congo, 58

Barone, Michael, 110–11
Barry, Marion, 19
"Being Gay at Jerry Falwell's University" (Ambrosino), 264n11
Benz, Karl, 161
Betras, Dave, 186
Bible, Gender, Sexuality (Brownson), 77
Biden, Joe, 234–35
Big Sort, The (Bishop), 14–15
Bishop, Bill, 14–15
Bishop, George, 9
Black Lives Matter, 46, 53, 57, 95
Blair, Tony, 219
Blalock, Hubert, 92
Bloomberg, Michael, 257n12
Blumenthal, Max, 210
Boehner, John, 133
"bonds of affection," 237
Bouie, Jamelle, 154
Brandeis, Louis, 199–200
Brandon, Willie, 109
Brazile, Donna, 134
Breakthrough (O'Keefe), 214, 215
Breitbart, Andrew, 209–11, 217, 218, 227, 228
Breitbart News, 19, 49, 92, 206, 208, 220, 227, 228, 230, 240, 243
Broadcast News (film), 205
Brooks, Albert, 205
Brooks, Arthur, 202, 203, 277n1
Broun, Paul, 144, 150, 273n2
Brownback, Sam, 199–202, 280n15
Brownson, James, 77
Bruce, Lenny, 53
Bryson, Bill, 28
Buckley, William F., Jr., 111
Bush, George W., 44, 45

Callahan, Robert, 174
Cantril, Hadley, 12–13
capitalism, 234
Carlson, Dick, 30

285

Carlson, Tucker, 30
Carson, Ben, 87, 144, 150
Case, Anne, 102, 103, 268n11
Cass, Oren, 135
Cassidy, Bill, 120
Cato Institute, 179, 244
Center for Neighborhood Enterprise, 193, 194
Chantilly, Va., 43, 47, 89–91
Chapman, Glenn, 58–59
Chapman, Rita, 58
Charles, Prince of Wales, 133
Charles River Associates, 138
Chicago, 28, 50
China, 134, 203, 230, 233–34
Chosen People Ministries, 59–60
Christianity Today, 70
Christie, Chris, 199
Clear Channel Communications, 218
climate change (AGW), 60, 116–41
    acceptance of human cause of, 132, 167
    alarmism/hysteria and, 133–41
    American attitudes about, 167–69
    American innovation and, 156, 164
    Appalachian workers and, 127
    auto industry and, 160–62, 276n20
    Bangladesh and, 140–41
    "the case for calm," 135
    celebrities of, 120
    Chinese response to, 134
    climate deniers, 118, 120
    "deep decarbonization" and, 160
    European Union and, 164–65
    free market economics and, 120–21
    extreme weather and, 120, 269n5
    Genesis 8:22 and, 118
    Germany's *Energiewende*, 164–65
    Inhofe and, 117–20, 121
    natural gas and, 157–59
    Obama and, 121, 125, 138, 156
    practical solutions, 141
    progressives and, 121, 134–35, 141, 168
    Republicans and, 122–41
    science on how to control, 168
    scientific evidence for, 119, 269n3
    Trump policy, 156
    UN Climate Summit, Copenhagen, 119
    UN IPCC reports, 135
    U.S. drop in emissions, 156, 158–60
    War on Coal, 125–27
    Yale's DICE model, 136
Clinton, Bill, 18, 188, 189, 201
Clinton, Hillary, 2, 4, 37–38, 44, 45, 46,
    87, 186, 221, 241
Clutterbuck, John, 30
coal industry, 104, 106–7, 115, 131, 124
    in Germany, 165–66
    Kentucky and, 104, 106–8, 122–31
    lost jobs, income, and health of
        miners, 127–28, 131, 271n20
    natural gas overtaking, 166–67
    War on Coal, 125–27, 130, 138
    workers as voters, 127
    See also Pikeville, Ky.
Coalition for the Homeless, 173–74
Coal Wars (Martin), 128–29
Cohn, Nate, 92
Colbert, Stephen, 91
Coming Apart (Murray), 55
Common Core, 10
confirmation bias, 17, 249
Consolidation Coal Co. (Consol), 122–24
conspiracy theories, 205–6
Continetti, Matthew, 219
Coulter, Ann, 267n6
creationism, 145–53, 273n2, 274n9
Creation Museum, 146–52, 274n7, 274n9,
    274n10
crime
        assault weapons and, 25
        Chicago murder rate, 28
        in England, 28–29
        falling rates of, 48–49
        gun control as ineffective, 24, 26,
            48–49
        gun homicides, 23–24, 48, 103,
            256n3
        gun ownership and, 49
        gun violence, 23, 33, 42, 259n17
        illegal immigrants and, 228–29
        Lott on reducing gun homicides, 42
        mass shootings, 23, 24, 25, 27, 33–34
        news media and perception of, 49
        OECD rating of U.S. homicide rate, 28
        right-to-carry laws (RTCs) and, 35–37
        in Switzerland, 29
        U.S. murder rate, 23
        weapons used in murders, 25
Croods, The (film), 146
Cruz, Ted, 58, 87

Daily Beacon, 219
Daily Caller, 30

Dalai Lama, 21
Daly, Jim, 75
Dave (film), 171
Dawson, Charles, 148–49
"Deacon Blues" (song), 89
"Death of a Douche" (Taibbi), 210–11
Deaton, Angus, 102, 103, 268n11
Defense Advanced Research Projects
    Agency (DARPA), 163
Democrats (liberals, progressives)
        abortion issue and, 244–45
        ACORN and, 211–12
        "afraid" of Republicans, 5–6
        author and, 2, 18
        bubble of, 17, 22
        climate change and, 118, 134–35,
        139, 141, 160, 168
        Common Core and, 10
        creationism, evolution, and, 153
        exaggeration by, 168
        facts ignored by, 11
        geographic sorting and, 14–15
        government seen as threat, 45, 260n25
        government solutions for problems, 121
        gun control issue and, 22, 36, 37, 42
        Hayek on, 115
        Hollywood and, 228
        loss of 2016 presidential election, 92
        Mount Pleasant support, 2, 4, 18
        neoliberals, 230
        problem of homelessness and, 173
        religious communities and, 57
        sanctimony of, 27
        single-parents, view on, 83
        uniform ideology and, 16
        view of Trump, 226
        vision for America, 97, 99, 111
        welfare reform and, 188
        words describing Republicans, 238
        working class and, 108, 168–69,
        234–35
Dixon, Walter, 106–7, 108
Dobson, James, 74–75
Doe Fund, 171–79, 186–87, 192–93
Dorn, David, 234
"Do You Live in a Bubble?" quiz (Murray),
    55–56, 71
drug and alcohol abuse
        in Appalachia, 128, 129, 130
        non-Hispanic whites and, 102, 268n11
        opioids, 103–4, 128

EastLake Community Church, 75, 77
Ebacher, Jason, 249, 250
Edelman, Peter, 188
Edin, Kathryn, 189–90, 191
Edward Jones Dome, 53
elites, cultural (coastal), 30, 57, 111, 114, 117,
        118, 127, 144, 155, 228, 229, 231, 233, 234
England, 28, 29
environmental issues
        fracking dangers, 158–59
        as low priority for voters, 96
        regulation of business and, 117
        Senate Committee on the Environ-
        ment and Public Works and, 117
        See also climate change
Environmental Protection Agency (EPA),
        117, 125, 127, 138–40, 159, 226
        Pruitt as head of, 167, 168, 226
Ernest, Joni, 133
evangelicals, 53–88, 146, 149
        Adams and, 60–65
        bubble of, 59
        change and, 74–77
        concern about the family, 80–84
        conservativism of, 57
        ethic of service, 64
        foster care efforts by, 67
        gay evangelical groups, 76
        homosexuality and, 56, 60–62, 73–80
        ignorance of, by liberal elites, 57
        importance of community, 87–88
        Inazu on, 56–57
        InterVarsity, 68–69
        leadership changes, 74–75
        Liberty University, 72–76
        marriage and divorce, 265n21
        media coverage of, 262n5
        megachurches, 75
        minorities as, 57, 262n2
        mission of, 58–59, 63
        number of, in U.S., 54, 261n1
        in Portland, 60–67
        social programs and, 75
        societal changes and, 149–50
        Urbana conclave, 53–54, 57–60, 68–69
        volunteerism and, 64
        voting Republican, 54
        worship services of, 84–87
        younger generation of, 56, 77–78
Everytown for Gun Safety, 257n12
"extreme ward," 14–15

Facebook, 78–79, 222, 223
facts
    climate change and, 119, 121
    conservative rejection of, 115, 121
    liberals ignoring of, 11
    Moynihan quote and, 12
    Princeton-Dartmouth football game
    and, 12–13
    slippery nature of, Internet and,
    213
    Trump administration and, 202–3
    views of, 12
fake news, 11, 206
Falwell, Jerry, Jr., 72, 73, 74
Falwell, Jerry, Sr., 72, 73, 74, 78, 82
Falwell, Kevin, 73
Farris, Floyd, 157
Feinstein, Dianne, 45
Ferguson, Mo., 46, 53
Fiorina, Morris, 16, 246, 255n16, 283n7
Florida, RTCs in, 41–42
Floyd, Ruby Stroud, 111
Focus on the Family, 74, 75
Ford, Roger, 124, 125–26, 128, 130, 237
Forrest, Nathan Bedford, 46–47
Fox, Mike, 162
Foxconn, 233
Fox News, 19, 30, 206, 208, 225
France, Brian, 99
Freedom Church, 86–88, 237
Frum, David, 232–33
Full Metal Jacket (film), 34

Gallup polls
    American views on abortion, 245
    on creationism, 145
    on federal government as a threat,
    44–45
Germany, environmental decision-making,
    164–66
Gerson, Michael, 97–98, 212
Gertz, Marc, 259n17
Giles, Hannah, 212
GMOs, 153–55, 275n12
Goering, Tom, 71–72
Goldfarb, Michael, 219
Gore, Al, 120, 133
government
    distrust of intervention by, 121
    merits of private sector versus, 164
    poverty programs, 180–85

    regulations, 107–8, 116, 117,
    138–40, 164
    Republicans on the welfare state, 180
    as roadblock to progress, 116–17
    Rooseveltian view of, 186
    seen as a threat, 44–45, 260n25
    seen as oppressive force, 107–8
    size of, 16
    social engineering and, 192
    subsidies for fracking, 158
    subsidies to Tesla, 163–64
Greatest Hoax, The (Inhofe), 117–18, 119
Great Society, 184, 192, 203
Green, Ake, 262n5
groupthink, 16, 221, 223, 225, 239
Guevara, Che, 209
Gun Owners of America, 259n17
gun regulation, 24, 26, 28, 29, 42–43
    Assault Weapons Ban, 26, 42, 43
    funding of advocates, 257n12
    gun control lobby, 259n17
    liberals and lawful gun owners, 42
    views on gun issues, 37–38
guns, 17, 21–52
    accidental deaths among children,
    24–25
    assault weapons, 25–26, 50
    concealed-handgun permits, 41, 51
    crime and, 23–24, 256n3, 259n17
    cultural bubble and, 22
    defensive gun use (DGU), 33,
    259n17
    District of Columbia v. Heller and, 50
    government as a threat and, 44, 45
    gun deaths, 23–25, 48, 103
    gun hoarders, 32–33
    issues that influence gun violence, 29
    more guns, less crime, 35, 36, 37
    number of gun owners, 32, 48–49
    open-carry rights, 35
    "prepper" movement and, 47
    right-to-carry laws (RTCs), 35–37
    sales, 27, 43, 48, 50–51, 256n3
    Second Amendment, 22–23, 44, 47
    shows, 27, 37, 41–48
    Small Arms Survey, 29
    social media responses and, 26–27
    stolen guns, 27, 256n3
    Switzerland's policy, 29
    Washington, D.C., law enforcement, 22
    who owns guns, 23, 50–51

Ham, Ken, 146, 147, 148, 150
Hancock, John, 207
Hannity, Sean, 208, 225
Hanson, Gordon, 234
Hastorf, Albert, 12–13
Hatmaker, Brandon, 78–79
Hatmaker, Jen, 78, 79
Haverford College, 18
Hayek, Friedrich, 115, 121, 168
Hayes, Robert, 173
Hellier, Ky., 130
Hemenway, David, 259n17
Heritage Action for America, 30
Heritage Foundation, 138
Hesburgh, Theodore, 74
Heston, Charlton, 47
Higgins, Michelle, 53
Hofstadter, Richard, 230
homosexuality and gay rights, 16, 70, 77, 95,
    263n7
        evangelicals and, 56, 68, 73, 74–80,
        264n11
        OCA attack on, in Oregon, 61–62
        same sex marriage, 77–78, 79, 80
Horwitz, Alexander, 179
Huckabee, Mike, 208
Huffington Post, research on political
    decision-making, 9–10

immigration, 16, 96
        American workers and, 231–33
        building the wall and, 91, 96–97, 267n6
        crime and illegals, 228–29
        Immigration Act of 1965, 232
        news media and perception of, 49
        refugee problem, 57–58
Inazu, John, 56–57, 59, 72, 85, 149
income inequality, 185, 230
Independence Ranch, Gonzales, Tx., 21–22,
    31, 32, 38–41, 205
InfoWars, 206
Inhofe, James Mountain, 116–20, 121
Internet and social media
        blogs, number of, 219
        Breitbart websites, 209–10
        "combat journalism" on, 219
        the "commentsphere," 219–20
        conservative bloggers, 206, 210
        "discussion networks," 221
        dystopian view of America, 223
        facts, slippery nature of, 213

groupthink and, 221, 223
        lack of regulations on, 219
        O'Keefe and, 213
        online political commentary, 219
        political provocateurs on, 209
        silence spiral, 222
        social media, 206, 223 (*see also* Facebook)
        trolls, 220, 247
        uncivility on, 220–21, 223, 239, 240
InterVarsity, 68–70
Iyengar, Shanto, 7–8

James River Coal Company, 107
Jenkins, Ky., 122–24, 270n8
Jindal, Bobby, 133, 199
Johnson, Lyndon, 181, 184, 185–86, 203
Jones, Van, 113–14
Journal of Legal Studies, Lott-Mustard paper
    on RTCs, 35–36

Kansas, 199–202, 280n15
Karr-McDonald, Harriet, 174
Kato, David, 263n7
Kazmaier, Dick, 12
Kennedy, John F., 10, 181
Kentucky, 104, 106–8, 122–31, 143, 145, 146
Kentucky Power, 125
King, Martin Luther, Jr., 83
Klar, Samara, 247–48
Kleck, Gary, 259n17
Kline, Kevin, 171
Kobach, Kris, 280n15
Koch, Charles, 206
Koper, Christopher, 26
Krosnick, Jon, 246, 283n7
Krugman, Paul, 134
Kubrick, Stanley, 34
Ku Klux Klan, 46–47
Kynect, 10

Laffer, Arthur, 199–200
Landrieu, Mary, 214, 215, 216, 217
"landslide counties," 15
Lee, Harper, 1
Le Pen, Jean-Marie, 235
Le Pen, Marine, 235
Levin, Mark, 19, 208, 219
Levin, Yuval, 243
Lexington Herald-Leader, 127
Liberty University, 72–76
Lichtman, Allan, 92

LifeWay Christian Stores, 78–79
Limbaugh, Rush, 180, 202, 206, 208
Lincoln, Abraham, 237
Lithgow, John, 57
Lively, Scott, 263n7
Lomax, Neil, 65–66
Los Angeles Times, 187, 282n7
Lott, John, 35–37 41–42, 49
Louisiana, weather events in, 120
Luther, Martin, 148

Maddow, Rachel, 119
Maher, Bill, 153
Manhattan Institute, 19, 244
manufacturing job loss, 98, 100, 108–10, 172, 228, 234
marriage, 80–81, 83–84, 104–5, 183–84
Martin, Richard, 128–29
Martinsville, Va., 98–99, 107–8, 111, 112, 244
Mason, Lilliana, 249, 255n16
McConnell, Mitch, 19, 133
McDonald, George, 171–79, 186, 277n1
McKibben, Bill, 120
McLean, Va., 71
McLean Bible Church, 84–85
media, 205–36
    as agenda driven, 49–50
    bubbles and bias, 225–26
    "the Complex," 209, 228
    conservative talk radio, 208–9, 248
    coverage of crime and, 49
    Fairness Doctrine eliminated, 218, 219
    FCC rule change, 218
    groupthink and, 221, 225
    mainstream, 50, 92, 118, 206, 208, 224
    outrage and, 218–19, 226
    partisanship in, 16, 208, 221
    Republican complaints of bias, 224
    Trump and, 90, 225–26, 281n6, 282n7
    See also Internet
Meeks, Ryan, 77
Milbank, Dana, 119
Miles's law, 168
Milwaukee, Wi., 14–15
Monsanto, 153, 155
Mount Pleasant, D.C., 1–4, 5, 6, 8, 18, 153
    Hobart Street, 1–4, 18, 22, 250
    "Hobart Street Pledge," 3–4, 17
Moynihan, Daniel Patrick, 12, 188
MSNBC, 118, 119

multiculturalism, 233
Murray, Charles, 55–56, 71
Musk, Elon, 161–62
Mustard, David, 35

NAFTA, 109, 230
NASCAR, 19, 99, 244
National Crime Victimization Survey (NCVS), 259n17
National Public Radio (NPR), 18, 22, 212–13, 224–25
National Research Council (NRC), review of Lott-Mustard article, 36–37
National Review, 110, 111, 226, 250
National Rifle Association (NRA), 29, 47, 257n12, 259n17
Nation's Gun Show, 43–48, 51
natural gas, 157–59, 164, 166–67
Needham, Michael, 30
New Life Church, 75
New York City
    Doe Fund and, 175–79
    elites of, 30
    homelessness in, 173–74
    inmates paroled into, 175–76
    poverty, crime, and, 172–73
    Ready, Willing & Able, 176–77, 178
    Supportive Work, 175, 176
New Yorker, on malcontent providers, 210
New York Times, 224
    bias/partisanship of, 226, 227, 248–49
    comment board, 221, 239–40
    "Daily Toll" articles, 42–43
    endorsement of gun control, 257n12
    Ethicist column, 240
    growth, Trump and, 226, 281n6
    liberal narrative of, 43
    Pineda op-ed, 238–39
Noelle-Neumann, Elisabeth, 221–22
Norton, Michael, 94–95
nuclear energy, 159–60
Nye, Bill, 120

Obama, Barack, 46, 105–6, 159
    climate change and, 121, 125, 138, 156, 167, 168
    EPA under, 226
    federal government as a threat and, 45
    on gun violence, 28
    view of Republicans, 179–80

vision for America, 97
War on Coal, 125, 126–27, 130
Occupational Safety and Health Administration (OSHA), 117
O'Connor, Larry, 210
O'Keefe, James, 211–18
Oklahoma, 118
See also Inhofe, James Mountain
Olbermann, Keith, 118–19, 219
Oregon, 61–62, 66
See also Portland, Or.
Oregon Citizens Alliance (OCA), 61–62, 64, 263n7
O'Reilly, Bill, 225
Organisation for Economic Co-operation and Development (OECD), 28, 80
O'Rourke, P. J., 146

Palau, Kevin, 62–68, 87

Palin, Sarah, 208, 227
"Paranoid Style in American Politics, The" (Hofstadter), 230
Paris Climate Accords, 133, 138–39
Paul, Ron, 249
Paulville, Tx., 249–50
Penn-Virginia Coal Company, 131
Perot, Ross, 229
Personal Responsibility and Work Opportunity Reconciliation Act (PRWORA), 188
Petersburg, Ky., 146
Pew Research Center
majority-minority nation prediction, 93
political polarization in America, 5, 6
poll on public perception of crime, 49
ranking of climate change as issue, 134
on "silence spiral" in social media, 222
study on religion in everyday life, 263n8
survey on gay marriage, 78
Phelps, Fred, 262n5
Pied Piper Pickles, 44
Pikeville, Ky., 104, 106–8, 124–26, 168–69
Hatfield–McCoy feud, 129–30
Pineda, K. N., 238–39, 240, 249
Planned Parenthood, 244–46
political decision-making, 8–11
signaling and, 8–9, 11
political polarization, 5, 6, 11, 204
Bishop's *The Big Sort* and, 14–15
bonds of affection and, 237

as clash of right versus wrong, 18
demonization and, 238–39, 241
"extreme ward," 14–15
fake news and, 11
fear of opposing party and, 5–6, 253n2
federal government as a threat and, 45
geographic sorting and, 14–15, 249–50
increasing, 5, 6, 16–17, 255n16
Internet and, 222–23
intolerance of competing views, 241
Iyengar-Westwood study, 7–8
key policy issues and, 16, 255n16
media and, 206
partisan bubbles, 15
party affiliation and marriage, 6, 254n6
political decision-making and, 8–10
as stronger than racial bigotry, 6–8
Tajfel studies on group loyalty, 241–42
"team spirit" and view of facts, 12
"warmth" gap and, 6, 253n4, 254n5
See also specific issues
populism, 227, 228, 229–32, 233, 235
Portland, Or., 60, 62
City Serve, 67
evangelical partnerships, 62–67
Roosevelt High School, 63–67
poverty, 17
annual spending on means-tested welfare programs, 181, 278n4
"birth lottery" and, 184
Brooks on, 202
Callahan v. Carey and, 173–74
child poverty, 83, 84, 183, 188–90
Columbia University research, 182–93
conservative approach, 186, 198–99, 201
defining "household" and, 191
economic growth and reduction in, 203
government program failure, 180–81, 185, 204
Hayes and, 173, 174
McDonald and, 171–79
number of government programs, 182
poverty levels, postwar years, 181
single-parent families and, 193
survey on public attitudes toward, 187
as a trap, 184
Trump White House and, 202–3

poverty (*cont.*)
    VFZ program, 195–98, 279n14
    War on Poverty, 182, 183–84, 185
    waste and abuse in programs, 194
    welfare reform and, 189–91
power threat theory, 92–93
presidential race, 2016
    "basket of deplorables," 89
    building the wall and, 91, 96–97
    correct predictions, 92
    Democrats, Mount Pleasant, 2, 4
    evangelical voters and, 54, 87
    failure of Clinton Campaign, 186
    gun regulation and, 37–38
    inaccurate predictions, 92
    lack of a shared experience and, 13–14
    "power threat theory" and, 92
    Republican platform, 244
    Trumpism and, 204
    Trump rally, Chantilly, Va., 89–91
    Trump voters, 91–92, 99, 108–10,
    112–13, 186
    Washington Post survey, 4–5
progressives. *See* Democrats
Pruitt, Scott, 167, 168, 226
public opinion, 221–22

race
    anti-white bias, 95
    bias, group most impacted by, 113
    changing composition of the U.S., 93
    diversity, 2, 4, 14–15
    Martinsville Seven, 111
    non-Hispanic whites, number of,
    99–100
    Norton-Sommers study, 95
    populism and, 235
    power threat theory and, 92–93
    rise in white mortality, 102–4, 268n11
    shifting perceptions about, 95
    white working-class despair, 23
    working class and racial animus, 113–14
    See also crime; immigration
Reagan, Ronald, 44, 185
Reed, Ralph, 58
religion, 53–88
    charity, social programs, and, 57, 59
    creationism, 145–53, 273n2
    Pew study, in everyday life, 263n8
    volunteerism and, 64
    See also evangelicals

Republicans and conservatives
    abortion issue and, 244
    "afraid" of Democrats, 5–6
    alternative-fact wing, 121
    anger at Democrats' vision, 98
    approach to poverty, 171–72
    climate change and, 117, 122–41, 167
    Common Core and, 10
    conservative bubble, 227
    conservative rejection of facts, 115, 121
    conservatives and transferring
    federal funds to state/local govern-
    ments, 198
    creationism, evolution, and, 153
    criticism of welfare, 180
    federal government as threat, 45, 260n25
    federal poverty programs and, 183–84
    geographic sorting and, 15
    Hobart Street unwelcoming to, 3–4, 6, 8
    immigration issue, 97
    jobs as coming first and, 186
    Jungian myth for, 116
    in local and state governments, 199–202
    news for, sources and content, 206–36
    in Oregon, 61
    as party that hates science, 143–69
    polarized views on gun issues, 37
    as political carnival, 235–36
    populist faction, 227, 228
    poverty agenda, 194–204
    seen as lacking compassion, 179–80
    seen as a threat by liberals, 5
    silencing of support for, 4
    think tanks or ideas factories, 19
    Trump and, 91–92, 235–36
    understanding, evangelicals and, 54
    uniform ideology and, 16
    words describing Democrats, 238
Republic Steel, 108
reverse polarization, 247–48
Right Online Conference, 206–8, 210,
    214, 217
Roller, Emma, 249
Romney, Mitt, 54, 92
Roose, Kevin, 76
Roosevelt, Franklin D., 186
Rubio, Marco, 133
Ryan, Paul, 182, 192, 194–95

Salyer, Jesse, 127
Sanders, Bernie, 127, 134, 168, 230

San Francisco Zoo, 274n10
Santorum, Rick, 259n17
Savage, Michael, 219
Sawhill, Isabel, 83
Schiller, Ron, 212–13
Schiller, Vivian, 213
Schwartz, Carol, 19
science, 143–69
  belief in, 144, 150
  climate change and, 144–45
  confluence of science and political
    ideology, 145, 156–69
  creationism, evolution, and, 145–53,
    273n2
  fakery in, 148–49
  golden age, current, 145
  liberal war against GMOs, 153–55
Second Amendment, 22–23, 44, 47, 73
Sellafield, England, nuclear facility, 160
Sentier Research, white men study, 100–102
Sexual Minorities Uganda Group, 263n7
Shaefer, Luke, 189–90, 191
Sherrod, Shirley, 228
Showmasters, 44
Silver, Nate, 92
Smith, Paul, 38–39, 205–6
social mobility, 184–85
Social Security, 96, 112, 130
Solomon, Lon, 84
Sommers, Samuel, 95
Sons of Liberty, The (TV show), 207
Spencer, Richard, 241
"spiral of silence," 222
Stanfield, Billy, 195–97, 198–99
steel industry, 100, 108
Steely Dan, "Deacon Blues," 89
Stein, Andrew, 171
Stern, Ken
  Bannon and, 230–35, 282n9
  bubble of, 55–56, 68, 71, 235
  evangelicals, politics, and, 53–88
  Facebook posts, 26–27
  guns, gun regulation, and, 21–52
  Hobart Street Pledge as wake-up call, 17
  learning to use a shotgun, 38–39
  as lifelong Democrat, 2, 18, 19
  looking for "real America," 30
  in the "muddled middle," 204
  at Nation's Gun Show, 43–48
  at NPR, 18, 22, 212, 213, 224
  pig hunting, 21–22, 30, 38–41, 51–52

  as polarized, 17
  quest to get outside his liberal bub-
    ble, 17, 19, 237, 243–44, 247, 250
  son Nate, 3, 18, 41, 54, 92, 111, 240
  wife, Beth, 3, 18, 51, 54, 111, 214–15
Steve (pastor, Freedom Church), 86–88, 237
Stewart, Jon, 120
Strain, John Paul, 46–47
suicide, 102, 268n11
Switzerland, "gun in every closet," 29

Taibbi, Matt, 210–11
Tajfel, Henri, 241–42, 243
Tea Party, 10, 19, 215, 219, 229, 243
Temporary Assistance for Needy Families
    (TANF) program, 187, 189, 201
Teresa of Calcutta, Saint, 70–71
Tesla Motors, 161–64
  Gigafactory, 164, 277n25
Texas, 30
  guns and, 21–22, 31–42
  mass shootings in, 33–34
  pig hunting in, 21–22, 30, 38–41,
    51–52
  as "real America," 30–31
Thomas, Adam, 83
Thomas, Clarence, 209
Thompson, Hunter S., 143
Time magazine, 212–13
To Kill a Mockingbird (Lee), 1
trade, 228, 233–34
Trimpa, Ted, 75
Trotta, Craig, 177–78
Trump, Donald, 2, 47, 73, 87
  Breitbart and, 208
  building the wall and, 91, 96, 97,
    267n6
  climate change and, 118, 132, 144,
    156, 167
  dismissal of Meals on Wheels, 202–3
  gun regulation and, 37–38
  jobs as coming first and, 186
  media and, 90, 225–26, 281n6, 282n7
  populism and, 230
  race issues and, 95, 113, 243
  rally, Chantilly, Va., 89–91
  rise of, 235–36
  voter fraud commission, 280n15
  voters for, 4, 54, 91–92, 99, 108,
    109–10, 112–13, 127, 186
Tufts University, research on media, 219

Turner, Ted, 227
$2.00 a Day (Edin and Shaefer), 189–90, 191

United Nations, 119, 135, 155
University of Chicago, General Social
    Survey, 105–6
University of Michigan
    institutional attacks on InterVarsity, 69
    poll on climate change, 132
    study on political views and facts, 12
University of Texas at Austin, clock tower
    shootings, 33–35
Urbana evangelical conclave, 54, 57–60,
    63, 68–69
U.S. Consumer Product Safety Commission
    (CPSC), accidental deaths of children
    under five, 24–25
U.S. Steel, 108
U.S. Supreme Court (SCOTUS)
    Brandeis and local government as
        the "laboratory of democracy," 200
    District of Columbia v. Heller, 50
    New State Ice Co. v. Liebmann, 200

Vallourec steel company, 100
Vanderbilt University, 69–71, 264n9
Vice (TV show), 134
Violence-Free Zone (VFZ), 195–99, 279n14
volunteerism, 64, 263n8

Wall Street Journal, 206
Washington, D.C., 2, 19, 30, 50
    Adams Morgan neighborhood, 139
    See also Mount Pleasant, D.C.
Washington Post, 119
    anti-Trump bias, 225–26
    Gerson column on O'Keefe, 212
    survey of Virginia voters, 2016, 4
Washington State, 159, 160
Weber, Steve (pastor, Freedom Church),
    86–88, 237
Wehner, Pete, 237, 251
Weiner, Anthony, 218, 228
welfare programs
    Bill Clinton and reform, 188, 189
    as poverty trap, 186
    PRWORA, 188, 201
    public attitudes toward, 187
    reform and poverty, 189–91
    Republican criticism, 180, 183–84

Republican's "A Better Way," 193
    TANF, 187, 189, 201
    work requirements and, 186–93, 201
Westboro Baptist Church, 61, 262n5
Western, Bruce, 178
West Virginia, 128, 129, 130, 131
Westwood, Sean, 7–8
Wheeler, Paul, 271n20
Whitman, Charles, 33–34
"Why I Am Not a Conservative" (Hayek), 115
Wilkow, Andrew, 248
Williams, Juan, 213
Williams, Robin, 21
Williamson, Kevin, 110–11, 114
Wilshire Baptist Church, 75, 79
Wilson, James Q., 37
Winship, Scott, 237
Woodson, Bob, 193–95, 197, 279n14
working class
    abandonment of, 94–95, 108, 131,
        168–69, 228
    anti-white bias perceived by, 95–96
    Democratic Party and, 234–35
    economic threats to, 100
    elitist view of, 110–11
    government programs and, 96
    immigration, effect of on, 231–33
    loss of jobs, China and, 234
    marriage and children, 104–5
    NASCAR and, 99
    as "new Gracchi," 230–31
    power threat theory and, 92–93
    previous generations, compared to
        current, 106
    rise in white mortality, 102–4
    study of white men, 100–102
    as Trump voters, 91–92, 99, 108,
        109–10, 112–13, 186
    See also race
World Resources Institute, 60, 63
World Trade Organization (WTO), 230, 233

Yale Law School, 18, 22, 31
Yale University, DICE model, 136
Yergin, Daniel, 158
Yiannopoulos, Milo, 220, 241
YouGov, 9
Youngstown, Ohio, 100, 108–10, 244
Youngstown Sheet & Tube, 108

ABOUT THE AUTHOR

Ken Stern is the president of Palisades Media Ventures and the author of *With Charity for All: Why Charities Are Failing and a Better Way to Give.* He was formerly the CEO of National Public Radio. He is also a frequent contributor to publications such as *Vanity Fair*, the *Atlantic*, *Slate*, the *Daily Beast*, the *Washington Post*, and the *Chronicle of Philanthropy*. He lives in Washington, D.C.